PRAISE FOR
AS THE SYCAMORE GROWS

"Jennie Helderman has taken a heart-breaking issue and boiled it down to human beings, of flesh and blood and lost days and fearful nights. It opens the door on a too-common human story and closes you in with it."

—**Rick Bragg,** *Pulitzer Prize*-winner and international bestselling author of *All Over But the Shouting* and many other *The New York Times* bestsellers

"Rarely has a story of a woman's courageous fight for freedom been told in such an eloquent and moving way. And, even more unusual, we get an open view into the twisted mentality of a man who was able, like so many abusers, to convince the outside world that he was normal. A hard book to put down."

—**Lundy Bancroft,** author of *Why Does He Do That?* and *In Custody*

"This story grabs hold of your heart and squeezes it dry. It is a tale so touching, so emotionally overwhelming, women will cringe and thank God they never had to walk in Ginger's shoes, and men will wish they could have met Ginger's husband in a dark alley. I applaud author Jennie Helderman's gift for writing, I marvel at Ginger's courage for sharing it."

—**Jedwin Smith,** two-time Pulitzer Prize nominee, author of *Our Brother's Keeper* and *Fatal Treasure.*

"With the careful eye of a journalist and the committed heart of a creative writer, Helderman provides witness to the kind of domestic violence and its after-effects that too many women suffer without the ability to express its tragedy. 'As the Sycamore Grows' becomes a fully realized and powerful account as Helderman twines her voice with that of Ginger, an abuse survivor. Such a story demands that it be told loud and clear, which is just what Helderman does."

—**Sue William Silverman,** author of *Because I Remember Terror, Father, I Remember You* and *Fearless Confessions: A Writer's Guide to Memoir*

"...a life-story of emancipation, personal fulfillment, and escape — not only from a padlocked cabin in the woods, but from a backwards anti-feminist culture into the broader world of contemporary human rights that is America's mainstream attitudes towards women's rights. Deftly written by an accomplished author..."

—*Midwest Book Review*

"A compelling story told with great courage and clarity that makes for an urgent read — it ends far too quickly leaving the reader wanting more! It may be the most important book I read this year."

—**Joe Carrel Daniel,** attorney, Florence, Alabama

"I certainly recommend this to the reader that is prepared for the journey, the real-life story of real people caught in the whirlwind of a heritage of abuse within their family tree. It takes strength and fortitude to grasp this book and then a bold step to open it."

—**Barbara Miller,** *Pacific Book Review*

"Jennie Helderman's thoroughly documented book proves the cycle of domestic violence can be broken, hope exists for the batterer and the abused, and the written word has the power to heal."

—**Lynn Hesse,** retired detective and author of
A Matter of Respect, Murder in Mobile Series, Book 2,
and other multi-genre mystery, suspense, and crime novels.

"I read 'As the Sycamore Grows' in one sitting....It illustrates how all domestic violence cases are similar and how each one is totally unique. Ginger's courage and strength, and her ultimate triumph, shine a light for other battered women seeking freedom from violence for themselves and their children."

—**Carol Gundlach,** Former Executive Director,
Alabama Coalition AgainstDomestic Violence

"[This] book is going to help countless women out there, but it's also helping me to reconnect to why I do this work after 16 years in the field and to reinvigorate my passion!"

—**Nicole Lesser,** Former Executive Director,
Georgia Coalition against Domestic Violence

"Amazing, powerful and raw...I highly recommend it."
—**Melissa Brown Levine,** *Independent Book Reviewers*

"...More than anything this book is a testimony to...the deep power of the human spirit to overcome and escape. It is a great triumph of hope....You won't be able to put this unique book down, even if it means finishing it at 4am in the morning...like I did."

—**Susannah Bales,** bookseller at Eagle Eye Book Store, Decatur, GA

"...chilling, yet heartwarming."
—**Jennie Hoover,** Alumnae magazine editor, Columbus, OH

"Good enough to take to the beach but it will come home on your heart."
—**Linda Tilley,** Former Executive Director, Voices for Alabama's Children

AS THE SYCAMORE GROWS
AWARDS

Winner of three 2011 Reader Views Literary Awards from among
publications from small, independent and academic presses:
First in Memoir/Biography
First overall categories in 14-state Southeast Region
Second in Narrative Nonfiction

Second in Women's Issues awarded by International Book Awards 2011
from among books of all publishers in 44 countries

Second in Women's Issues awarded by USA Best Books 2011

Voted 2011 Bonus Book of the Year by a network of
525 book clubs in the U.S. and 11 other countries

Nominated for 2011 Best Nonfiction Book of the Year
by Southern Independent Booksellers Association

Jennie Miller Helderman presented with
Alumnae Achievement Award in 2012,
the highest honor given by Kappa Kappa Gamma,
based on her work as an author and community leader

· A SPECIAL UPDATED EDITION ·

JENNIE MILLER HELDERMAN

AS THE

SYCAMORE

GROWS

A HIDDEN CABIN, THE BIBLE and a .38

LU(ID
HOUSE
PUBLISHING

LU(CID
HOUSE
PUBLISHING

Published in Marietta, Georgia, United States of America by Lucid House Publishing, LLC
www.LucidHousePublishing.com
© 2010 by Jennie Miller Helderman
All rights reserved. Special Updated 2nd Edition.
This title is also available as an e-book and audiobook via Lucid House Publishing, LLC
Cover design: Troy King
Interior Design: Jan Sharrow
Author photo: Kevin N. Garrett www.KevinGarrett.com

Publisher's Note: This multi-award-winning book is a cross-genre blend of memoir and a journalist's determined reporting that gives a rare look at a domestic violence survivor's story from all sides, including her abuser's and that of family members of both parties. Although *As the Sycamore Grows* often reads like a suspense thriller, Ginger MacNeil's story is true. If you or someone you know is experiencing partner abuse, please call the National Domestic Violence Hotline at 1-800-799-7233 or visit www.thehotline.org

Library of Congress Cataloging-in-Publication Data:

Helderman, Jennie Miller, 1939-
As the sycamore grows/a hidden cabin, the Bible, and a .38/ by Jennie Miller
Helderman—2nd edition.
Library of Congress Control Number: 2010931872
Print ISBN: 978-1-950495337

1. Memoir 2. Domestic violence 3. Spiritual abuse 4. Verbal and emotional abuse
5. Sexual Assault 6. Family abandonment 7. Suicide 8. Victim isolation
9. Psychological torture 10. Financial hostage 11. Women's shelter 12. Women's rights
FAM001030
BIO022000
BIO038000

To Ginger,

For her courage, honesty, and trust in me,

and to all those who provide the safe places.

CONTENTS

PROLOGUE

Alabama, September 2005

My assignment: A magazine story about poverty in Alabama. Real names, real people. Due in two weeks. Fifteen hundred words.

High stepping, but I knew where to look. I'd worked at walk-in social service agencies, taught school in rural Alabama, and clerked at debtors' court. I cast a big net. Soon, the director of a women's shelter suggested I meet someone on her staff.

That's how I came to know Ginger McNeil.

We met at a sandwich shop. A woman dressed in lime green and brown linen dashed through the door. I spotted her briefcase and guessed she was Ginger, hurrying from court in the next county.

The woman stopped short. The tentative expression that crossed her face as she scanned the room turned into a broad smile when she saw me waving from a back corner. Her brown page boy bounced against her collar as she made her way toward me, hand out, half-way through an introduction even before she reached my table.

"I'm late," she said, dropping into her chair, "but at least I'm not in jail."

I did a doubletake.

"Auto theft."

She dropped that bomb with a straight face.

"In the courthouse parking lot. Under the nose of the sheriff."

Her eyes were the color of coffee. I spotted mischief in them and smiled.

She leaned forward in her seat and lowered her voice.

"As I was racing to come here, my key wouldn't fit in the ignition. Then I heard a tap on the window and there stood the judge. I was in her car, not mine. I ran before the law came." She threw her head back and laughed at herself.

Her words flowed but she hung on to mine. She talked about her work with abused women, and I could read on her face the satisfaction she found in it. I ate my chicken salad.

But abuse isn't about poverty, I thought but didn't interrupt.

We talked through lunch and refills of iced tea. Pleasant chatter, but the clock was ticking toward my deadline. I needed to find a source for my story.

Just as I thought we were finished, Ginger said, "I'm a former client of the shelter. I didn't have two dimes the day they took me in."

I settled back into my chair.

"I lived in a cabin in the woods, too poor to afford electricity, and too afraid of my husband to leave. I even made my own soap."

"You made soap?"

"From hog fat. You have to butcher the hog first."

She told me she slaughtered, butchered and canned, shingled roofs, and bushhogged land—whatever it took for her and her two sons to survive.

"And you were afraid?"

"He hit me."

This woman with a briefcase. What I heard clashed against the image before me.

She drew a map to the cabin, twenty miles north up the Natchez Trace, left on one dirt road, right on the next. I promised to meet her there the following Saturday.

The first road I found quickly, then I topped a rise and looked for the second. Nothing but scrub oaks, piney woods, and red dirt lay ahead. Three times I drove back and forth before I spotted tire ruts between two scrawny oaks. Then the open gate appeared against the undergrowth.

The road wasn't hidden, but nothing marked or announced it. Had I not known there was a road and a house and once a family living back in the trees...that thought played in my mind even after I returned home late that afternoon.

The road dipped, rose, and circled through the trees to a small clearing amid sheds and a cabin. Ginger had heard my car and she bounded toward me. No briefcase today. Instead, she wore jeans and heavy boots. The cabin behind her was a cracker box with a tin roof and board and batten walls. Leggy red geraniums strained out of a clay pot by its front door.

Ginger ushered me inside, past the black wall-to-wall wood stove that dominated the first room, and through two bedrooms hardly larger than their beds. Cozy. Neat. We popped cans of Diet Coke and stepped out into a dry day with no breeze on this last weekend of September.

"I've made changes," Ginger said. "What you see as a clearing used to be so thick with vines and thorn bushes, someone could be within thirty yards of the cabin and never see it. That's how Mike planned it. He didn't want company coming."

We strolled along the dirt road and picked through tall grass to a metal contraption attached to a hickory tree.

"See this winch? After Mike slaughtered a hog, we hoisted it here to cure. Later I ground the meat into sausage."

I pointed to a mound of gray ashes. "And that fire pit. Is that where you boiled lye with the fat to make soap?"

"No, boiling fat is too dangerous with children around. I dissolved the lye in water, the cold method, you know."

All I knew was that I'd never made soap from any method.

I'd visualized the cabin tucked behind tall trees in a deep forest, solitary and haunting, not cluttered with sheds and tools. I hadn't taken into account the realities of living off nothing, the making-do with whatever could be caught, grown, or bartered.

We stopped beside what looked to me like a concrete block chimney.

"This is a final exam." Ginger touched her hand to it. "It's a smokehouse. My boys were barely teens when they built it. Practical application for the solid geometry, math, and physics they'd learned."

The boys had passed their test. I failed mine.

I tried to operate the chicken plucker but, without a chicken, I didn't catch on. All I got was a red face while Ginger got a good laugh.

I was ready for shade. We opened more Cokes and settled into lawn chairs under hickory trees.

"You lived like pioneers or survivalists," I said. "Did you choose this way of life? How did you get here?"

"How long do you have?" Ginger said.

She laughed, then her face grew serious. "Was there a choice? Yes. I made my choice when I married Mike. He chose this way of life for us, and I bowed to his decision. I never expected it to lead to such poverty."

She pushed her hair off her face and took a swallow of her Coke. "Strange as it may seem, poverty can be a choice, especially when it allows one person to control another."

We talked for more than an hour. When I stood up to leave, Ginger pointed to a path. "The root cellar is up there. You're welcome to see it. I don't go there."

"Not me. I'm claustrophobic."

I didn't question why Ginger shied away from the root cellar until I was in the car on my way home. I had an hour's drive to marvel at her skills and the strength and energy they required. And to ponder why they had lived as they did in a place so hard to find.

I wrote fifteen hundred words, but the story begged for more. Much more.

When I approached Ginger about a book, she mulled it over for several weeks, talking with her family over the Thanksgiving holiday, exploring her feelings and theirs.

Ginger and I met again at the sandwich shop. She was somber and thoughtful.

"When I sought safety at the shelter," she said, "my bed was waiting, the sheets already turned down. I had my own kitchen with a refrigerator and gas stove, and food, shelves and shelves of food, canned goods, and food in boxes. Everything I needed. Somebody had prepared all that just for me and my kids."

She paused, her eyes focused over my left shoulder, locked on something I would never see. A slight smile crossed her face.

"They didn't know my name or that I'd be coming, but they did this for me," she said. "They anticipated what I would need. I'm still overcome with gratitude for this person...these people. I've wondered how to repay them."

She placed both palms on the table, and her eyes suddenly shone with tears. "Telling this story is what I can do. It's worth whatever the cost is to me."

Whatever the cost. Those words had little meaning for me. I had no measure then of how great the risks would be for Ginger.

We began regular conversations wherever we found a quiet private place, her house, a secluded corner at the public library, an artist friend's studio. Sometimes we pored over photos, journals, and letters, some dating back to childhood, some from her children to her, including the son she lost.

Ginger was unflinchingly honest, even when probing scarlet pain and remorse.

"Everything I was taught and believed and have done, it's all part of me. It's what made me a sitting duck for a man like Mike. And it's where I drew my strength in the end."

~~~~~~

Long before the magazine article turned into a book, I knew I had to speak with Mike. I had to allow him to tell his side of the story. So, I phoned him, asked if he would meet with me. He agreed.

I was apprehensive. I had no idea what to expect of him, especially when I'd have to confront him with questions about physical abuse. Was I courting danger? I didn't know.

We met at a Waffle House in the late afternoon. His choice, his territory. He's a regular there. But it was a public place, which I hoped meant a safe place for me.

I stepped inside the doorway and stopped. Several men were hunched over their coffee and ashtrays at a gray counter. In booths opposite the counter, other men and a few women talked in twos and threes. Two men sat alone in two booths, the first with his nose in a book.

I approached the second, a man with gray-blonde hair, a white mustache, and bushy eyebrows who was scrambling to a half-stance in the booth.

"Mike?"

"You got me."

He smiled. His eyes were Paul Newman-clear-blue and his face was pleasant. He slid back to his seat even as we shook hands.

Firm handshake Strong hands. Medium height, fit enough for a man in his fifties. Wearing a white dress shirt like he'd rather not, unbuttoned at the neck, the sleeves rolled up, and no undershirt.

"Have a seat."

I did and ordered coffee. I never glanced at the man reading the book. He was my husband, ready to come to my aid if needed.

There was no need.

Mike fidgeted. He smoked nine Winston Reds to three cups of black coffee. But he spoke candidly.

"Ginger was always out to please. Nobody in her growing up gave her approval, and I had to turn all that around. Most of my life I spent battling to get her to take up for herself. "

He talked about picking peas and going to church, at no time showing any animosity toward his former wife, a woman whose public speeches identified him as a batterer.

Neither of us had mentioned the subject, though it was the reason I'd asked for this meeting.

"Ginger told me there was abuse, physical abuse. Was there?" I tensed, ready to flinch or duck.

"Yeah, there was." He thought for a minute. "One time I hauled off and slapped the fool out of her. She said I shoved her other times. But you have to remember, this was over twenty years."

"So you acknowledge there was abuse that included physical abuse?"

"That's what I said."

Matter-of-fact. Without apology.

I wrapped up the conversation, thanked him, and was five steps toward the door when he called out to me.

"Hey! You didn't pay for your coffee."

Heads turned in my direction. I felt my face flush. "You're right. Sorry."

I settled my bill and left. Mike won our first encounter.

Two months later, with the article growing into a book, Mike emailed me that he wanted to participate. I didn't know why and didn't ask, afraid he'd reconsider and bolt.

We continued to meet at the Waffle House until its clatter chased us to quieter spots. By then I was less uneasy around him. He never denied any of the bad times. "Men will understand. Men know what the program is."

He has no remorse. "I wouldn't change a thing if I could go back."

To Mike's thinking, he and Ginger couldn't be where they are now without having experienced it all.

Mike has a story too. It trickled out as if from a medicine dropper. He announced early on he would have "his say," and one day he did just that. Mike took me inside his skin or let me think he did.

Either way, I came to appreciate what it revealed of him, even the parts that to this day I can't fully comprehend.

This story has many voices. Ginger and Mike speak, as do their family, friends, coworkers, and court officials. They tell what they remember, or what they chose to divulge, about things that happened a long time back, then comment on them in the present time. In some cases, I've changed names and physical characteristics to protect their privacy.

2005. That's when I came in. Not that I intended to do more than listen, record, and tell. But my questions took people back to old places, sometimes dark places, and this time I was along when they relived the memory. Sometimes they uncovered something new.

And so I joined the journey.

This is Ginger's story, and Mike's. It didn't begin with them and, despite Ginger's prayers, it may not end with them.

chapter one

A noise. Ginger awoke, listened. The hum of a motor, the scrunch of tires creeping along the road outside the cabin. She reached over to her husband's side of the bed. Empty. Where he was heading in the thin light of dawn, she didn't know. Mike McNeil didn't offer explanations for his comings and goings. She knew better than to ask.

She rolled back onto her pillow, wide awake now. She could see the black handle of Mike's .38 at the edge of the closet shelf. Mike seldom strapped the gun to his belt anymore. He had made his point. She wouldn't take it again and he knew it.

The light was still too dim to see the photos fastened with thumb tacks to the rough-sawn boards next to the closet. It didn't matter. She pictured them in her mind. She and Mike had squeezed into the metal kiosk at a truck stop that day and posed fast before their quarter ran out. Mike had just trimmed his beard. A good memory.

Birds chirped outside.

Time to rise. She rolled out of bed.

In the boys' room, she stood over her sons and smiled. Casey's feet hung off the foot of his bed. He'd hit a growing spell the day he turned thirteen. She kissed his forehead, then his brother's.

"Wake up, both of you. Casey, I'm going to put a brick on your head or you'll outgrow everything you own." She laughed and gave twelve-year-old Cody a nudge.

In the next room, she built a fire in the woodstove to chase off the morning chill. Atop the stove, water for coffee heated in a blue enamel pot while the last of the oatmeal cooked in a dented stewer. The boys would have the oatmeal. She wasn't hungry.

She laced up her boots and trudged up the hill to milk the cow while they ate breakfast.

It was an ordinary morning at the cabin in the woods where she lived with Mike and their two sons.

There was nothing different or ominous, nothing to suggest that before noon Ginger would make her escape.

She forced a needle through pigskin for a rifle pad while each boy pulled on his one pair of jeans. *Better pick beans today before the sun gets up in the sky.* Summer didn't like to let go here at the bottom of Tennessee, and this day would be hot by noon. She twisted her hair through her fingers, wishing she could pull it up off her neck. Or cut it.

Casey crossed the kitchen in two steps, gathered his homework under one arm and dashed out the door. All knees, elbows, and perpetual motion, he disappeared up the hill. Cody lumbered in from the bedroom and fumbled with his papers, a scowl on his face.

Still my little freckle-faced boy.

Cody and Casey had entered school for the first time this year, a small church school just across the state line in Alabama. She'd hoped they would like a regular school but so far it was a split decision. It was early, just three weeks into the school year. There was plenty of time yet to adjust.

She gave Cody a quick squeeze before hurrying him toward Casey and her old Honda. They had ten miles to drive to school.

Mike spotted the blue of Ginger's car in the distance as he returned home. He checked his watch and calculated when she'd be back. At the cabin, he opened his Bible to Revelations and read until it was time to go. He tromped down their dirt road to the blacktop where he ducked into the trees to watch for her car. Leaning against a pine, he lit a Winston Gold, then another as soon as it burned to the filter.

The last time she left, he'd watched her. He could see to the bottom of the hill where, that time, she'd stopped for a few minutes, backed up the road, then stopped again. She was trying to pick up a signal on that car phone, way out here.

He was on to her.

Ginger slowed to turn between two scrub oaks onto their road. The galvanized metal gate stood open. Mike didn't always padlock it now like he once did. He'd made that point, too.

Her tires crunched against the road as she headed the quarter mile toward the cabin, hidden by honeysuckle vines and briars. Mike didn't want anybody in his business. If somehow anybody slipped past the padlock and wandered up the road, they could pass within thirty yards of the cabin and never know it was there. That was part of the plan.

They'd built the cabin back in 1996, when they had to vacate the rental house in a hurry. She and Mike sawed and hammered while the boys, young as they were, toted and hauled. It had five hundred square feet divided into two rooms, no electricity, no phone, by design.

Mike's car sat in tall grass just off the road. She parked beside him and called his name when she got out of the car. No answer.

Backtracking down the road, Ginger walked to Trent's tree, a young syc-amore named in memory of her oldest son. She'd first planted an apple tree for Trent, but ants made a bed at its base. When she poisoned the ants, she killed the tree. The sycamore was a sapling that came up in the compost pile. A smile spread across her face. The sycamore was thriving. She'd kept a close watch on it.

She hurried to the garden. *Time to pick beans.*

Later, listening to the beans simmer, she eased a thimble onto her sore thumb to resume stitching the rifle pad. Wayne, a neighbor from two miles up the blacktop, had hollered from the gate with an armload of corn a few weeks back. Mike didn't encourage visitors, and Wayne respected his dis-tance, which allowed them to be friends, if at arm's length. Wayne was half Mike's age, clean-shaven and buzz cut, and to him neighbors were next to kin. Mike had been oiling his rifle and their talk turned to guns.

"Ever seen a pigskin rifle pad?" Wayne said. "That's what I want, but I guess I'll have to get it special made."

"Tell me what you want and I'll make it," Ginger said, watching Mike's face as she spoke. As much food as Wayne's garden put on their table, it was the least she could do.

For two weeks she'd struggled with the rifle pad, from drying white sand in the woodstove to fill the cushions, to forcing a needle in and out through three layers of leather. Her thumb and forefinger smarted at the touch, but as soon as she whipped the last seams together, the pad would be finished.

She heard stomping feet outside.

Mike called out, "How about bringing me a cup of coffee?"

Ginger spread the rifle pad across the kitchen table and took Mike his coffee.

He lolled in the swing under the hickory tree within earshot of the cabin door. His beard, blonde like his hair, reached to his belt. He tucked his Bible under a thigh so the loose pages wouldn't fall out and reached for the cup.

Ginger joined him in the swing, sweeping the skirt of her denim jumper to one side. She ran her arm under her hair, lifting it off her neck. "My hair's making me hot. If I don't get it cut, I'll soon be sitting on it."

She exaggerated, a joke to test Mike's mood. Her hair fell below her shoulder blades, not her waist.

Mike leaned forward to scratch Samson, his blue heeler, cupping the dog's snout in his hand.

"You're not cutting your hair." His voice was low but firm.

"If I cut it, Mike, it'll still be long."

They'd had this conversation before. This time he spoke into her face, emphasizing each word with a downward thrust of his fist, index finger pointed.

"I said—you're—not—cutting—your—hair."

He still kept his voice low, because he didn't need to yell.

He jutted his head forward and stared into Ginger's eyes. "You don't have the authority to decide what you want."

She clenched her jaw, holding tight inside what she dared not say aloud: *Move over, God, Mike's in charge. He knows what's best, and I no longer exist apart from him.*

Mike's words tossed in her head, picking up energy with each tumble until they exploded like marbles fired from a pinball machine, her anger and indignation rising with each ricochet. She could sit still no longer. Stalking into the cabin, she let the screen door bang shut behind her.

The swing stopped. She watched Mike plant his boots hard against the ground.

He stood up and marched straight toward the cabin, controlled, careful not to spill a drop of the steaming coffee.

Ginger leaned against the kitchen table, her fingertips brushing against the rifle pad. Seeing his face, she dropped her arms to her sides.

He eased the cup onto the table. Snatched up the rifle pad. Pushed the screen door open with one hand and slung the pad onto the ground outside.

"I'm sick and tired of this crap."

The pad hit with a splat. Its seams burst open and white sand spilled onto gray dirt. Samson skittered out of the way.

Tears rolled down Ginger's cheeks. Mike knew how many hours she had put into the pad, knew how hard she had worked, knew the needle hurt. Wayne was his friend, and they owed him. Besides, Wayne had paid for the materials. She had to account for them.

For a while, she busied herself about the cabin. When she thought Mike had turned his attention elsewhere, she carefully circled past him and slipped out to retrieve the pieces of the rifle pad.

She sensed heavy steps behind her before she heard them, sensed the weight of his presence as his hands grabbed her arms and shoved her aside.

"I said no more of this crap."

He kicked the rifle pad. It slid like a deflated football six feet away, leaving a thin trail of the white sand. Facing Ginger, feet planted apart, he swiped his fist across his chin. "Now you get in the house."

What's he going to do?

Ginger dropped her head, her eyes avoiding Mike's glare. "I don't want to go into the house."

Mike charged. He grasped Ginger by her arms, lifted her off her feet, dragged her to the porch. He let go and she stumbled. Before she could get her balance, he shoved her hard through the open door.

She shuffle-stepped, her arms flailing like a rag doll's, grasping for a handhold in the air. Her knees smacked against a wooden arm of the couch, and she fell onto its cushions. The screen door slammed shut.

She lay still. She needed to catch her breath, yet not look his way. She had to steady herself, to think. To make up her mind.

Mike positioned himself in the bedroom doorway next to the couch, one elbow propped against the doorframe.

Ginger pulled up. Five steps took her across the tiny room to the sink, her refuge. First, she washed her hands, then the breakfast dishes, then her hands again, soaping to her elbows and rinsing. It was what she did when she needed to go to a private place, and she needed that now, needed to wash away her indecision. She needed to wash away Mike and everything else that bound her to this place.

Behind her, she heard him pick up his coffee cup from the table. Heard him step toward her. She spun to face him. And gasped.

With his arm crooked over her head, Mike dumped the coffee over her. She squeezed her eyes shut. The brown liquid rolled down her forehead. She felt it puddle in one ear and run down the back of her neck.

It didn't burn; it was lukewarm, but it scorched her heart.

She shook her head, slinging droplets, then dipped her head under the faucet to rinse away the coffee.

When she reached for a dishtowel, Mike grabbed her by the arms and pulled her face to his, his nose almost pressing her nose. She squeezed her eyes shut. *If he looks into my eyes, he'll see that it's over, and I'm afraid to let him see that now. Afraid of what he'll do rather than lose me.* She thought of the root cellar with its prison-thick walls.

"Get the crap out of here before I hurt you," Mike yelled down her throat. "I don't want you around me anymore."

Drops of warm spit sprayed onto her face.

She picked up her purse—it held no money, nothing but her keys and driver's license—and hurried to her car, the ten-year-old Honda that was wrecked when they bought it. She hoped the junker would start.

It did.

At first, she inched forward; she had to be sure. She stopped at the syca-more tree. Trent's tree. *Can I abandon Trent again?* She whispered a long goodbye, her heart aching.

A rock hit the car. Mike was pelting the car with rocks and yelling, "Go! Get out of here. Git!"

She accelerated toward the open gate, its padlock hanging from a post, and raced to the blacktop. Cold water trickled between her shoulder blades, and she told herself that was why she was shivering so hard.

She had left before, and those memories washed over her now. One day she drove two miles up the blacktop to a country cemetery. Hiding among the tombstones, she knitted a sock. Each clack of the needles measured the moments until the toe shaped to its fit and she would go back. She had no money and nowhere else to go.

This time, maybe it would be different. Two years ago, she'd seen a bill-board advertising Safeplace, a women's shelter across the state line in Ala-bama. She had chiseled its phone number into her memory.

Her mind screamed *It has to be different this time!* as she screeched up to the curb by the school playground. Her boys were huddled together, not quite in the midst of the other children.

Ginger called to them from the car, "Come on, boys. Hurry, hurry!"

She saw them glance at the other children, the classmates they scarcely knew, before they rushed to her.

She gave them their choice. They could go with her or stay with their father.

"I'm going with you," Casey said. "I don't know what happened this time, but I know if we don't go with you, you'll come back."

"Me, too," Cody said.

While Ginger drove, she thought of the first time Mike threw coffee at her. She had left then, too, her face bruised by a blow. That escape had started just like this one, with coffee poured on her by a man who swore to love and honor her, but never had. Or maybe he did, but in a twisted way she would never be able to understand.

This time can't end the same way. It just can't!

She yanked her mind away from the memory and kept the Honda speeding toward the shelter thirty miles away, watching the rearview mirror for Mike's brown Chevy Caprice. As she drove, her sons bombarded her with questions.

"Are we going to tell Dad where we are?" Casey asked.

"Are we going back to school?" Cody asked.

She had no answers for them. She had no answers for herself.

When the car buzzed into The Shoals, Ginger ducked behind a service station to call the number she'd memorized. She followed their instructions, keenly aware of the secrecy the shelter insisted upon. A matter of life and death, they had said. *Yes, thank you.* She checked her rearview mirror one more time.

Not until the shelter's gates clanged shut behind her did she feel safe.

The staff gathered them behind the closed doors of a pale, yellow room, hugging them, welcoming them.

I feel like I've come home to family, yet I don't know a single one of them. At the same time, she felt hollow, exhausted as if she'd been up all night, knowing she had stepped from one planet to another. Safe, yes. Also afraid and guilty and weighed down with the responsibility of what she had done.

She blinked back tears. Turning her face away from her sons, she wiped at her eyes. *Can't let them think I'm having second thoughts, not after coming this far!*

"Would you boys like a snack here in the rec room while we talk with your mother?" a staff member asked.

Casey stood in front of Cody at the threshold, each of them taking in all the rec room had to offer, hesitant. Their entire cabin could fit inside its walls. Soft brown chairs semi circled a TV set, and a boy about their age slouched in the largest one. He glanced up, smiled, and turned back to his program. Nearby a Monopoly board was open across a game table with four chairs. Blue bookshelves lined the back wall, up to a toy box spilling over with Nerf balls and little kid toys.

Cody asked for a glass of milk.

Laine, the counselor on duty, showed Ginger into a cubicle where they could talk privately. When Ginger tried to fill in the paperwork, her hands trembled so much that Laine took the pen and filled in the blanks for her.

"And you live in a cabin where? What's your 911 address?"

"911? We don't even have a mailbox."

Laine looked up from the papers at Ginger.

"I'm a mess," Ginger said. Limp brown hair hung loose halfway to her waist. Her eyes sunk into hollows. Her face was pale, yet her arms had a farmer's tan, brown past the elbows then white where her shirt sleeve fell. She knew she was lean and sinewy but probably looked malnourished—just downright old and haggard.

"Do you know what you weigh? How tall are you?"

The questions weren't on the forms. Laine was just concerned.

"About a hundred and six. Five feet seven."

Laine made notes, then pushed her chair back and took off her glasses.

"Tell me about yourself."

Ginger stammered and muttered at first. Then the words spilled out on top of each other. "No phone. No electricity. I had my babies at home…. I butchered hogs, made sausage, rendered the fat and made my own soap—my husband threw rocks—poured coffee on my head…. I don't have any money."

Laine led Ginger, Casey, and Cody down fresh-smelling hallways to their room. Three single beds, a desk, and dresser left little walking around space. Ruffled curtains, hooked rug, and pastoral landscapes on light blue walls brightened the room. Blue plaid spreads covered the beds.

Next, she showed them through the shelter.

Each family had its own kitchen space within a larger room, with a stove, refrigerator, and a pantry. Ginger let out a little cry when she saw the refrigerator and freezer, another one when she opened the pantry door: shelves and shelves of canned meats and vegetables, packaged cereals, grains, bread, cookies, frozen foods, more than they could want.

She was too overcome with gratitude to say a word.

I can't believe this. Someone prepared this for me. They don't even know me, but here it is, ready for me now, when I need it.

"Did you bring a bag with you? A change of clothes?" Laine asked.

Ginger glanced down at her jumper with its coffee stains, suddenly aware of feeling sticky. "No, only this dress. And the boys' schoolbooks."

"I'll call," a staff member told Laine. She phoned the agency that provided clothing.

"They were locking up for the weekend," she said, "but they've reopened. Let's go."

January 2006

I parked behind Ginger's ranch-style house. Just home from work, she waited for me under a flood light. Darkness had fallen in the late afternoon that Monday in January.

"From now on, you're a back door friend," she said as we wound through the garage and into a pine-paneled kitchen. She clutched two grocery sacks in her arms. I carried a take-out order from The Speedy Pig for the first of our working suppers.

Nowadays she races from court to court in six counties, a counselor employed by the shelter that once gave her sanctuary, bolstering other women who seek its safety. A professional woman with confidence, skill, and a briefcase.

The transformation wasn't easy.

She and two boys with teenage appetites had lived on $543 a month Supplementary Security Income in a house owned by the shelter. At forty-two years old and working part-time, she entered college. That led to a B.S. in behavioral science and a job with the shelter.

"Abuse is about control. I heard that over and over at the shelter and later in class." She kicked off her heels and shoved them out of her way.

"Isolation and dependence are tools of an abuser."

"You could have taught those lessons," I said. They hadn't even had a mailbox. She had to go through Mike to send or receive mail.

"Isolation and poverty formed the backbone of my marriage," she said as she sliced store-bought tomatoes for our barbecue sandwiches. She opened a jar of homemade pickles and put a second jar on the red Formica counter for me to take home.

"I didn't even think about it then," she continued when we sat at a maple table to eat. She had traded her suit jacket for a nubby sweater while I put a log in the fireplace. "The less we had, the more I stretched. Stretching became my weapon, my way to fight back. Stretching was my strength."

She put her sandwich on her plate. She needed her hands to help find her thoughts.

"Stretching meant—or I believed it meant—I was a competent wife and mother who could overcome whatever hurdles I faced—"

She stopped.

"Do you know what I just realized?"

I had a mouthful of barbecue, so I shook my head.

"I built my own prison. I used my strength to wall myself in."

"How was that?"

"If I hadn't stretched our money, watered the soup or whatever, if I'd just let it all collapse, then Mike would have had to go to work. Or else we'd have fallen apart much sooner. I never thought of that."

She shook her head, thinking about what she'd just figured out.

"Mike's primary tool was economic abuse. And I made it possible."

After supper, we leafed through Ginger's high school yearbook and a box of photos and letters she kept under a bed in a spare room.

Ginger didn't know poverty before marrying Mike, nor did she expect it of the marriage. She did know about control. That she learned well growing up in Baycross, Texas, in the 1960s and 1970s.

chapter two

A one-picture-show town, Baycross was known in Texas for big county fairs and a hanging. Forty-three churches served its people in the 1960s. Ginger Mitchell grew up in the shadow of one of them.

Thus, the shrimp boat anchored in her back yard had to be Noah's Ark.

The boat swallowed the yard and rivaled their house in size. Its hull rounded out from a narrow keel and reached high into the sky, allowing space underneath for forts and doll houses.

How a Biblical ark came to be in the Texas flatlands south of Houston was a mystery, since everybody knew the ark landed on Mount Ararat. But Sam, Ginger's older brother at age eight and the smart one in the family, figured their yard must have once been on top of a mountain named Ararat. Pronouncing Ararat was challenge enough for the younger siblings. They didn't wrestle with the mystery of the disappearing mountain.

Often Ginger lay on her back and wondered what Noah had seen from the deck towering above her. She was a climber. She could scale its wide wooden planks, even where they bowed out. But she didn't dare. Playing on the boat was forbidden. Claude Mitchell's four children did not disobey him.

Sam, the oldest—the smart one—was followed by Mileah, the little mama. Ginger, three years younger than Mileah, jabbered as the chatterbox or roughhoused as the tomboy. She was bright, but she felt dumb by comparison. Besides, Sam was the bright one, and the distinction was exclusive, only one to a family. Pete, eighteen months after Ginger, was always the baby.

In their neighborhood families visited back and forth and borrowed sugar and tools. The children ran barefoot in the summertime, sold lemonade from stands, and caught fireflies in Mason jars.

"Hey, Sam, look. Here's Stitches again."

Ginger held out a wriggling frog for her brother to see. She and Pete had declared themselves the Frog Police. Once a month they patrolled the cast iron water valve boxes buried at every house on their street and "rescued" any frogs that had taken up residence. Back home they played with the frogs until they lost interest, then let them go.

Except for the day Sam borrowed one of their frogs. With the encyclopedia open to a diagram of a frog's internal organs, Sam sliced into the frog. Ginger bent close to watch, then shrieked and squealed, both curious and repulsed. When he finished, Sam stitched the frog together and released him in the yard. "Stitches," as the kids named him, survived. Pete and Ginger caught him time and again on their patrols, always identifiable by the zigzag scar on his underside.

Sometimes Ginger slipped away to a private place. A thick stand of bamboo circled a telephone pole at the back corner of their yard and its center stalks supported her when she shimmied up and leaned back against their fronds. She liked to watch clouds, imagining them as flocks of sheep or angels watching down from heaven. Heaven was a very real place for Ginger. She knew a lot about heaven.

As newlyweds, her parents had chosen to "obey the gospel" which meant total acceptance of the tenets of their Church of Christ. They embraced this vow fully, fervently, and with unswerving devotion.

When the church doors opened, the Mitchell family filed in, Bibles in hand, to sit still throughout the service. No wiggling or squirming. No nursery for Claude Mitchell's children, even as toddlers.

At school Ginger and her peers recited the ABCs. On Sundays, she stood in her finest dress, its sash tied in a bow in the back and recited the books of the Bible. All sixty-six of them. And after that, the twelve tribes of Israel.

After services each Sunday, her father counted the offering and rolled coins for the bank deposit while the family waited quietly at home. Their sit-down dinner, like all their meals, could begin only after he took his chair and asked the blessing. Always her father, never her mother. Women didn't pray aloud before men, even if the men were their own little boys. Her mother deferred to her sons once they reached their eighth birthday, as the church taught. The children ate what was put before them, no picking and choosing, no complaining. Then they went back to church Sunday night and again each Wednesday night.

Nothing interfered with church. Not even Thomas, their cat, who lay sleeping on the driveway until her father backed over him and kept going.

The church literally extended into their home. The fourth bedroom had an outside entrance, perfect for the preacher to use as his office, provided the children doubled up in the remaining bedrooms.

Morals and Christian values overlaid family life like the roof over the house. There was always a lesson to be learned, some deliberately taught and others Ginger picked up on her own.

Her mother often rolled Ginger's hair into sausage curls.

"Hop up on my chair," she'd say, patting the tufted gold cushion on her brass vanity chair.

Ginger was age three the day she crawled onto the "princess" chair and smiled at the curly blonde girl looking back from the mirror.

"I like you, Ginger, you're so pretty," she said to her reflection.

Her mother overheard from the next room.

"Shame on you. You're a vain little thing."

She put her hand on Ginger's shoulder. "Pretty is as pretty does. Good deeds lead to beauty."

Ginger pins her later dowdiness to this oft-repeated lesson.

By her eighth birthday, Ginger's blonde curls gave way to limp mousey-colored strings that hung down her back. They tangled on tree limbs and snarled into rats' nests on her pillow at night. A tender-headed tomboy, Ginger yelled when her mother tried to brush her hair.

"You're getting your hair cut," her mother said.

She made an appointment with a hairdresser, and Ginger returned home all smiles, proud of her pixie cut.

Until her father came home from work.

He burst into the kitchen from the carport and ran smack into Ginger.

"What the—"

Ginger's grin dropped off her face when she saw the expression on his.

Brushing past Ginger without another glance, he headed for his bedroom.

"Helen!" he called to his wife.

Ginger stood in the den, frozen in place. Even through their closed door and up the long corridor, their voices rose. And rose. Never had she heard them have such a blow-up. She stood in the den, trembling. She'd brought this on. It was her fault.

After long minutes, her mother emerged from the bedroom, her face tight.

"Your daddy pitched a hissy fit about your hair."

It was all she said. She was angry, but no words poured out. She pressed her lips together, hard. Ginger could see the veins standing out in her throat.

Often in the fall, on her half-day off from work, Ginger's mother took the children to pick pecans. They hung burlap sacks from their necks and knee-walked through the pecan groves picking nuts off the ground. Afterwards they sold them at the feed store. Ginger learned that by being quick she could earn $6 to $10, a lot of money for an eight-year-old.

Her mother kept the nuts she gathered to bake pecan pies. Whenever she tied on her apron, Ginger would pull a stool up to the kitchen counter and beg to help.

Her first efforts dusted the kitchen with flour but eventually she could crisscross two dinner knives through flour and lard until the ingredients were evenly mixed. When she learned to flute the edges of the crust, her mother said, "You've mastered the art of pie-making,"

This was high praise from a mother who believed in doing things right.

Mileah and her friends played with their dolls while Ginger often played alone. She felt she was a friend to everybody else but had no real friend of her own.

Often, she sat, knees to her chin, on the concrete stoop at Debbie's house next door. Other than being Ginger's age, Debbie was everything Ginger was not: blonde, cute, bouncy, popular, and an elementary-school cheerleader. And if that didn't make Debbie special enough in Ginger's eyes, her big sister led cheers at the high school.

"Two, four, six, eight," Debbie yelled. She waved her arms in short, staccato moves emphasized by the pompoms in her hands and the red and white pleated skirt of her uniform bounced with her body. Her big sister had even bigger, more magnificent pompoms.

"Here, let me show you," Debbie said and SuSu, their classmate who lived on the other side of Ginger, hopped up to learn the routine.

Ginger hugged her knees to make herself smaller. She no longer needed to say anything. She wasn't allowed, and they knew it. She couldn't be a cheerleader, nor could she even pretend to be a cheerleader practicing the moves with her playmates.

She couldn't go to their slumber parties nor do many of the thing girls her age did. They belonged to the in- crowd at school, and Ginger didn't.

Many years later, when she was an adult, she came across a set of pompoms at a yard sale. She bought them. She gave them to the boys to play with, but at last she owned pompoms.

Baycross, April 2006

Couldn't even pretend to be a cheerleader?

I had to go to Texas. Baycross, with its small-town Texas culture, was the backdrop of Ginger's childhood. What she learned and experienced there shot to the center of who she would become and how she would lead her life. I had to see for myself the places and people so central to her.

Baycross sprawls in the flatlands forty miles south of Houston and so close to the Gulf I smelled salt on the evening breeze.

Helen, Ginger's mother, referred to their neighborhood as "silk-stocking hill" although she acknowledged they lived on its blue-collar end. I didn't find any hill at all as I approached. In fact, the entire landscape felt flat, like a view through a wide-angle lens—open pasture enroute to Baycross, one- and two-story stores, some with covered sidewalks in front. Then I topped an overpass. Below it one silver Erector-set building followed another—petrochemical plants extending sixteen miles to the brown beaches at Freeport.

Dow Chemical Company had been first. Its plant in 1953 lit a firecracker under the little cattle and farming town. Its good-paying jobs had enticed Ginger's father to Baycross, and he toiled there as a shift foreman until he retired. With Helen's income as a nurse, they bought the four-bedroom house where Ginger grew up.

Helen said their house barely squeaked into the neighborhood, and she was right. It sat at the end of the last street, a 1950s yellow-shingled ranch style with a carport and concrete front stoop.

She greeted me on the stoop wearing navy pants, a white overblouse, and horn-rimmed glasses. Her hair was wet and rolled in pin curls. She ushered me back to a pine-paneled kitchen-den to meet Claude.

Claude was tall with big ears and a deep baritone voice. He was jovial, easy with conversation, and he absorbed all the space around him. His children had warned me he had a steel side and those who knew him didn't go there. They also told me Claude's parents' marriage rocked along until his conception, then split. He bounced from one family member to another as a child.

Claude took charge. He pointed me over to the couch facing the kitchen. Helen sat opposite me at the wooden table where they take their meals. Claude settled into his brown easy chair and began to talk about himself.

"I marched straight out of high school into the Navy in 1948."

He reared back in his chair, tossed his head back.

"I danced the jitterbug. I sowed my oats. Let me tell you, I sowed my oats."

Once he accompanied a Texas buddy home on furlough to meet the buddy's sister, yet it was the younger sister with brown curls, sixteen-year-old Helen Baranov who caught his eye.

Ginger had told me about Helen. The daughter of immigrant Czech farmers, she didn't speak English until she was five. She had worked in the fields with her siblings and had no intention of spending her life there. Nurs-ing would be her profession.

Helen has a quiet confidence about her. A submissive Biblical wife, she knew how to reach compromise. In her household, that was important knowledge. Ginger had described her as a worker bee, a dutiful but not a doting mother, not one who read to them or helped with homework. Like cooking, childcare was part of her day-to-day household chores. The chores included managing the check book, a role Ginger expected once she married.

"Ginger said she was terrified of me," Claude said soon after he began talking. "I don't know why."

He looked puzzled, as if he expected an answer from me. When I didn't respond, he continued.

"Her mother and I didn't grow up in affectionate families. We didn't do that lovey-dovey, huggy-kissy business."

Helen laughed and turned to Claude.

"Remember that Christmas when you gave me the fur coat?"

She turned to me to explain.

"I put on the coat and then gave Claude a kiss, and the children were shocked—they were all grown by then—they said they'd never seen us kiss before."

No hugging, no kissing, very little touching in their family. No saying, "I love you," others said later.

"What did you want for your children?" I asked. "What were your hopes?"

"The girls I wanted to be good cooks and truthful ladies," Claude said, "and the boys to be pro baseball pitchers. Sam's left-handed. I spent hours practicing with him from the time he was seven."

Sam had already told me about crying to his mother when his arm hurt from the pitch practices. Nevertheless, Sam became the star pitcher—for his Little League team.

"We wanted them to be well-rounded young people," Helen said. "Not to conform to most. To lead good stable lives."

"Do their best," Claude said.

"And what did you expect from them?"

"Obedience."

Claude's answer was a pronouncement.

"We provided for them, and I expected obedience in return."

He sat against the back of his chair with his arms folded across his chest. His face wore no expression, but his voice rang with authority, and his eyes made me feel like a twelve-year-old. When Ginger later told me about the power of his stare, I knew what she meant.

The children quickly learned the consequences of disobedience. Helen said she taught them on that part of the anatomy which the Lord provided. Claude told a story about spanking Pete, the baby.

"Pete was a little fellow, two or three. His mother warned him to sit still at church but he wiggled and squirmed. I snatched him up, took him outside, and blistered him. He had on short pants, and I just blistered up and down one leg. When it was over, I said 'Now, I'll have no sniffling or sobbing. I don't want to hear a peep out of you, or we'll be back out here.'

"And back we were, a second time. When I yanked him up the third time, a woman on the pew behind us leaned forward and grabbed my arm. 'Claude Mitchell,' she said, 'you're the cruelest man I know.'

"I glared at her until she turned loose of my arm, then I took Pete out and did what I promised him I'd do."

I asked Ginger later and she doesn't remember this incident. She would have been no more than three or four herself. She does remember sitting during church services with her back tight against the pew, her knees and ankles pressed together, holding her breath whenever her father looked her way.

Claude told another story, this one about Sam in the garage. I had already heard about it. Everybody had a version.

As the oldest, Sam's every misstep meant two transgressions, one for whatever he had done or not done and the second for failing to be a good example for the younger children.

Sam was fifteen and working in the garage. Ginger was eleven and acting the pest. Fed up with her, Sam twisted her arm behind her back. Ginger let out a howl worthy of an *Academy Award*, that much all agree on.

"What? What's this?"

Claude said he threw open the door from the kitchen into the garage.

"Why, I'll show you how it feels to be pushed around by somebody bigger and stronger than you are."

Sam recalled Claude charging into him so hard that he hit against the wall. For the next ten minutes, Sam said Claude threw him around the garage, from the walls to the cars to the walls again.

"I've never been so afraid."

Pete and Ginger cowered behind the kitchen door, crying.

"At the time, I thought he was going to kill Sam," Pete said, "but now I can see it was tough love."

Sam said his dad told him, "You've outgrown my belt. From here on out, you'll feel my fists."

Claude remembered teaching Sam a lesson; he didn't remember it being so severe or frightening. It was "just discipline."

For Ginger, the lesson was complex, as she told me after I returned to Alabama. She saw what lengths her father would go to as her protector, but that wasn't all she saw. She vowed never to be on the receiving end of his anger. Claude didn't have to get physical with her. Drilling her with his cold eyes was enough.

Someone had described Claude to me as a shell of a man, hollow and without feelings. I found him boastful of his misdeeds while swaddled in self-righteousness, but full of feelings, a veritable bundle of nerve endings, all encased in cement.

When Claude finally relinquished the conversation to Helen, she showed me drawers and drawers filled with fine needlework she had sewn. I examined several pieces, turning them to the back side. Just as Ginger had told me, the back looked as neat as the front.

"Do it right or do it over," Helen said.

Seldom did the children disobey or sneak around rules. But there were times.

A big pasture with tall oak trees bordered their subdivision, and Ginger and two sixth-grade girl friends discovered a secret hideaway under the trees. The mother of one friend smoked. She never missed the unfiltered Lucky Strikes the girls puffed on after school. One day, they slipped into a vacant house and smeared a wall with black cigarette marks.

They swore each other to secrecy, but the crime burned a hole in Ginger's heart. Eventually her guilt burst out in big sobs as she confessed to her mother, who made her tell her father. He didn't punish her. The homeowner assured her parents that the marks had washed off, but Ginger didn't know. She wanted so desperately to be forgiven of this horrible crime, to have it wiped off her slate. The event led to her baptism.

Baptism in the Church of Christ is by immersion, a symbolic washing away of sin and a prerequisite for becoming a member of the Lord's body, the church.

Ginger began to think of herself as the good Ginger and the bad Ginger. The good Ginger atoned for the cigarette sin, but the bad Ginger couldn't ask for forgiveness.

Summer sizzles in the nineties, even beyond a hundred degrees, in south Texas, and Ginger, like many children, cooled off in the spray of a garden hose, running through its stream, holding the nozzle against her body to feel the water's pressure. Something about the water tingled. She aimed the nozzle straight up so the water rained down on her. She held the nozzle against her again. She moved it until she found the tingle. And she held it there, between her legs. All that week, she returned to the tingle until the tingles multiplied into her first orgasm.

"I was totally addicted. From then on, it was everyday, in the yard, in the bathtub, vary the water pressure, and vary the temperature. A severe lack of self-esteem encourages masturbation; it produces endorphins, which feel good. And I learned to feel good."

But she also felt wrenching guilt.

"I was on the path to hell because it felt good, and it was *down there*. It was sex and what I knew about sex was from the Bible: carnal knowledge and people being struck dead from lust. My periods didn't start until I was fourteen-years-old, so I thought I had broken something. There was nobody to ask. Who could I tell what I had been doing? I didn't learn until after the birth of my second baby that I hadn't damaged myself."

The summer of Ginger's twelfth birthday, the family went camping near the beach. One night when her brothers were playing ball, her father said, "Since the boys aren't here, Ginger, you come on. Let's gig some flounder."

They waded out into the bay with a lantern, a stringer, and flounder gigs—three-pronged sticks they'd thrust into any fish they spotted. Ginger looked across a gold carpet atop the water to a yellow moon. She heard the soft slap of waves against the beach. Her father looked around from time to time, but all Ginger could see was water. She felt it rising against her chest and knew the tide was coming in. *How's Daddy going to get us back to shore, back where we began?*

"Daddy, do you know where we are?"

"Don't worry. I know."

Daddy'll protect me. She walked beside her father. *No matter what else, he'll always keep me safe.*

She lifted one foot—ummmmph! She felt a hard push from behind. She fell, swallowing salt water as her head went under. Then there was another push to her side. She flailed her arms, fighting to bring her feet underneath her, to regain her footing.

She stood up, sputtering and spitting sea water. *Daddy shoved me. He made me fall.*

"Stand back. Stand back. Give me room."

Her father pulled the gig out of the water. The biggest flounder she had ever seen struggled against its prongs.

"Whooo boy, lookie here, he's the king," her father said. "You nearly stepped on him, Ginger."

"I didn't see him, Daddy. Man, he *is* a prize." *That's why he shoved me, to catch the big fish.*

"And we caught him."

We? Of course we did.

They hurried back to the camp site to show off their catch. Ginger skipped alongside her dad, a smile all over her face. *We caught it. Dad and me. That's worth being dunked.*

Gigging that flounder is one of the fondest memories Ginger has of her father. For once, she had him all to herself. And she felt safe in his company.

Daddy as protector overrode the shoving. It was the abiding feeling. It was the feeling she would fall back on the next time she was shoved.

Ordinarily, puberty and the early teen years herald the beginnings of independence. Parental controls fall away as teens, like nestlings, flap their wings and take a few spills before they fly away.

Not so for Ginger or her siblings. According to Sam, they could eat, sleep, and breathe, anything else was a sin. Like mud, sin clung to their wings.

"For me, those years were miserable, miserable, miserable. You couldn't draw my dead body through them again," Ginger said.

They weren't allowed to participate in after-school activities. No social clubs. No cheerleading. No baton twirling. Very few movies. No dancing, even at school, even at the prom. A boy invited Ginger to the victory dance following a football game, and she had to tell him no. Word spread. After that, no one bothered to ask her.

No genuflecting, even as part of a theatrical production. In the tenth grade, Ginger won the part of a nun in *The Sound of Music*. The play went into rehearsal, and the nuns were told when to genuflect. Ginger followed the instructions, until her parents learned about it.

"You're Church of Christ!" her father yelled. "You're not Catholic, you don't worship idols, and you won't pretend you do on stage at the high school or anywhere else. That's it."

He forced her to give up the part.

Consternation resulted with Ginger at its center, humiliated at the unwanted attention. All the parts had already been assigned, the students had memorized their lines, and no one wanted to swap roles. The play went on short one nun and with Ginger standing in the wings.

No mini-skirts was another rule.

"Stand straight, arms by your sides, fingers extended. If our skirts were shorter than our fingertips, we didn't leave the house. It was the Sixties, and we dressed like old ladies," Ginger recalls.

Bell bottom pants passed muster, but not long hair for Ginger's brothers.

"If your hair so much as touches your ears," Claude said to Sam, "you'll wear ruffles on your underwear."

Ginger and her mother shopped for a bathing suit so she could teach swimming in a private backyard pool. She fingered through the racks. Nothing but bikinis. Even if the Queen of England wore a bikini, she knew better than to covet one.

"They may as well be naked," Helen said. "Don't you have anything else? No one-piece suits?"

"One piece? Oh, Mom, nobody wears a one-piece anymore," Ginger said.

They tried another store and found a one-piece suit with a ruffled skirt. *Something for Granny.*

"No, it's not youthful," Helen said.

Ginger sighed with relief. *Mom's trying.*

The third store was the last ladies clothing store in Baycross and its most upscale. They found a two-piece Bali suit, expensive but cute enough to please Ginger and decorous enough to satisfy Helen. After all, it was intended for a backyard, not the town square. The top cost $50, which Ginger paid with babysitting money. Her mother chipped in for the bottom.

That night after supper, Helen said, "Go put on your bathing suit. Let your dad see what we bought."

"Mom…I don't want to put on a bathing suit." Ginger tried to plead with her eyes.

"Go ahead. Do it." Helen motioned her toward her bedroom.

"Your dad needs to approve. Go, go on."

Claude sat in his recliner, reading his paper. He hadn't even looked during their exchange.

Ginger slunk back to her room. She took as long as she dared pulling on the suit, hoping an earthquake, a UFO sighting, something would spare her this ordeal. With the suit on, she padded with bare feet down the hall and leaned into the den.

"Oh, here you are," Helen said. "Come on, Claude, look at Ginger's new bathing suit."

Ginger took a deep breath and a few steps into the room. She felt totally naked.

Claude folded down one corner of the newspaper and stared at Ginger. His nose curled as he looked her up and down.

"You call that conservative?"

He snapped the newspaper. It blocked Ginger from his view, and him from Ginger, a barrier as weightless as a feather and as impenetrable as a wall of steel.

"But Claude," Helen said. "It was the most...."

Her voice trailed off in his silence.

Ginger wore the bathing suit that summer. Among her age group, she felt conspicuously covered up. Deep in her heart she burned with guilt and shame. Whatever Claude intended, his disapproval left an indelible mark. Ginger has never since owned a two-piece suit or even considered a bikini.

A little Christian girl. Ginger heard these words from her father again and again like a mantra, whether it was the sock hop in the school gym or the prom or whatever else her classmates were doing: "What other children do doesn't matter. You're different. You're a Christian girl."

And so alone.

"My picture of the Heavenly Father was drafted by my father. He intimidated us as children, but I didn't see him as abusive. He instructed us that we should never cause shame on the name of the Lord. That extended to the whole church community. We couldn't be just good, we must be above reproach. I transferred his rigidity to God."

Whatever the church sanctioned, and only what it sanctioned, was allowed.

It sanctioned marriage as one man and one woman, united forever. Claude told Helen he'd kill her if she ever left him. She smiled when he repeated his vow. She wasn't going anywhere. She was as committed to marriage as he was.

Divorce might be allowed under very narrow circumstances, but remarriage was absolutely forbidden.

The church centered on reading and interpreting the Bible. The minister preached every sermon above an undercurrent of pages riffling as his congregation looked up each scriptural reference he cited. At Bible study, a man, never a woman, clothed in sincerity and tradition, if not academic training, selected two or three verses to dissect word by word. The people read the words for themselves, but the leaders told them what they meant.

No one ever raised questions. Who could question the Bible?

If women had questions, they were to ask their husbands.

Encouraged to seek her friends at church, that's where Ginger found her first love, and she tumbled head over heels. She was fourteen and he was seventeen, and they kissed and petted. He broke her heart by breaking up with her on her birthday at a baseball game at the Astrodome. But she'd had her first taste of passion and other boyfriends followed.

They could go on dates to church or out to eat and then back to the living room at Ginger's house, which to her surprise was quite private, even with the door cracked.

"I never let them get near anything that mattered. I tried to be chaste, and I was, but I was so afraid, so emotionally needy."

What started as a close friendship with Bruce, a tall, gangly boy at church, erupted into abiding love, but only on Ginger's part. For her, church revolved around him. They met there, sat together through services, and confided in each other for two years, but never dated.

"Right now, we need to be friends, nothing more," he said. "We've got all the time in the world for love when we get older."

Two days after his car crashed into a telephone pole, he died in a Houston hospital. Ginger tried to donate blood, but the hospital turned her away because of her age.

For Ginger, the support was pulled out of her world, and she was in free fall. All his cards, the notes they passed during church, every reminder of him, she placed in a box and tied it with a ribbon for safekeeping.

At school, a body occupied her chair.

At home, she drifted through her chores, grieving all the while.

Several weeks passed, and she remained despondent. One afternoon, she lay across her bed, crying. Her father burst in, the first time she remembered him ever coming into her room. He snatched up the photograph of Bruce on the sewing machine, opened a drawer and slammed the picture face down inside, then closed the drawer.

"That's enough. I don't want to hear anymore," he said, and left.

~~~~~~

The Superdome in New Orleans opened in April 1975, with the Purple Pride high school choir of Baycross, including Ginger Mitchell as alto, singing the national anthem. Later that year, her senior year, Ginger was asked to list her school honors and activities for the yearbook. Some of her classmates wrote nearly a page.

Choir. One word. That was all she had to show for four years of high school.

The school posted the class rankings on a bulletin board outside the principal's office. Ginger heard a crowd of students oohing and teasing when they found their own and their friends' names. She pretended to look at a trophy case until they'd all left. Then she scrolled down the list of the top ten percent and was shocked to see her name

I made As, but I didn't know…does this mean I'm smart?

~~~~~~

"I didn't chart my own course. I always sought the validation and consent of others," Ginger had told me while studying pages in her old yearbook. "I remember being struck with the tragedy of the waste, with what I might have done, had things been different, had the church not frowned on so many activities, had my parents not forbidden them."

What about her siblings? What was their childhood like?

"I don't remember much about my childhood," Pete told me in 2006. "You forget things that are painful."

Nevertheless, the way he was raised made him more severe with his boys.

"Right or not, it was very effective."

Mileah takes a somewhat different view.

"We had a good childhood. Our parents loved us. They were stricter than our church friends' parents, but it taught us resilience. It gave us personal strength."

She pushed a coffee cup around a black laminated table at the Busy Bee Café in Calvin, Texas, less than an hour from Baycross. Rick, her husband, leaned back in the chair opposite her. His crutches rested on the vinyl seat of a nearby booth. He shifted positions again, tugged at his pants leg, trying to find a comfortable place for his recently amputated leg. Mileah hadn't told her parents about the amputation. It hadn't occurred to either of them that this was the kind of information families usually share.

"My life began when I got married," Mileah said. "That's when I found my voice. The years up to that were building my foundation. That's the way it should be."

Ginger shakes her head.

"I wasn't given freedom of space to develop. I felt like a Chinese girl with my feet bound."

chapter three

In the fall of 1976, following high school graduation in June and an eighteenth birthday in July, Sam invited Ginger to tag along to a stock car race in Pearland, just outside Houston.

"Stock cars?" she said. "Thanks, but no thanks."

That is, until Sam's friend Turner showed up.

Turner was twenty-two with a mischievous face under lacquered reddish-blonde hair, and a boyish build that belied his strength. He stood several inches taller than Ginger. She knew who he was and that he raced cars, but she hadn't paid him any attention before. Something clicked this night, and she hopped into the front seat of his car headed for the races.

He didn't ask if her shoes were clean. She later learned that everyone else who rode with Turner knew to kick off their shoes, that he tolerated no dirt in his cream-colored Cutlass Supreme with the Armor All-ed black vinyl top.

Ginger talked about Son of Sam, the serial killer up in New York, and the Viking probes landing on Mars, and stories on the news. Turner, who was known to be taciturn at times, was downright lively in his response.

"You're fun to be with," he said. "You put me at ease."

He asked her out the next night.

"I have a reputation," he said.

A lock of hair fell over his forehead as he sat slumped in a chair in Ginger's living room on their second date. He gave her a sideways grin.

"I confess. In school I studied hard and made good grades. Now I work hard and make good money, and on the weekends, I party just as hard. I mean really hard drinking and racing cars."

Ginger knew his reputation, as did her parents. She and Turner began to date, but strictly within the rules, going out to eat and then back to Ginger's house or his house. No partying.

Turner lived with his parents, good, ordinary people, who had adopted him at age five. He worked for his father's auto parts business and, with his aptitude for math and mechanics, earned upward of $30,000 a year.

After dating just over a month, he and Ginger drove up to Lake Livingston one evening and parked on a knoll by the water. The smell of rain rode a cool breeze and the moon pushed apart dark clouds. Turner leaned his head against the door on the passenger's side, his legs stretched across the floorboard toward the accelerator, his left arm around Ginger. She rested her head on his shoulder while he told her about himself.

"Mom and Dad think I don't remember before they adopted me, but I'll never forget...all that. Being poor. And, write this down, I'll never be cold or hungry again. I'm not afraid of hard work. I'm going to be somebody.

"I don't take anything off anybody," he said. "I can take care of myself and anything that belongs to me. Anybody who wrongs me better watch out."

"What would you do?" Ginger asked. She snuggled against him.

"Get even. Without that person ever knowing what happened."

She sat up to face him.

"It's easy to put a spoonful of sugar in someone's gas tank. It caramelizes in the pistons and locks up the motor. There's no way to get it out and no way to know how it happened."

He didn't tell her he organized his sock drawer, or that his pocketed knit shirts had to be folded exactly in half, sleeves tucked in, just as they came from the box.

He called Ginger his angel on a pedestal and that's what she heard above all the rest.

Finally, he took Ginger's chin in his hand.

"I want to grow old with you."

"Is that a proposal? Are you asking me to marry you?"

At eighteen, Ginger held no thoughts of growing old. She saw in Turner a hard worker and good provider, a stable man who would protect her—just like her father—and someone who adored her. Someone totally smitten with her.

She said yes. They decided on a date in January two months ahead.

When Mileah, Ginger's older sister, married at nineteen, Claude hesitated to give his consent, muttering some fatherly notions about not realizing his little girl had grown up. But he and Helen jumped into Ginger's wedding preparations, despite Turner's wild reputation. Claude still talked about sowing his oats as a young man, so he could overlook the partying.

"Mom and Dad were eager to marry me off," Ginger said. "To them, I was sprinting toward promiscuity and marriage would end that worry."

Helen had basis for her concern.

Ginger had lost her virginity the previous summer in a whirlwind beach romance. Back home the next week, she hurried to the bathroom to urinate, time and again, but a painful hot clamp shut off the flow before relief came.

Soon drops of red blood tinted the water in the toilet bowl. She had cystitis, or the "honeymooner's disease," a common inflammation of the bladder, sometimes associated with sex. She'd never heard of cystitis, but she had heard all about the wages of sin. Hurting, bleeding, and frightened about her body and soul, she sat on the toilet and sobbed.

Her mother heard her crying and entered the bathroom. The nurse sized up the trouble within seconds.

"You haven't been doing things you shouldn't, have you?"

Ginger's marriage answered Helen's prayers.

She got a big hug from her father, the first time he'd ever hugged her, on the day he gave her away to another man.

The newlyweds bumped through the first year getting acquainted. Then the marriage peaked and plummeted like a roller coaster.

They honeymooned at the Houston Zoo, a portentous outing. Dinner followed at the Steak and Ale restaurant where rice sprinkled from Ginger's hair onto the red carpet. She drank a margarita, her first mixed drink, and fell asleep in the car on the way home. The next day, they drove to a lake to spend three days in a camper, despite the drop in temperature to fourteen degrees.

Later they argued over groceries.

"We have $6,000 in a checking account, and you're pitching a fit over a pound of hamburger meat," Ginger said.

She shopped for groceries with checks Turner wrote for each shopping occasion. They held a joint bank account and she worked as a secretary for an accounting firm, but Turner marshaled the checkbook. Her mother had paid the household bills. Ginger assumed this would be her duty, but Turner said no.

Doesn't he know I can add and subtract?

She made the grocery list, and he approved it.

He liked Charmin toilet paper, and she'd better not buy another brand.

"Hand me the list," he'd say when she returned with the grocery bags. As she put the groceries away, he checked off the list.

"One can of tuna. You bought two cans."

He held out the list to show her.

"There was a special. The second can was half price."

"But the list called for one. One can. Not two," he yelled, slamming his hand against the tabletop. "You can't be trusted with money."

What does Turner want? Does he think I'm incapable, unreliable, dumb?

Each slight, innuendo, or accusation poured Miracle-Gro onto the resentment welling up inside her and ate like acid at her self-confidence.

Nell, Ginger's high school friend and a newlywed, observed that nothing Ginger did seemed to be right or enough with Turner. One day, she washed his car to surprise him. He berated her for not vacuuming it too.

"Ginger didn't say much." Nell said. "We'd do girl things together, fun things, hide-away-the-tears things."

Turner worked on cars and each tool he used had its own separate storage spot. Ginger spent hours sitting on the edge of a car's hood holding a drop light, learning about cams, pistons, rings, transmission, and u-joints, or fetching a certain lug nut from the bottom drawer, fourth row—or a shallow socket wrench from the second cabinet on the right. When he finished with the tools, he wiped each one clean, slowly and meticulously, no matter if dinner was growing cold on the table, perhaps especially if dinner was growing cold, or it was hours past bedtime.

During their brief courtship, Turner acted warm and loving. He shared his most intimate hopes and dreams and listened while Ginger spilled her heart to him. But he discarded these traits like yesterday's newspaper when he stood before the altar. For periods of four to six weeks, he might not speak to Ginger or acknowledge her presence. She couldn't understand what she did to cause these cold spells.

Or, the old dating-days-Turner might rise with the sun one morning, and they'd laugh and play together. By nightfall, he'd be gone. Ginger couldn't fathom what brought out the old persona or what drove it away.

Turner owned a boat, and they water skied. But they didn't party. No drinking, no dancing, none of the things that had earned Turner his reputation.

"I don't feel the need any longer," Turner said when Ginger pleaded with him to go dancing. "You're the turning point in my life. You're all I want."

They began Bible classes.

"Turner, I can already recite the Sermon on the Mount and the names of the twelve disciples," she teased. "You want to hear the twelve tribes of Israel?"

She aimed the hand mixer at a stick of butter in the mixing bowl on the kitchen counter. Turner sat at the kitchen table, flipping through the newspaper.

"Reuben, Levi, Judah."

She began to tap her foot and lift her shoulders in a little dance while the mixer bumped against the butter.

"Ben-ja-min, Zeb-u-lon, Jo-seph—"

"Ginger!"

Play period over, Ginger switched off the mixer.

"Please, Turner, let's—"

"I'm just your vehicle to escape home," Turner said. "I'm the bad boy who did all the things you want to do, and you resent that I quit doing them."

"I don't want to be bad. I want to be normal," Ginger said. "I'm eighteen and life is dry crackers."

They separated.

Whatever her reasons for marrying Turner, she had walked down the aisle into a cage locked as tight as those at the Houston Zoo, the first stop on their honeymoon.

The church said marriage was forever, one man, one woman; so they reconciled. They had to reconcile. Ginger couldn't go home, not even for consolation.

"Once you leave home, you're gone," her dad said over and over. "You can't come back here." He later said he didn't mean it, but all the children understood that he meant it. They still think he meant it.

Her mother couldn't understand why she was unhappy.

"Does he mistreat you? Does he hurt you? He bought you a new car. Don't you appreciate how good he is to you?"

Guilt flooded the resentment.

What is so wrong with me? Why do I toss one way and then the other in my mind? Why can't I find satisfaction?

She vowed to try harder. She saw no other choice.

They coasted along happily enough for Ginger to become pregnant during their third year.

When Ginger suspected she might be pregnant, she chose to be tested at the clinic where her mother worked. Helen and Claude had no grandchildren. This baby, if Ginger were pregnant, would be their first. Ginger imagined how excited they'd be.

Her mother gave her the news when she returned for the results several days later.

"The test was positive," Helen said. "You're pregnant. But don't tell anybody because you'll probably lose it."

Ginger dashed away.

Turner jumped and shouted, ecstatic at the prospect of being a father, as did his parents when they learned they'd be grandparents.

Weeks later, Ginger popped in on her mother at home. Helen sat on the couch in the den crocheting a baby blanket.

Ginger reached out to admire the blanket.

"Are you making this for me?"

Her mother pulled it back.

"Lots of people have babies."

Ginger felt her face flush. She made some excuse for her visit and went on her way.

A month passed.

Mileah parked her car against the curb at Ginger's house. Ginger watched from her window as Mileah gathered something from the passenger seat and tucked it into one arm.

The baby blanket.

She recognized it from across the yard.

That's strange. I wonder why Mileah is bringing the blanket to me.

She stepped outside to greet her.

Mileah smiled.

"Meet your new nephew."

She held out a baby to Ginger, a little boy swaddled in the blanket her mother had crocheted.

Ginger reeled in disbelief.

Mileah and her husband had adopted a baby, a plan they'd kept secret from everyone except her parents. Their baby was the first grandchild, not the baby in Ginger's womb.

In retrospect, Ginger understood. Her mother knew Mileah's baby would arrive before Ginger's, and she didn't want Ginger to steal Mileah's thunder. But understanding didn't ease the pain of her mother's callous words or being excluded from her sister's confidence.

Jubilant over their first grandchild, her parents lavished time and gifts upon him, all the while paying no attention to Ginger's protruding belly.

Fortunately, Turner and his parents' exuberance offset her family's indifference. Turner's mother shopped with her for maternity clothes at a new store called Wal-Mart. She and Turner grew close studying baby books, going to Lamaze classes, and making preparations.

On September 10, 1980, Ginger gave birth to a baby boy they named Trenton.

Trent was the new star in the sky for everyone in the family including Helen and Claude, who transferred their devotion to the new baby.

Despite their intentions, the new family got off to a rough first few months. Trent didn't take to nursing well. Each feeding took hours, exhausting and frustrating mom and dad, who got little sleep, and baby, who cried too often. Ginger held him to her, kissing his head, his fingers, his toes. Sometimes he cooed and smiled, but often he cried. She didn't know what more to do.

Grandparents rushed to assist.

Helen fretted that Trent wasn't getting enough to eat.

"You shouldn't breast feed—that baby's hungry. . . . Is something wrong with your breast milk? Do you think Trent is allergic to it?"

Her questions heaped doubts atop the usual insecurity a new mother feels with her first baby.

There's something wrong with the milk my body is producing? Am I starving my baby?

Helen often watched Trent while Ginger did her errands, seizing the opportunity to feed him cereal, beef, and lamb—samplings of the grocery store's baby food shelf—something she neglected to tell Ginger.

All the while, Ginger worried that he refused to nurse, not suspecting his tummy was full. How could he be gaining weight?

Eventually she conceded. She couldn't breastfeed her baby. Mothers from Eve forward had breastfed their babies, but Ginger couldn't do for her son what came so naturally to others. She failed at the most basic function of motherhood, not for lack of will or effort, but because of something outside her control.

Her mother, the nurse, bound Ginger's breasts with a diaper for four days to make her milk go away.

Bobbie, Turner's mother and Trent's other grandmother, possessed the magic touch. If Trent were crying, no matter how hard Ginger tried to rock, pat, or comfort him, he calmed the minute Bobbie picked him up.

Bobbie and Turner's father hovered over Trent. They visited, took him for outings, even kept him for two or three days at a time. Trent gurgled when they arrived and cried when they left.

～～～～～～～～～～～～～～～～～～～～～～～～～～～～～～～～

"Trent came first for both of us," Turner told me. We sat at a linen-covered banquet table in an empty meeting room at the Holiday Inn in Baycross in April 2006. A pile of used cloth napkins lay on the table beside a dozen salt and pepper shakers. Turner was still the man/boy, even at fifty. Very little gray in his sandy hair. A disarming grin. But he was fully serious and tearful when he talked about Trent.

"Ginger was a good mother. He was the sole focus of her attention."

～～～～～～～～～～～～～～～～～～～～～～～～～～～～～～～～

A good mother in Turner's eyes, but not in her own.

I wanted this baby. I want to be a mother, but I have to learn how.

She had set out with confidence propped up on book learning, and she deflated liked a popped balloon when Trent didn't respond like the babies in the books.

As she had done in the past when she felt someone else could do a task better than she could, she handed over the reins. Bobbie and Helen could visit, entertain, feed their grandchild, her baby, as often as they liked. Ginger looked on from the sidelines, loving, willing, eager, while they chipped away at her confidence until it was gone.

The emptiness within her grew, and she wondered if infancy would ever end. Her mind drifted into a harrowing place where she stood over a deep hole until she began to sink.

Long black days crawled one after the other, days when her ears buzzed and her skin stung, and she could see no way out of the quagmire she'd made for herself.

She phoned JoAnn, a childhood friend. Once very close, they'd grown apart when Ginger married and JoAnn went away to college. JoAnn recognized the anguish in her friend's voice. She hurried to Ginger's side and sat with her all day in the bathroom, beside a tub of water and a box of single-edged razor blades.

She came every time Ginger called.

~~~~~~

Ginger's parents found out how mired she was in depression. Her father's response?

"How could she heap sin upon sin? God won't forgive a suicide. She knows that."

She sought out the minister who married them but found no help there.

The marriage, in the meantime, still rode the roller coaster up and down. Neither Turner nor Ginger changed when Trent arrived. They were just sleepier and more on edge. Turner still charted every penny Ginger spent and every step she took, and she paced her confines like a caged animal.

The day before Ginger's twenty-third birthday, Turner's parents swooped by unannounced. They were off on a two-day trip and wanted to take eleven-month-old Trent along. Ginger and Turner would have two days to themselves. She wanted to celebrate her birthday by going to a club and listening to its music.

Turner declined. He had something else he planned to do, something that didn't include Ginger.

Anger is a high-octane fuel. If her husband wouldn't accompany her to the club, then, by golly, she'd go alone.

She wore jeans and a ruffled shirt, sat by herself in a leatherette booth, and ordered a large Coke. When her eyes adjusted to the smoke and dim lights, she glanced about, hoping not to see anyone she knew.

She didn't.

The club was much as she imagined, much like the ones she'd seen in movies on television: lots of mirrors and shine, a row of banquettes at the rear, where she sat, the remainder of the room filled with small circular tables, two or three black chairs at each, all under a dark canopy that sparkled with shimmering silver lights. Down one side of the room stretched a bar with round stools. A few women, mostly men, leaned over the tables. More men sat with their elbows on the bar, heads down, cigarettes in their hands. Glamorous. Sophisticated. Ginger smiled, pleased with herself for coming. The band began to play, and she drifted into the music.

A waitress flashed by her table and plopped down a tall icy glass.

"Courtesy of that man at the corner table."

Ginger pushed the drink away. She didn't dare look toward the corner.

She declined the next drink offer as well. Sometime later, the waitress handed Ginger a torn sheet of paper.

"Somebody's passing you a note. I'll wait if you want to answer."

Ginger read the note. Someone asked her to join him at the bar. His name had a familiar ring, a Czech name that she recognized from her mother's hometown.

The waitress said, "Hey, all you got to do is nod yes or no."

Ginger popped up and marched over to the bar to the man with the Cheshire cat grin.

"You looking for company?"

"Looking for your company, baby."

He stood and twisted a bar stool toward her.

"I don't think so."

She called him by name.

"Please give my regards to Arlene, Patty, and the twins," she said, referring to his wife and three children.

The grin dropped off the man's face. He wheeled the bar stool away.

"Well, excuse me, Miss. Just trying to be neighborly. Looks like I picked the wrong bar tramp."

Ginger flushed and hurried back to her table. She burrowed into its high cushions, sensing people staring at her, overhearing some crude remarks. She was angry at Turner, angry at this brazen man, and angry at herself. Tears welled in her eyes, and she pulled the last of the Coke through her straw.

The band took its break, and she signaled the waitress for her bill so she could leave.

"I saw you fending away the wolves. You really came for the music, didn't you?" said a tall man with a smile that broke across his face like Robert Redford's. It was the lead singer with the band.

"May I sit with you while I drink my Coke?"

She ordered another Coke, and another, as he returned to her table at each break. They talked until the lights came on and everyone left to go home. Trent was with his grandparents; she didn't need to hurry back to him. Even if Turner had come home, he'd be in his own world. Lonely and depressed, she left with the singer.

This man wasn't the first, or the last, Ginger would seek solace with before she and Turner divorced.

Two years before Trent was born, Turner had traveled on business for three weeks, but he had been away behind his wall for even longer. During his absence, Ginger served on jury duty, and she found comfort in the arms of another juror. The trial ended, as did the affair, before Turner returned home. Ginger stood penitent in the front yard as Turner unloaded his car. She confessed with big sobs and begged his forgiveness. Too upset to eat, her guilt had cost her twelve pounds in two weeks.

~~~~~~

Turner felt a punch to the solar plexus. How could his angel fall to this? He felt sick. Anger flashed and then ebbed into a flood of tears, both of them crying and vowing eternal love and forgiveness. He tucked the raw edges of his pain in the secret place behind his wall and locked Ginger out.

~~~~~~

Intimacy was what Ginger craved, and her husband denied her that. He was a provider and protector, like her father and, like her father, distant and unaffectionate. When she'd felt lonely and unloved as a child, she'd learned to compensate.

The next time she cheated, and the next, Turner pondered why she confessed to him. Was it her honesty? Did she want to hurt him? Or did she want out of the marriage? He wasn't going to kick her out or let her go. She belonged to him.

He couldn't see what Ginger needed or her unhappiness. All he wanted was to return to the status quo.

"I was blind," he realized later.

"I was a mess," Ginger said. "I was divided, torn between two equidistant prongs, one very strong and the other weak. I was trying to reconcile both sides of me: the one that tried to be so good, the little mother, the little church-goer, and then the side that longed for what had always been labeled bad things—which really weren't so bad. I had to meld, I had to pull myself together, and I couldn't do it.

"Looking back, if Turner could have just said: 'Young as she is, my wife's never been to a prom. By golly, we're going to dress up and go dancing. Or my wife's never been to a club. She wants to see what happens there, and I'm going to take her.'

"If he could have said these things, if he could have understood, we'd still be together today. The commitment I made to Turner I meant.

"I wasn't running away from motherhood. I wanted to be a mother to Trent, but I failed."

They sought out psychologists twice, each time men who were Church of Christ members. The second one told Turner to take back Ginger's credit cards and kiss her goodbye.

Eventually, the roller coaster crashed.

"Why don't you just get your shit together and get out?" Turner shouted.

He jerked the steering wheel of his car around a curve.

"I'm two steps ahead of you," Ginger said. "My things are nearly packed now."

She found an apartment behind Kroger's and a job waiting tables at the Barbecue Shack.

Trent was on vacation with Turner's parents when Ginger moved out, and he remained with his father at first when they got back. Ginger knew Turner's mother would give Trent the most loving care a mother could want, far better than she herself could give.

Soon she and Turner began to alternate weeks keeping Trent. One Friday when Turner was to return him to Ginger, he phoned.

"Mom and Dad want to take Trent to the fair tonight. They'll bring him to you tomorrow. Okay?"

"Sure."

The next morning she answered the knock on her door, arms extended, expecting her little boy to wrap his arms around her neck. Instead, a deputy sheriff handed her a peace warrant. Turner had sworn that Trent might fall to harm in Ginger's care. She was forbidden to go near her son until some future date when a judge would hold a hearing.

~~~~~~

Ginger acknowledges her responsibility. She was twenty-three going on twelve.

"I was in full-blown rebellion, a delayed teenager, and Trent was a casualty of it, a huge casualty.

"There's sorrow, huge, huge sorrow, oceans of sorrow, but what can I do? It's over, said, and done."

~~~~~~

Dancing, of course, had been forbidden as Ginger grew up. When new friends introduced her to kikk dancing, two-stepping in a clockwise circle around a big dance floor, she took to it like a convert at a revival. She earned enough money waiting tables and cleaning up construction sites to buy kikker clothes: a pair of beige Dan Post boots with wood grained heels to go with her high-waisted Jordache jeans. She'd known kikkers in high school. They were the Future Farmers of America, the country kids who listened to radio station KIKK, not the "in" crowd at high school. That didn't matter, as Ginger had never been "in" herself. After work, she met groups of friends or families with children at the Armadillo, a large dance hall.

Kikk dancing was something to do as a group. It didn't require a partner, but someone could find a partner there, if they were so inclined.

Being on her own was exciting, for nearly six weeks. Then the lights came on, and she could see the dance floor at the end of the dance, the smashed paper cups, dirty footprints, and cigarette ashes. She remembered the first club where she met the singer and how it looked when the lights came up, the exposed ductwork and pipes overhead, initials carved into tables, the floor wet where drinks sloshed over, cigarette butts swimming in beer, the club's glamour gone with the flick of a light switch.

The glitter was just glitter.

She was struggling, living hand-to-mouth on tips and less than minimum wage, and she felt so alone in her apartment. Empty, forlorn, and heartsick. She missed Trent terribly, but she couldn't see him. She wasn't welcome at Turner's house, or at his parents or hers.

"An alley cat's a better mother than you. Trent does very well without you," her mother told her.

Ginger echoed what she heard from others until she believed it herself. *I'm not a good mother. I'm bad for him, a bad mother. He's better off without me.*

She couldn't return to the marriage. She didn't want to. But nothing satisfied her, and everything was so messed up.

Misery lashed at her until she had to escape its sting. Returning to the glitter was the only way she knew.

~~~~~~

"Ginger needed someone to put their arms around her, even if it was just for a little while," Mileah said.

"You may have outgrown this marriage like a pair of old shoes, but you won't take this child with you," Turner said. "I'll drag you through mud; I'll make your life public."

Ginger knew they weren't idle threats. He'd warned her the night he proposed, talking about what a spoonful of sugar would do to a gas tank.

They both wanted a divorce and they both wanted Trent.

I can't give up my baby, I'll learn to be a good mother. Please, please give me another chance.

"Every town has one lawyer who's meaner than all the rest, and that's the one I hired to represent me," Turner told me when we met at the Holiday Inn.

Ginger knew nothing about lawyers. She chose the one name in the phone book that she'd heard somewhere before. His office was a small brick building that faced the old courthouse. Her chair had no arms.

"Tell me what's on your mind," he said.

She did and answered every question he had.

"You say you wait tables down at the Barbecue Shack? That right? And you want a divorce from your husband and custody of your little boy?" He drawled his words with a deep baritone voice.

"Yes, sir."

He rocked back in his leather chair. "I can't take your case. My advice to you, little lady, is that you turn around and head home."

Ginger stammered. "I...what, I don't understand."

"Have you got $15,000?"

"No, sir." Ginger felt her face flush.

"I get $15,000 for a retainer fee, and that's where it starts. Fact of the matter is, you can't afford me, and you can't afford to take this case to court, even if you had the money."

"If it's not the money, then how do you mean I can't afford it?" Ginger asked.

He rolled back to the desk and put his elbows on its glass top.

"You might get your custody despite all your shenanigans. But do you really want to smear…stinky stuff…all over yourself, on your fine church-going family, have it drip down on your little boy? And even if that's what you want, honey, you can't pay the bill. Your husband can drag this out and he will. And the lawyers' meters will just tick right on up."

He stood up and put his hands in his pockets.

"Now you go on home and think about it."

Ginger had no breath. She couldn't speak. She left without closing the door behind her and ran to her car.

Hours later she knocked on the door of the house where she'd lived with Turner. Her eyes were red and swollen. When Turner answered the door, she asked for Trent's baby book.

"I just want it for a few minutes. I promise."

She waited on the stoop while Turner fetched the book, listening for sounds of Trent's voice. She didn't hear him. *He's probably with his grand-mother, laughing and playing.*

Turner's face looked puzzled when he handed her the baby book, but he said nothing.

Ginger sat in her car and turned the pages of the book while crying softly. She had done mental battle with the lawyer until she was exhausted. She didn't have $15,000. She didn't have $50.

She found a blank page and began to write:

> He's happy and little
> and fit as a fiddle.
> He runs and plays
> to fill up his days.

He finds it so easy
to spin till he's dizzy.
He comes to a stop
and then is off with a hop.
He picks out a toy
that shows he's a boy
and hunts for a place
with plenty of space.
His head isn't muddled.
He seldom gets troubled.
And I hope he'll know
however things go
he'll always be fine.
And he'll always
be mine.

Six weeks later Turner and his attorney made their case before the domestic case judge.

"Where's your wife? Where's the mother of the child?" the judge asked.

"She's not here, your honor," Turner said.

"Custody granted to the father. The mother will have visitation rights on occasional weekends and for two months each summer." The judge tapped his gavel.

~~~~~~

"I didn't ask for custody," Ginger said. "I didn't even go to court for the divorce. Turner called me the morning of our hearing and told me it was postponed to another day. He called back the next day and said he'd been mistaken, and the divorce was final. It didn't matter. I was spineless. There was nothing I could do anyway. I didn't even fight for my baby."

Ginger's parents disowned her.

"You're no longer welcome in our home."

They appeared before the elders of the church where she had worshipped all her life and asked that the church withdraw from her.

Withdrawal is a formal procedure within the Church of Christ. It's based on scripture that says the church should admonish a wrong-doer and, if the person persists, withdraws fellowship just as a gardener prunes a dead limb from a vine.

Ginger opened the door of her apartment to admit Joe, a longtime family friend and the father of JoAnn, her friend who'd spent the dark days with her by the bathtub.

"I know why you're here," she said. "I've been expecting someone from the church."

With his head bowed, Joe quoted scripture from the third chapter of 1st Timothy and added, "In the name of God and the church, heed this warning."

"I know what comes next," Ginger told him. "Do what you have to do."

The next Sunday night the church elders announced that fellowship had been withdrawn from Ginger. She was publicly denounced and severed from the body of the Lord as if she were a dead tree limb.

"Ginger was engaged in some things I couldn't encourage," Joe said in 2007, "like the cowboy scene and the dance hall scene. It was unfortunate. And it wasn't all her fault. Helen and Claude put a lot of demands on their children. I think they see now that things could have been different.

"The church had to withdraw from her. That's what the Bible says."

Cut off from her baby, her family, and her church, Ginger drifted in a sea of despair. She threw herself into her work.

One rainy day as she dashed from a building supply store juggling two sheets of plywood, a sandy-haired man with a mustache lifted the load from her arms and helped her out of the rain.

"I'm Mike McNeil," he said, when they got around to exchanging names.

chapter four

Waffle House, February 2006

S now flurries fell from a gray sky on that first Sunday afternoon at the Waffle House. Mike drank three cups of coffee to my one. Over time we would measure coffee by the gallons. There's no way could I have counted the cigarettes he smoked while he told me about his childhood.

"I grew up just six blocks from Ginger. Did you know that? Her father coached me in Little League. But we didn't know each other."

Six years separated them. Other differences mattered more.

All small towns have a railroad track, a river, a road, something to denote the right side of town. In Baycross, Northridge Drive marked the boundaries. Ginger lived within its confines, albeit at the tip end. Mike lived four blocks away, on the wrong side of Northridge.

Both their fathers were authoritarian, but Ginger's father quoted scripture. Mike's father taught his boys to steal pecans from the neighbors' trees, then he'd sell the pecans.

The McNeils lived in a two-bedroom tract house on a quarter-acre lot, with three boys and one girl, each two years apart. Mike, born in 1952, was the oldest but his younger brother, Roy, Jr., bore his father's name. Then came Carol and Lawson.

Roy McNeil, Mike's father, spoke with a speech impediment layered over a deep southern accent, which caused some people to underestimate his intelligence. He was smart but tenacious as a pit bull and mean as a snake. What was his, was his, and what he wanted, he took without regard for boundaries.

"Nobody stepped on his grass, not even his own kids," Mike said. "And to be sure the neighborhood kids didn't cut through his yard; he laced its hedges with barbed wire. Yet he'd take down someone else's fence if he wanted. We got chased off for trespassing more times than I can count.

"I watched him, every month, disconnect the power meter from the house and turn it upside down to make it run in reverse. When it showed we hadn't used much power, he'd reconnect it. He paid $2 a month for our power until he got caught. Then it cost him a $10,000 fine, and he almost landed in prison.

"I knew it was wrong. Even as a little kid, I knew it was wrong, and I didn't want to be like him. But I guess some of it rubbed off on me. If you lay down with dogs, you're going to get fleas."

Mike said he came from the "hard school of knocks." His father ruled and he got knocked on the floor—and knocked in the head. He doesn't hear with his left ear because of his father's blows. Sometimes Roy would punch Mike on the arm in one spot, over and over and over again until Mike's arm was so sore, he couldn't move it.

"I never saw him hit my mother," Mike said, "but I was so young, I don't know. I saw her crying sometimes. I had vibes."

One summer Roy decided to build ponds to grow minnows for bait in his back yard. He dug three ponds, each eight feet long by eight feet deep and the width of the lot, by hand with a shovel.

Mike's job at age twelve was to haul the dirt to spread in the front yard, one wheelbarrow after the next, all the hot summer long while the rest of the kids were out playing.

The heavy-duty chores always fell to Mike. Roy, Jr. had a congenital heart defect, so he was spared all things strenuous. Anger, resentment, and embarrassment, whatever Mike felt while slaving away all summer in sight of his carefree peers, he squashed away. Protesting would have been risky and fruitless.

Like Ginger's father, Roy worked at Dow, but his job was in dispatch, the low end of the pay scale. Rumor at Dow said he purloined enough goods from the company to build a house when he finally retired.

Thelma, Mike's mother, married down from a prominent family in Beaumont.

"Way down," Mike told Ginger when they were getting to know each other. "She wasn't the class end of the family."

Her family sent boxes of hand-me-downs. Mike remembers men's wing tip shoes with decorative holes punched in elegant patterns.

"Roy and I pretended they were trucks and played with them in the yard."

Mike told Ginger about visits to his Beaumont relatives.

"They lived in a mansion with curly scrollwork and a wide porch with poles on half a downtown block. Inside was plastered all over with Civil War uniforms and metal photographs, stacks of newspapers from the early 1900s, stamps from all over the world. I'll show it to you."

They set out by car to drive the hundred miles northeast to Beaumont.

"Twelve-foot ceilings, ten-foot windows," Mike said while he drove. "The dining table was twelve feet long. Lots of places to hide in that house."

He stood outside the house, shaking his head at gutters hanging loose and cracks in the brick. The doors and windows had been boarded over, but somebody had pulled the boards loose from a side door. He and Ginger squeezed through the opening into the empty room that had been the dining room. The odor of dust and mildew filled their nostrils. An old mattress lay on the floor in one corner, with a wad of blankets against the wall, all dirty, stained, and musty.

"My grandmother was fancy-schmancy, all about ethics and etiquette and which fork to use. I was the first grandchild. She dressed me up in lace collars and I had to sit straight at the dining table with dozens of forks and spoons beside each plate."

He scratched his chin, still dismayed at the deterioration of the house in the thirty years since he'd last seen it. "She'd turn over in her grave if she saw her house like this. Maybe it serves her right, I don't know. My granddaddy wasn't like her."

His grandfather would sit at the head of the table and hiccup and wink at him or stick his finger in his whiskery ears when Mike's grandmother wasn't looking. Later he'd turn Mike upside down and walk him like a wheelbarrow until they toppled on the grass laughing.

"When I was about three, I climbed up on my granddaddy's bed, one of those big antiques with posts. Thing sat so high off the floor it had little steps to climb."

"My granddaddy held out his arms and told me to jump. He said he'd catch me. And I jumped."

His grandfather stepped back and dropped his arms. Mike hit the floor with a splat.

At first, he didn't cry. Then a drop of red blood fell to the rug and his chin began to sting. He screwed up his face, the beginnings of a whimper, when his grandfather scooped him up and held him tight to his chest.

"Don't ever trust anybody all the way, boy. Let that be a lesson to you. Don't ever trust anybody all the way."

He never let Mike forget.

Despite the incident, they grew close. He took Mike to work with him at the cemetery where he directed burials and sold used cars and cemetery lots. Mike's job was to retrieve coins that had fallen between the car seats.

"My grandfather was my anchor," Mike told Ginger as they drove back to Baycross. "You could feel affection, concern, and love in his voice when he talked to you."

"Some people said he was an alcoholic, but I never saw it or smelled it. Maybe he was a recovering alcoholic, I don't know. But if he ever drank, she drove him to it."

He was nine when his grandfather died. He had been inside the funeral chapel before—it was across from where he played while his grandfather worked—but never with other people present, packed shoulder to shoulder. He stood over the coffin, looking down on his first dead person. His grandfather seemed to be asleep, but his chest didn't move, and he wasn't snoring. Mike touched his cheek and jerked back. His grandfather's face was cold wax.

Back at the big house after the service, cars lined up around the block. Mike's grandmother received family and guests, often introducing Mike.

"You don't know your cousins, but these are the people who send you clothes," she said.

Mike wanted no more. He vowed never to go to another funeral.

He found no excuses for Pawpaw, Roy's father, who lived in Vidor, Texas. Vidor had a reputation as a "sunset" town, a place that threatened to hang Blacks if they were caught there after dark.

"Pawpaw was hard-nosed and crude like my dad. I hated when he'd go fishing with us. He had the filthiest mouth, the most vulgar, repulsive train of thought, even for being out with the guys, and my dad would match him word for word. Thank goodness we didn't see him much."

Waffle House, March 2006

Mike left his cup in the car and went back in the rain to get it. Once he had his coffee, he went on with his story.

He said he learned why he received the brunt of his father's abuse when he was fifteen.

"I played ball for a coach named Reuben Welch. Mr. Welch was president of the baseball league, but he was a photographer at Dow and also a Missionary Baptist preacher.

"We didn't go to church. None of that Bible business at our house. We went fishing. But somehow his family and ours knew each other. And every now and then my mother'd go to his church.

"Mr. Welch took me under his wing. He knew what was happening at home, and he tried to protect me. He'd devise ways to get me out of the house to pass out circulars or do some other work for him. He leveled with me."

One Saturday, Mike cut the grass at church while Mr. Welch clipped the shrubbery. Afterward, they sat in the shade, drank cold water, and talked.

"Your mother was working when she got pregnant," Mr. Welch said. "Your dad's always suspected he's not your father. That's why he's so hard on you."

The words stung, but they fit. They offered some explanation for his father's hostility toward him, although he didn't believe for one minute there was any truth to it.

His mother wasn't made like him. She was hostage to cooking and cleaning, bound to her situation, and she knew she'd be there all her life.

One day Mike's father backhanded him around a few times, then hit him in the face with his fist. Mike knew he was hurt, so he sneaked off to Mr. Welch as soon as he could.

"What's the matter with you, boy?"

Mr. Welch was tacking notices on the bulletin board at the church.

"I need to see a doctor."

"Get in the car. Let's go."

He drove Mike straight to his doctor and paid for the treatment. Mike's jaw was badly bruised but not broken.

Soon after that, Mr. Welch finagled a way for Mike to go to church camp. One night, they were walking down a dirt road, and he put his arm around Mike.

"Mike, I don't want you to let anything your dad's said or done hide what I'm about to tell you. You've got a mind that can reason things out. And you've got more potential than any kid I know. Remember that."

Mike remembered.

He returned to school in the fall and tried out for the football team. That was the year the 4A Baycross High School freshman team scored its first undefeated season, with Mike starring at right end.

That was the year he ran away from home.

~~~~~~

"Going through school without getting in scrapes is tough for a boy," Mike told Ginger when they were dating. "Some kid elbowed me in the ribs and called me dirty names. I lit into him, and that's when the teacher looked up. I got kicked out of school for fighting.

"My dad always said he'd kill me if I got thrown out of school, so I slipped home when he wasn't there, got my things and took off for California. That was in the tenth grade, and I never went back to school. Finishing high school was the last thing my granddaddy had asked of me before he died, but I never did."

He had just turned sixteen.

For two years, he worked here and there, demolition in California, printing milk cartons in Garland, Texas, always hiding from the law, afraid he'd be picked up as a run-away and sent back to his parents.

Eighteen and legal at last, he returned to Baycross for a visit on Halloween, 1970. At a party, he met the prettiest red head he'd ever seen. They talked until four in the morning.

Within three months they eloped and were married by a justice of the peace.

~~~~~~

"What do you mean, you're pregnant? Dang, I got to make more money," Mike said months later when his wife Belinda told him the news. He signed on with the State Department of Transportation, proud to be earning $2.01 an hour when their son Mickey was born in 1971.

Then a back door opened in Baycross.

In 1972 union workers walked out on strike at the Dow Chemical plant, threatening to shut it down. The company had contracted with Volkswagen to add magnesium to steel to prevent rust. They would take a strike, but they weren't going to close their furnaces. They offered strikebreakers good money. Mike saw opportunity and jumped at it, even though it meant working in the magnesium cells.

The mag cells. He'd heard about them. *The starting out place.*

He pulled on his fire-retardant overalls, put a long-sleeved jumper over them and opened the door to Plant A. Hot air smacked him in the face. He threw his arm up to protect his head and walked in.

"Hey, you, watch where you're going," a man yelled at him. "Floors are full of furnaces and they'll crisp you in nothing flat."

Overhead black cylinders hung from the ceiling, carbon anodes that carried electricity.

"Touch one of them and it'll knock you to Oklahoma," another worker warned.

"Sea water's pumped in there." The foreman pointed to a large pipe.

"These here boxes are filled with water and electrical coils. Magnesium floats to the top and all the rest, the sludge, sinks to the bottom. Your job is to clean out the sludge."

"They gave me a protective suit with gloves and a head covering and, hot, man, it was hot. I've never sweated like that," he told Belinda that night while she fed the baby.

Hot, dirty, and dangerous but he earned an incredible $4.56 an hour.

The money paid bills. It didn't buy happiness.

"Everything's gone to hell around here since the baby came. Any woman knows how to tend a baby, but you won't even get out of bed. Baby blues, hmmmph. I didn't know you were that kind of person."

Two years later Belinda was still despondent when Jeffrey, another son, was born.

Mike's back door entry to Dow paid off. The hot job cleaning the magnesium cells led to motor transportation, then to driving a crane and flex truck, to equipment operator, and on to scales and a salaried position as dispatcher.

"That's it," he told Belinda. "Can't go any higher on my schooling."

But he earned nearly $15,000 a year. With a lot of time off. He opened a hamburger business on the side. Then a lube shop. And later a car wash.

The next investment nearly got him killed. His first day at managing a Pizza Hut, two men just out of jail attacked him. He swung with a kitchen knife. Their wounds were still healing when they marched back to their prison cells.

~~~~~~

Mike was thirty-two years old and single, at least in his view, when he spied a goose egg on a tire belonging to a brown-eyed woman. He sent his workers to repair it.

Three days later, he noticed the woman again. She was loading four-by-eight sheets of plywood onto a pickup truck in a pouring rain.

"Here."

He took the plywood from her arms and stacked it in the bed of the truck. Then he opened the door by the driver's seat.

"Get in. You're getting wet."

~~~~~~

"And I did," Ginger told me. "He took charge. He was broad-shouldered and older than me, which I took as strong and mature. I'd been trying so hard on my own, and faced with a protector telling me what to do, I backed into my familiar corner."

chapter five

Ginger and Mike walked on the beach at Freeport on their first date, away from the neon lights and jukebox music of eateries on the shoreline. Hermit crabs skittered before them, and their feet sank into sand wet from the outgoing tide.

Mike held out his hand to help Ginger skirt a tidal pool.

"I've gone as high as I can at Dow, but I want more. I've got some businesses on the side. Little here, little there."

He looked down, then across the dark water.

"Got two boys I'm raising by myself."

Ginger stopped to face him.

"By yourself, Mike? Where's their mother?"

"She may as well live in the hospital, she stays there depressed all the time. Actually, she's mentally ill. We're separated, in a way. We divorced once. Only reason I took her back was because of the boys."

He picked up a beer bottle on the beach and slung it over the surf.

"I been depressed a time or two myself."

Of course he's been depressed. I know something about depression.

Overall, Ginger regarded him as hard-working and enterprising. His friends were business and professional men. He dressed and talked like a businessman. He drove a T-bird that had a telephone in it. He wrote poetry.

She found a yellow sticky note attached to her door:

> If all we had
> were our endless dreams
> it would be so sad
> like fishless streams.
> Our existence depends
> on the ones we grab.

"I don't like the company you keep," he told her.

That was that. He became the company she kept.

One night after Thanksgiving they shared a pizza at Ginger's apartment. Mike let drop that Belinda was back home, AWOL from the hospital. She'd come for the holiday on a pass and refused to go back.

Ginger lowered her slice.

"She's back to stay?" she said. "Then you're not exactly separated, are you?" She pushed the pizza away.

"That explains why you've popped in here and left by seven o'clock every night the past week. You've been slipping around to see me, then going home to her."

"What do you expect me to do?"

Mike thrust his head toward her, his eyebrows rising with his voice. "You can't throw a crazy woman out on the street."

He sat back in his chair and rubbed his forehead.

"Besides, she's the mother of my boys," he said in a lower voice.

Ginger stood up.

"You can't live with her and see me. That's not right. If you're separated, if the marriage is over, then one of you needs to find somewhere else to live. Your choice but decide right now."

She stormed out of the room.

From her bedroom, she heard the door slam when Mike left.

Her knee bumped against a half-opened dresser drawer. She yanked the drawer out, emptied it onto the bed, and began throwing away whatever could be discarded. The rest she stacked back into the drawer before attacking the bureau drawers. A long hot shower sounded like a good idea, so she stepped into the shower and poured shampoo over her hair.

She heard a noise when she was toweling off, listened, but didn't hear it again, so she turned on the blow dryer. Halfway through drying her hair, she felt more than heard a thud. Something heavy shook the floor. She switched off the dryer. Two more thuds.

"Ginger, it's me," Mike called.

She pulled on her robe and peeped out the bedroom door. Mike stood in the middle of her den with boxes and clothes, all his things. He'd found another place to live.

Warning bells clanged in her ears. They wouldn't shut off. It was wrong, all wrong. She knew it; she felt it.

"Look, you can stay a few days…until you find something else."

The words didn't come out forcefully as she intended, and he didn't really seem to hear them anyway.

Her stomach acted up until she couldn't hold anything down, which lasted two weeks. Mike nursed her gently, told her again and again how indebted he was to her for letting him share her apartment, and took charge of the household.

They moved to another apartment at the end of Mike's first month with her. The new apartment wasn't larger or finer; there was no reason to move.

He's displaced me, Ginger realized too late. *This place is "ours," not mine. What have I done?*

She caught on more quickly to Mike's penchant for mind games.

As a passenger in his car, she could be mid-sentence in a story when he'd shout, "Look!" and point out her window. She'd turn to see what grabbed his attention.

"What? What were you pointing at? I don't see anything."

"I didn't point at anything."

"Yes, you did. Just now. You yelled for me to look."

"Nope. Don't know what you're talking about."

"Mike, you did."

"You must be daydreaming."

At first, she lost track of her story and doubted her own mind. Then she caught on. To that trick.

The first month they were together, she thought she smelled something peculiar in her car. Mike couldn't smell anything. She'd clean the car out, search under the hood, but never find anything—until she caught Mike slipping a room deodorizer against the radiator. Mike guffawed at his joke, alerting Ginger to trust what her senses told her.

Within six weeks after they took their apartment, a bank called a note on one of Mike's businesses, and then another bank called a note on a second business, until they all collapsed like a stack of cards, leaving him with nothing.

"Bankers ganged up on me. They're in collusion," he said, "all because of my divorce. Small town, full of gossip."

He insisted they move away from Baycross, from family, friends, and his job at the chemical company.

Waffle House, April 2006

"I was depressed, and I wallowed in it the next year or more," he said to me, "waiting for the healing to set in."

Ginger had taken a job waiting tables in Conroe, Texas.

"She was a real trooper," Mike said. "She took up the slack."

"I resented every minute of it," Ginger told me later. "My father was the breadwinner. Turner was the breadwinner. The men I knew worked, and here was Mike wearing his slippers all day, sitting at home waiting on my paycheck. He'd signed a lease, we had bills, and he wouldn't work. Trent spent weeks with me, except he was at home with Mike, and I'd be out waiting tables. It didn't make sense to me."

She had raged like a magpie for six months until he took one job and quit, then another, moving them further away with each job and leaving them less to live on.

Mind games, isolation, and dependence: the tools of a batterer, Ginger would learn years later.

With still another move, they took work together selling high-end mobile homes. One day, Ginger showed a customer through the model while Mike waited in the living room. When the customer left, she closed the door behind him.

"You took your sweet time showing him around," Mike said from the blue tweed sofa where he sat. "What were you doing back there?"

"Showing him the bedroom," Ginger said. "How big it is."

She still stood by the front door, one hand on her hip.

"Why?"

"Because you were flirting with him. That's why."

"Flirting?" She scrunched her face in disbelief. "That's ridiculous."

"I heard you, both of you back there laughing." He stood up and put his hands on his hips. "I know what I heard."

"Of course, I was laughing with him. I was trying to make a sale." She cocked her head and smiled.

"You wouldn't spend a wad of money with a sourpuss, would you?"

Mike bounded across the room. He clamped one hand on Ginger's shoulder and shoved her out of his path. She stumbled into the coffee table, which overturned with a thud, and landed on her knees beside it. Mike didn't stop until the door slammed behind him.

Ginger twisted around to sit on the floor. She watched for the door to open and Mike to come back in. Her knee stung, and a blood stain spread on her pants leg. She rolled her pants up to expose a skinned knee. For a long while, she sat on the floor, pants rolled up, staring at her knee.

At home that night, Mike acted pleasant, congenial, as though nothing had happened.

"Why did you do that, Mike? You shoved me into the coffee table."

She stood in the kitchen, car keys in her hand.

"I didn't shove you. All I did was walk out and walk home."

Mike fumbled through the cabinet searching for matches, his back to Ginger.

"Mike, you shoved me. Look."

She rolled up her pants leg to show the skinned knee. "Look what you did."

Mike closed one cabinet door and opened another.

"I didn't shove you. I didn't even touch you."

"Mike, look."

"Do you know where we put that new box of kitchen matches?"

He closed the cabinet and left the room without looking Ginger's way. Nor did he ever look at her knee.

The next week, he conceded that after thinking about it, he might have brushed past her as he left, but he did *not* push her.

She began to believe he really didn't intend to shove her so hard. After all, he was so sure of himself. Had her knee not been skinned, she might have questioned whether it had even happened.

She sat it aside. It was two years before it happened again.

By then, 1986, Mike and Ginger were married, and their first son Casey was born.

Ginger sat on the side of the bathtub while Mike lathered his face. She watched as he maneuvered the razor around his mustache and sideburns, his arms bent at the elbow, the skin on his back rising and falling with the rotation of his shoulder blades. When he rinsed off the razor and dried his face, she pressed against his bare back and wrapped her arms around him.

"Hey, what? Back off. Back off!"

He shook loose of her.

"I'm just trying to hug you, that's all."

She reached for him again.

"Well, don't. It's too hot in here."

He twisted away and went into the bedroom to dress.

She gave him several steps lead before she followed. She crawled onto the bed and tucked her legs under her. Mike stood across the room with his back to her while he buttoned his shirt.

"Do you not like to be hugged?"

"Sure."

"But you always push me away."

He didn't respond.

"I want you to hug me, Mike. I need to be hugged. It doesn't have to be anything but a hug."

She grinned. *Keep this light. Don't let him see how much it means.*

He unzipped his jeans and tucked his shirt in.

"We'll get around to it. Don't worry. I'll surprise you."

"If you're talking about making love, that *will* be a surprise. And a good one," she quickly added.

He threaded his belt through the loops on his pants, put on his watch, gathered change into his pockets.

"We used to have fun making love. We made time for it. What's happened? We're not getting old, are we?"

She smiled again, keeping it light.

"We give it what time it takes. It just doesn't take long."

Mike faced her, feet apart, hands on his hips.

"It used to." Her voice was soft.

"That was then. Doesn't need to anymore."

He dropped his arms to his side.

"What do you mean by that?" She curled her legs in tighter, drew herself into a ball.

"Look. If you need a car and you don't have one, then you're going to do what it takes to get that car," he said. "But if you look out in the driveway and there sits a car, then you don't need to do anything but get in and ride off when you're ready."

"Oh, Mike, don't put it like that."

Ginger frowned.

"That's the way it is."

Ginger returned home one day with her hair cut just above her shoulders. Mike steamed up like a pressure cooker.

"Why did you do that?" He wrinkled his forehead until his eyebrows met in one bushy line. "Why'd you let them do that?"

"It needed to be trimmed. It was uneven."

Ginger stood beside the dresser in their bedroom dressed in her black waitress' uniform.

"I know how I like it, and it's not the way it looks right now."

"Mike, I'm not a hairdresser. I try to tell them what I want, and then they cut my hair. That's how it is. And I don't know how to tell them different."

"Well, I know how to tell them."

Two months passed before she mentioned a haircut again.

"I'm going with you," Mike said.

She walked into the Conroe Cut 'N Curl ahead of him, a pink and black beauty parlor with two stations. A mirrored wall topped a black laminate countertop. She took her place in her hairdresser's chair.

Mike took one of the chrome-and-black leatherette chairs lining the back wall. He stretched his legs, crossed his feet, and locked his arms behind his head. He didn't say anything, just watched.

The hairdresser draped a black plastic cape around Ginger's shoulders and began to comb her hair.

Ginger gazed at her reflection in the mirror. She rehearsed in her mind, once again, the directions she'd give the hairdresser.

I'm going to get this right.

And we'll leave and he's going to be unhappy.

She couldn't see Mike's face in the mirror without twisting in the chair, but she didn't need to see him.

"How do you want it?" the hairdresser asked Ginger's reflection.

Ginger stared at the mirror.

"Ask him," she said. "He'll tell you."

And he did. He instructed the stylist just how he wanted it and watched as she snipped the ends of Ginger's hair.

From that time on, Mike presided over every haircut.

"Ask him. He'll tell you."

A woman doesn't have the final say about her hair. Ginger learned that as a girl when her pixie cut infuriated her father.

"I was the body. Mike was in charge."

Waffle House, February 2007

"Oh, it was only two or three times," Mike said. "I tried to tell her if her hair grew an inch and she had an inch and a half cut off every month, she'd soon be bald. Just because the hairdresser said 'cut,' didn't mean she had to cut."

Ginger didn't know how to stand up for herself, according to Mike. "Ginger was a left-handed achiever, always out to please. No one in her growing up gave her approval so she sought it everywhere."

Mike told me how Ginger bought peas for canning through an ad in a tabloid, which led to someone with a pea sheller on a porch. That person asked her to help pick more peas, then shell them, then put them up in jars—for no money, just a few jars of her own, and she did it. The next day, someone called their house wanting to speak to the woman who picked peas. Mike hit the ceiling.

"She wasn't of a right mind, but she didn't know it. Her confidence was so low. I had to stay on her all the time. Most of my life was spent battling to get her to take up for herself. For us to survive, I had to become like her dad. She put me in that position."

Mike continued to change jobs almost as often as he changed shirts, and each new job usually meant a change of address. Money was always tight, and they often argued about it.

Ginger's credit record was unblemished, so Mike insisted she take out a credit card in her name.

She came home from waiting tables one day to discover Mike astride a chair at the kitchen table, counting out $500 in cash. "

"Where'd the money come from?"

He wasn't working. She knew he hadn't earned it.

"That machine over there," he said, pointing toward the ATM machine at the bank across the street.

"How'd you—you used *my credit card?*"

Mike held the card up and wiggled it back and forth. "Open sesame."

"You withdrew $500 and charged it to my card?" Her voice rose. "I don't have $500. *We* don't have five hundred dollars."

He just watched her.

"Do you think this money's a gift? That we don't have to pay it back? Just you watch how quick the credit card company comes after us."

Mike slid the twenty-dollar bills into his wallet. He picked up a magazine and began turning its pages.

Ginger fumed. She snorted. She started toward the bedroom. A canvas duffel bag had been sitting on the floor for days, and she caught her foot on it.

They'd moved so often, their mail had to catch up with them. The duffel bag gaped open, showing circulars, junk mail, and letters. Mike had let it pile up, not even opening the envelopes.

"Sort this mail before I break my neck tripping over it." She shoved the bag toward him.

"Just trash it all."

"You can't do that." She slapped an armload of mail on top of his magazine.

He sat back in his chair, stared at the mail, looked up at Ginger and gave in. He flipped through the pile on the table and emptied the canvas bag. Most of it he tossed out.

Ginger thumbed through his discard pile, knowing how little attention he'd paid.

"Whoopee," she shouted. "Look what I found. A check for $2500."

The check was a pay-off for Mike from an old investment, a godsend he'd almost thrown away. It more than covered the credit card balance.

She paid off the balance on the credit card and put the card in a safe place, for her use only. *My good credit I'll always have, should I ever need it.*

She and Mike didn't see eye to eye about other money issues.

She had added his name to her bank account, and he bounced four checks. It wasn't intentional.

He was in the habit of writing checks on money yet to be deposited, fully expecting the account to have enough money to cover the checks by the time they were presented. It allowed him to pay bills on time with money he didn't quite have.

Sometimes he'd run a magnet over the check to lift its magnet reader. Then the bank would have to set it aside to process by hand. It gained him a little time.

Once, though, he miscalculated, and the checks beat the deposit to the bank. Their account was penalized $80.

Ginger was outraged. Not only was her name on the bad checks, but it was just wrong. Wrong, she declared silently and aloud. Rigid and righteous, stiff with her Sunday school teachings, she puffed it up into a red alert moral crisis.

"I'll just cash money orders, and we'll live like white trash." She hoofed it straight to the bank and closed out the account.

She didn't trust Mike with their money, even while she handed him her own paychecks and asked his permission if she wanted to buy anything.

~~~~~~

Mike was selling ads on commission for a shopper, a free newspaper, when Casey was due, and again money was scarce. It was Mike's decision that Ginger deliver the baby at home. Doctors tell you what to do, he'd said, and it's our baby.

He had heard about Deeny, a midwife who would charge $250, and they went together to interview her. She wore a head covering and had no television in her home.

"Strange," Ginger whispered to Mike.

Mike hired her.

~~~~~~

Casey was born on February 10, 1986. Mike lay in bed behind Ginger, holding her, but he left whenever he wanted a cigarette. He had time for a lot of cigarettes. Casey's head was large, and the delivery was long and difficult with a lot of tearing.

Afterward, Deeny opened the kitchen cupboard to make something for Ginger to eat. The shelves were bare. She found two potatoes in a bin, enough to make a pot of soup.

"The best soup I ever ate," Ginger told her.

The soup gave Ginger strength to get to the hospital, where the emergency room doctor sutured the tears. The home delivery ended up costing far more than $250.

Ginger held her new baby and thought about Trent and how she missed him. He was six years old now, learning to read and write. He'd answered her last letter with a Valentine saying in big block letters, "I love you, Mom, Trent."

Mom. Turner had remarried the year before. Erika, his new wife, insisted that Trent call her "Mom." Trent said she spanked him when he refused.

After several spankings, he compromised. Her name was "Momma." Ginger was "Mom."

Trent was supposed to visit every other week, but all too often Ginger lacked gas money to drive eighty-five miles to Baycross to get him. Now with another baby, she wondered how long it would be before she'd see him.

She missed her own parents too. She hadn't spoken with them in two years, not since they told her she wasn't welcome in their home and the church withdrew fellowship from her. The loss of family and church left a void in her life, an ache that wouldn't go away.

She longed to reconcile with her parents but didn't hold out that hope.

Mike telephoned them.

"They need to know they have a new grandson," he said. He gave them the news and answered their questions about the baby.

"Here," he said, holding the phone toward Ginger. "They want to speak to you."

She took a deep breath.

"Hello, Mom."

When Ginger spoke to Mileah on the telephone two weeks later, she confided that they had very little money.

"I'm skimping and saving every way I know how," Ginger said. "We use cloth diapers and wash them in a bucket. And I'm using old diapers as sanitary pads."

"You've just had a baby and you can't afford to buy sanitary napkins?" Mileah said.

"Well, I guess—"

"Does Mike still smoke?" Mileah asked.

"Several packs a day."

And never gives one thought to what his cigarettes cost. The more she thought about it, the madder she got.

She stood by the dryer in the narrow back hall waiting like a shotgun with both barrels loaded, ready to blast him with her words.

Mike yanked opened the back door.

"How can you burn up money in cigarettes when your family—"

The look on his face as he came toward her shut her up. He bent her backward over the dryer and pinned her with his left elbow against her chest. He balled his right fist and drew back as if to hit her in the mouth.

"I just—"

He leaned into her face.

"Close your mouth. If you say one more word, I'll knock your teeth down your throat."

She took a breath to say something.

"One word."

He means it. He's going to hurt me. She pressed her lips together.

It was a conscious decision. It let Mike know all he need do was threaten and she would collapse.

"It was a disastrous mistake on my part." Ginger said. "I should have left him then."

chapter six

Mike answered the telephone.

"Hi, you want to go fishing?" It was Roy McNeil, his father. Out of the blue, as though they talked every day.

He couldn't remember the last time he'd spoken with his dad, didn't want to remember it.

"There's property across the street, right near the lake, son, and I'd like you to come live there. I'll even help you build a house."

Roy had moved to his retirement home, the one his coworkers called "the house that Dow built," on Lake Sam Rayburn near Hackleberg, Texas. The lake was the largest in Texas, covering more than 115,000 acres, so it was popular for fishing and boating.

Mike considered hanging up the phone, but he let his dad talk on.

Roy had suffered a heart attack. "Opened my eyes," he was saying. It led him to Jesus. Besides, he was growing old, and he wanted to make amends.

"I want my family close by, son."

Mike was reluctant. Old wounds had scarred over, but they remained near the surface.

"Oh, Mike," Ginger said, "yes, he's reaching out to you, let this be a healing." She knew her own need for family bonds and how much it could mean for both families to be restored. "Please, let's accept his offer."

They packed up what baby gear they owned and moved to Hackleberg. Casey was four weeks old.

Roy McNeil's subdivision lay eight miles outside of Hackleberg. A road led two miles through it to the lake, with other roads branching off from the main road, all with one acre lots. Some held houses, some held mobile homes, but most were still thicketed in underbrush.

Roy and Thelma, Mike's mom, lived on two lots bordering the lake at the end of a cul-de-sac. They had total privacy. All the adjoining property stood wooded and unclaimed.

Mike, Ginger, and Casey moved in with them. Mike found work selling ads for a radio station and they put $100 down on the lot next to Roy.

After work each day, Mike and Roy tore down an old house in exchange for its lumber, which Mike intended to recycle in building his house. Roy showed Ginger how to pull nails from the lumber.

Roy was meticulous. Ginger had to do it just right. Couldn't drop a nail, had to put them all in a can. She spent all day pulling nails, stopping only to nurse the baby.

Nursing came easy this time. Ginger mothered her baby, and he responded. There was no one to tell her she was doing it wrong, or that she couldn't do it at all.

Vines and brush covered their lot so thick that there wasn't space to plant two feet. She, Roy, and Mike attacked it with a machete and chain saw, clearing away enough underbrush for a small house and yard.

Ginger basked in the family unity, although she found Thelma rather peculiar. Mike's mother was a white-haired tomboy, a horrible cook, and the only woman Ginger knew who was completely oblivious to a crying baby.

She didn't seem to be aware of Casey's presence, except that he and his parents disrupted her tidy house, not that she minded. She vacuumed the entire house every day and emptied the bag. Ginger heard her mumbling, "Um hum, that's good, that's good," as she examined its contents. Ginger and Mike chuckled about his mother's eccentricities.

Contact with both families restored, Ginger sought out a nearby church. Without church, she'd felt like one leg was missing. They were in a new town, so she'd make a new beginning.

Ginger's family had never seen Casey, who was now four months old. She yearned to see them and show them their new grandson.

Besides, she and Mike needed money to begin work on the house, and she didn't want to pawn her gold ring again, the last of her jewelry. She'd redeemed it once already, unlike her engagement ring from Turner. Mike had pawned that ring, and it was gone. They decided to ask her parents for a loan of $500 to $1,000 with the ring as collateral. She knew this ring would be safe until she could repay the loan.

Ginger had never asked them for money before.

Mike handed her the phone.

She took a deep breath and dialed their number. She intended to approach her mother, not her father, even though she knew what her mother's stock answer would be. Still, she preferred to do a dry run with her mother.

She began with news of Casey, then her new church, until there was nothing more to talk about. Mike stood beside her, rolling his hand to hurry her along.

"Mother, I want to talk with you and Dad about a business proposition."

As she expected, her mother deferred to her father.

"We'll talk about it when you bring Casey to see us," Helen said.

And that's what happened. Her parents agreed to the loan, all very business-like. They would hold the ring. That done, they made one request: that Ginger go to their church and repent so she could be reinstated.

"But I'm going to church in Hackleberg," Ginger said. "I'm in a church I like. It's right where I live. It isn't necessary—"

"But we want you to make redemption with our church." her father said.

Ginger thought about how terribly she had missed her family. If reinstatement in the church that had in effect kicked her out was the price for reconciling with her parents, she was willing to pay.

"Then I will," she said.

She went to church with Claude and Helen that very night and sat in the pew where her family always sat, four rows from the front on the left side. Mike opted to stay home.

At the end of the sermon, during the invitation hymn, Ginger would walk to the front of the church and write on a card that she repented of her sins and wished to be reinstated. That was the procedure.

She sat still as stone, hands in her lap.

It all looked the same, the faces in the congregation, the beams in the ceiling, the pecan-colored pews, the dais where the preacher stood, and the purple velvet curtains covering the baptistery behind him. She had the strong sense she'd never been away, despite the time that had passed.

She listened hard to the sermon, absorbed in it to escape the torment of waiting, but she also savored the familiarity of being at this church.

The preacher reached the end and Ginger tensed. The hymn came next, her signal to come forward. The congregation stood to sing, and she turned to slide into the aisle.

"Page sixty-seven," the preacher said. "*Just As I Am.*"

Ginger stopped. It was the song the congregation sang when she first walked the aisle to join the church. Tears filled her eyes. She took a deep breath, exhaled slowly, and walked down the aisle, singing the familiar words with the congregation:

Just as I am, and waiting not
To rid my soul of one dark blot,
To Thee whose blood can cleanse each spot,
O Lamb of God, I come, I come.
Just as I am, though tossed about
With many a conflict, many a doubt,
Fightings and fears within, without,
O Lamb of God, I come, I come.

And Ginger came. Tears streamed down her face, the aisle seemed endless, but she came.

The preacher handed her the card. With eyes so blurry with tears, she could hardly see where to write. With her hand shaking so much the writing was barely legible, she wrote out her repentance and request for reinstatement in the church.

The preacher called on a man in the congregation to pray, and it was done. Ginger was reinstated.

Everyone welcomed her, old friends hugging and crying with her, and telling her they loved her. She felt whole again. No one remembered anyone ever asking to be reinstated before.

She looked for her parents, who stood in the back, smiling, and showing Casey off to their friends. They both hugged her before they rode home together.

For the first time in their marriage, Ginger and Mike danced in good graces with both sets of parents.

Claude and Helen let them borrow a 24-foot Shasta camper trailer that they parked on the lot and moved into, baby and all. It held a full-sized bed, toilet facilities, and a compact kitchen, leaving little space to walk around. Ginger could lie in bed and stir a pot on the stove.

Mike took a job building a prison in nearby Lufkin, earning $210 a week. Over the next two years, he hung 110 high security doors while working for Timberline Construction.

He dug a ditch and Ginger laid pipe from Roy's house 220 feet away, and they paid him $10 a month for their water. They dug a pit for a sewer and a field line for the drainage pipe.

The house came next.

They framed up one 14-foot square room, smack against the camper, and nailed silver foil-covered insulation between the studs. Sheets of thick black plastic covered the exterior. Mike weatherized the opening from the camper so they could walk back and forth. When the sub-roof went up over the room, they moved in, despite having no real interior or exterior walls.

When Ginger pushed between the studs, the insulation had enough give that she could reach out onto the ground. At night, they heard critters sniffing and scratching just inches from their heads, but they never got inside.

The house was tight as a drum and warm. Air didn't stir since there were no windows. They jerry-rigged a mobile home-type air-conditioner for the hot summers.

Ginger learned how to cut corners. She had to. She planted a big garden. Pregnant again when Casey was only eight months old, she had to squat with her legs out to the sides to pick green bush beans.

Groceries she bought in bulk, a month at time, and packed them under the beds and in every nook. She bought ground beef in quantity and squeezed it flat into packages for the camper freezer. She never paid more than 89 cents a pound, and she fed the family on those pennies.

Yard sales offered better bargains than Wal-Mart—$5 could stretch into a carload of reusable goods.

Stretching became a way of life, and in many ways, a satisfying one.

In Ginger's mind, she was doing what she knew to do, what she had been prepared all her life to do. She supported her husband, cared for their children, and accepted her lot in life. Of course, she gave Mike the biggest piece of pie, and the children the last piece of pie. Wives and mothers always put their families ahead of themselves. Never mind that they lived in a black plastic cube and slept with critters sniffing inches from their heads. This was temporary. They would finish the house. Their lives would improve. In the meantime, she knew how to stretch. Stretching was her strength. She felt proud and affirmed.

Ginger made a friend at church, another mother with a young baby. One Sunday in late fall of 1986 as the two women rocked their babies in the nursery, Ginger burst into tears.

"What's wrong?" her friend asked. She leaned over to pat Ginger's arm. "You can tell me."

"I don't know how to undo my life," Ginger blurted out, sobbing.

The preacher had given a sermon on marriage, divorce, and remarriage that morning, and his words tossed about in Ginger's head. Divorce might be justified, he said, but anyone who remarries is living in sin.

"I don't know how to undo my life," she repeated. "I was married, divorced, and now I'm married to Mike and we're expecting another baby."

She spilled everything to this woman. The woman consoled her, patted her, put her arms around her, until Ginger stopped crying.

They didn't mention it again.

In time, Mike began to attend the church. The congregation welcomed him so ardently that one Sunday he decided to join. When the invitation hymn began, he walked down the center aisle, smiling, head high, singing along. At the front, he took a seat while the minister huddled over him, whispering. He nodded. The minister stood to announce that Mike had made his confession of faith. He told the people to keep singing while he prepared Mike for baptism.

The baptistery was behind the podium much like the one at the church in Baycross. Velvet curtains concealed it from the congregation when not in use. Behind the curtains were steps leading down into a waterproof enclosure large enough for two or three people to stand in waist-deep water. When the curtains opened, the minister and Mike stood in the water, Mike now dressed in a white cotton gown. The minister recited scripture and he dipped Mike under the water and up again. Mike was baptized.

After the service, members of the congregation hugged Mike and extended fellowship to their new member. Ginger sailed home on clouds, only a little more euphoric than Mike. Mike rode home fully dressed, except for his underwear which lay soaking wet in a plastic bag stashed under the car seat.

Four days later, a man from the church phoned asking for Mike while he was at work in Lufkin.

"Tell your husband to call me," he told Ginger. "There's a meeting you're both to come to next Thursday."

"What's this about?" Ginger asked.

He declined to tell her. Men discussed business with other men.

Her skin prickled. Something was wrong. People weren't summonsed before the church without some reason. All afternoon she fretted, anticipating what the elders would say, knowing in her heart what lay ahead.

By the time Mike got home, Ginger was beside herself, worried sick.

Mike phoned the man.

"We need to discuss your marriage in regard to your salvation," he said, and gave the date for the meeting.

Mike relayed the message to Ginger.

"No! They can't do this!" Lightening was about to strike her a second time, and she became inconsolable.

"I told you not to let your guard down," Mike said. Anger simmered in his stomach while he called back.

"Let's get it over with. Let's do it right now."

"Our people have jobs," the man said. "They can't come at the drop of a hat."

"Listen here. You're calling us on the carpet about our life, ripping us up, so you dang better be ready to take it up right now."

The man set the meeting for the next day at the preacher's office in the church.

Mike stayed awake all night studying the Bible so he could speak to these men of God.

The door to the office stood open when Mike and Ginger arrived. It was a small, paneled room lit by a fluorescent light. The preacher sat in a swivel chair against the back wall, his desk in front of him. Metal folding chairs lined every inch of the remaining walls, and in them sat eight "devout men of the church," a term akin to deacons or elders.

Mike and Ginger took the two empty chairs obviously meant for them. Ginger pulled one-year-old Casey against her pregnant belly and looked into the faces of their judges.

One was so obese he spilled off both sides of his chair. Another was a man prominent in the area, a large landowner and the husband of the friend in whom she'd confided.

They said Mike and Ginger were living in sin in an unholy marriage. The bulge in Ginger's belly was proof. Their salvation was at risk.

They were adamant, citing scripture, invoking Jesus, shaking fingers. The husband of Ginger's friend was clearly their leader. The friend had reported everything Ginger confided to her in the nursery three months earlier. He and "the devout men" did nothing then since they held no authority over Mike, but once Mike was baptized, he fell under the church's mantle.

There were only two courses open to them, the men said, and one was to live as brother and sister.

Mike's face reddened. "I can't do that. No man could." His voice shook with anger. "You may as well ask me to paint my windshield black and go for a drive. I'd be bound to crash."

He turned to face Ginger. "Look at this woman. She's my wife and I love her. To expect me as a man not to have sex with her is bull."

Tears streaked Ginger's face. *Mike can't relate to what's happening as I can, and I feel so alone. I'm ashamed of his strident tone—but so grateful he has the courage to say what I can't.*

The other alternative was divorce.

The preacher, who'd had little to say until now, leaned forward, his hands pressed together as if in prayer.

"Ginger, if you'll leave Mike, the church will support you and your children."

How shameful you say that to me. It's as if the new convert can fend for himself while the church shelters the lifelong member. She shook her head, not daring to speak her thoughts.

"What if we just come to church anyway?" Mike asked.

"We'd have to post a sentry at the door," one man said. Another muttered something about calling the police.

"You're nothing but a cult." Mike steered Ginger and Casey toward the door.

Their exit ended the meeting.

The church never contacted Ginger or Mike again, nor did they contact the church.

Ginger cried so hard the following week she worried she'd lose the baby.

"You'd of thought they cut your heart out," Mike told her.

She had gone through withdrawal before. She knew its shame and she feared its power. This was so unfair, so unreasonable. She couldn't believe a God of love would demand such a thing. She had never questioned the teachings of the church before, but now she questioned everything.

To her, it was a horrible, wrenching ordeal that scarred her in many ways she can't describe to this day.

Mike spit and spewed outwardly at what he viewed as a betrayal of his baptism, betrayal of Ginger's trust, and just downright meanness. Inwardly, anger chewed at his heart.

Who were these men to tell him what God intended? How could this church stand between him and God? If God was a Father, what father would treat his children the way his family had been treated?

Ginger knew the Bible inside and out. He didn't. He wasn't raised in a church like she was. But he didn't need some church or its holy elders to tell him what it said. If the Bible was where they drew their power, then he could do the same. But he could read it for himself.

And he did, pouring over its pages every day. For hours.

The McNeils celebrated Independence Day with sparklers, fireworks and the birth of Cody, their new son. The baby arrived at dawn July 4, 1987, delivered at home by a midwife Mike had hired. This time, Ginger's mother was on hand. So were three big brothers: Casey, at seventeen months; Trent, at seven years; and Mickey, Mike's son by his first marriage, at fourteen. Mickey lived with Mike and Ginger off and on. Trent spent two months every summer.

The baby was born in the one-room unfinished house. The sub-roof was ready to be shingled. Electrical wires and ducts threaded through blue insulation between the stud walls. Shirts, dresses, and jeans hung from nails around the room, the only wall-coverings. The room held a bed, a television, and a pot-bellied stove in one corner. A curtain shielded a bathroom in another corner. The camper served as both kitchen and bedroom for Mickey and Trent. Ginger's mother slept on a cot in the space partitioned for the future kitchen. Every inch of space was in use, but the family was together and joyous over the new baby.

As soon as Ginger recovered enough to climb a ladder, she pounded shingles onto the roof, descending every two hours to nurse Cody.

Mike had more wire to run.

Roy offered to trade Mike a roll of 10–2 wire with a ground for a roll of lighter weight 14–2 wire.

"I've got no use for that heavy wire. The difference ought to come to about a hundred dollars. Just pay me later," he said.

He had thrown up an outbuilding with barn doors on his land, about 25 feet square resting on concrete blocks, which he used as a storage catch-all. About three weeks after the wire deal, he decided to add a proper foundation to make the barn more permanent. That meant removing everything stored inside and digging footings for concrete. Mike and fourteen-year-old Mickey offered to help.

Bright and early that Saturday morning, about seven o'clock so it'd be cool, they were ready to get started. Mike's mother stood in the yard hoeing weeds from her flower beds.

Roy, Mike and Mickey started emptying the barn of sacks of grass seed and fertilizer, wheelbarrows, an old sawhorse, all the stuff that collects when there's a place to hide it away.

"When you going to pay me for my wire?" Roy asked about an hour later.

"Dad, I told you this is a new job and I don't get paid until the end of the month," Mike said, lowering an armload of fishing gear onto the driveway.

"You've always got an excuse, don't you? Did you move up here just to remind me how worthless you are?" Roy stepped toward Mike.

"You begged us to move here."

Thelma put down her hoe. Mickey came to a halt.

"I didn't want niggers living next to me, that's why. But I guess I'd as soon have a nigger as you."

He hauled off and hit Mike square in the mouth, bursting his lip.

Mike reeled. His father had never hit him in the mouth before, not even when he was a kid. He had hit him on the jaw, or the cheek, where it didn't show so bad. Or on the temple. He was so shocked he laughed, and when he did, blood sprayed onto his father.

Roy swiped at the bloody spit, infuriated.

"Now, Roy. Now, Roy!" Thelma headed toward her husband.

Roy whipped around.

A few feet away lay a pile of garden tools. He grabbed up a shovel and spun back toward Mike, swinging the shovel like a baseball bat—landing it square across Thelma's face as she stepped into his path.

The blow knocked her to the ground.

Mickey ran to her as Mike bent over her. A white knot popped up on her cheek, blue at its base, and split down the middle as if her skin were an overripe tomato. Blood rimmed the gash and spilled down her face. Her nose swelled, a red cut across its bridge. Two bloody rivulets streamed from her nostrils.

They hovered over her. Mike mopped at her face with a bandana and tried to get her to lie still, but she struggled to her feet. They both steadied her.

Roy lay draped over a garden tractor they had pulled from the barn. He looked at Thelma and dropped to his knees, sobbing, his head on the ground, his arms folded into his heaving chest.

Thelma twisted away from Mike and wobbled her way to Roy. She knelt beside him with her arm around his back. When she looked up, a deep red paste had covered her swelling face.

"Look what you've done," she said to Mike. "You want him to have a heart attack, don't you?"

Mike heard her voice. *Had his mother said what he thought she said?*

He nodded to Mickey. The two went home.

Ginger had never seen Mike so angry. His eyes were the color of ketchup. He went into the bathroom and threw up.

The following Monday, after Mike left for work, Casey chased a baby duck through the yard while Ginger filled the empty black molasses lick tub with fresh water for the duck. Just past the half-way level, the water petered to a stop. *That's funny.* She went inside and turned the tap at the sink. Water flowed for a few seconds and stopped.

Cody, who was not yet a month old, lay sleeping in his bassinet. He needed his bath, and Ginger had diapers to wash.

"Hey, Ginger!" Roy called from across the road.

She leaned out the screen door. Roy stood on his property, waving a garden hose, spraying silver figure eights of water through the air before they splashed onto his grass.

"Water, water everywhere," he said, laughing and dancing a jig.

He had shut off their water supply.

Cody outranked the duck. Ginger bathed the baby in the clean water in the tub that day, the first of many baths the family would take in the molasses tub. After a week without water, they rigged a garden hose two hundred yards through the underbrush behind the house to a sympathetic neighbor on another street. Ginger would heat the water on the stove, or they'd fill the tub and let it sit in the sun to heat, then they'd bathe outside after dark. Sometimes, when the weather was pleasant, they took a bar of soap down to the lake.

"I hired a water witch," Mike announced one evening. They had to find a permanent source for water. "Be here in the morning."

The next day a man walked back and forth across their lot holding a forked stick in front of him. When the stick turned in his hand, he said, "Dig right here. Here's your water."

"No, that's in the middle of my garden," Ginger said.

"You better start digging you another garden," Mike said.

The well had hardly been finished when Ginger yelled, "Hurry, Mike! Come quick!"

Mike saw her leaning over its wall, looking down, so he ran toward her. *Oh, surely Casey hasn't fallen—.* Casey was standing beside his mother, his face wrapped up in her skirt.

"Casey dropped the car keys down the well," Ginger called out as Mike approached.

"Dang, that's all? You scared me," Mike said. He peered into the well. Total darkness. "Nothing we can do. No way to fish them out."

They didn't have another set.

Mike hotwired the car. "See, you've got to hold the wires tight, like this," he said, showing Ginger what to do.

Another month passed and they returned home one day from buying groceries to find a trench dug over the width of their driveway two feet deep. Although they had no proof, they figured it was Roy's handiwork.

Mike called the sheriff.

"Nothing I can do," he said.

"What do you mean there's nothing you can do?" Mike heated up. "You mean if I went down to Wal-Mart's parking lot and trenched over the entrance, there's nothing you could do?"

"Now I didn't say that," the sheriff said.

He didn't do anything.

Roy mulched his flower beds and mounded his trees with leaves he raked up in the fall. Bugs and worms burrow under dead leaves.

Mike and Ginger kept chickens. They gathered the eggs and occasionally killed one for the table, but that was hard to do—the chickens had names and were almost pets.

Mike's chickens pecked at Roy's mulch. Roy shot all the chickens with a rifle and threw their carcasses into Mike's yard.

Mike bought more chickens and a box of .22 bullets. He put the bullets in Roy's mailbox with a note saying, "Don't stop now."

"I want to give him enough rope to hang himself," he told Ginger.

Time passed. Ginger set out pine seedlings by the road and Roy mowed them down. He ran cows through their yard. He came into their yard taunting their sons, and Mike chased him away with his gun.

Mike reached his limit. He phoned the Baptist church where Roy landed after his heart attack conversion.

"My name is Mike McNeil, and I have a serious issue with one of your members. He happens to be my father. Somebody's going to be shot at the OK Corral before it's over, so you better intervene. Do your job."

They did. The church monitored a meeting with both feuding families, including Mike's brother and sister, and some of the deacons. By its end, Roy broke down and apologized. They declared a truce, an end to hostilities, but the rift between the families was deeper than the trench across the driveway.

The harassment had spanned several years. It began when Casey was a toddler and lasted long enough for him to remember crawling through pampas grass to spy on the Old Goat, as they all referred to Roy.

"Mama, the Old Goat's coming!" "Mama, the Old Goat kicked our jack-o-lantern!"

Casey was seven-years-old and Cody five before they learned the Old Goat was their grandfather.

"I burned my fingers again," Ginger said, holding out her hand to show Mike. She sat in the front seat of the car. "I already have scars."

"Twist the wires harder. You let them get hot." He demonstrated one more time. "I know you hate this car but there's no way we can afford a new ignition."

They couldn't afford anything, and that was gnawing on Mike.

"We're stuck here." He slapped his hand against the fender of the car. "We're obligated to pay $77 a month for ten years for this stupid acre of land at the dead end of nowhere. Every extra penny we squeezed we've plowed back into this house. We're trapped."

The joy they'd felt when they were reconciled with family and church had popped like overfilled balloons.

At least Ginger's family still embraced them.

They would struggle there another five years—with the house, bills, and with each other—before leaving Hackleberg for good.

chapter seven

Discord between Mike and Ginger rose and fell with their bank account. Or, at least, money was what they argued most about. But not exclusively.

Just before Labor Day of 1990, they emptied the house of furniture and piled everybody back into the camper so they could lay flooring.

They pounded three-inch pine boards to the subfloor. Ginger came back with a sander, smoothing the boards but charging the air with fine wood particles. Lacquer came next, heavy coats for a gymnasium finish, which they slapped on with wide paint brushes.

September is hot in Texas, with humidity as oppressive as a steam roller. The fumes from the lacquer had Ginger sneezing and wheezing until her throat closed and she could hardly breathe. The doctor diagnosed her with asthma and filled her with steroids.

Medusa flared up, grouchy and nasty and lashing out at nothing, a reaction to the steroids as fast as flipping a switch from off to on.

Ginger always fought stress at the kitchen sink, washing dishes, wiping down the shelves, sometimes starting over if she hadn't washed what bothered her out of her system. It wasn't a good time or place to provoke her, but one evening she and Mike bickered from the kitchen to the living room.

Ginger asked a question and Mike didn't answer. She walked to the threshold.

"Are you listening to me?"

He kept staring at the television.

She wadded the dishrag in her hand and sailed it at him.

It smacked him in the face.

"That hurt!" he yelled.

"A dish rag?"

"It hit me in the eye." He covered his eye with his hand.

"A wet dish rag's heavy."

"Uh huh." She picked the rag up from the floor where it had landed and returned to the dishes.

~~~~~~

Mike said Ginger was on steroids once, but claimed Medusa came visiting like clockwork every month.

"Once I was standing in the camper, and she balled up her fists and started pounding me on the chest. I took her by the arms and threw her across the floor. She got all upset because the carpet burned her knees, but I had to do something to stop her."

~~~~~~

Medusa visited Mike, too. When an ad for condoms flashed across the TV screen one night. Mike jerked the TV from the wall. He banged into the front door getting it open, then hurled the television set into the yard. It hit with a thud and pop.

Casey drew his legs under him and crouched against the sofa. Ginger came running from the kitchen.

"My boys aren't going to see that garbage," Mike said.

No more television from then on.

Another time he tossed a computer out a window. Throwing things into the yard became a way to discharge anger and a family euphemism.

"Don't like it?" they all said to each other, "then just throw it in the yard."

Three years after they started the house, it was complete enough to detach the camper. At last Ginger had a kitchen with a for-real range. She'd cooked three Thanksgiving turkeys on the doll-sized camper stove, sawed in half to fit in the miniature oven, cooked one half at a time. She pressed them back together to serve, but one half would be hot and the other half cold. She'd laughed about starting a new tradition.

All together, they spent eight years building the house. First the one room, then another, for a total of seven rooms on the ground level. Stairs led up to one bedroom centered above the others. A door from the top bedroom opened onto the roof of the front porch. Sheet rock in various colors covered the interior walls, plywood the exterior walls.

Ginger made fishhooks for a manufacturer, some-thing she could do at home while the babies were little. She filled a tiny plastic skirt to each hook and hung them like fringe to the rim of a wooden Coke case well out of reach of the children. Later she packaged each one separately and stapled it to a card. For this she earned a nickel per hook.

Putting lead on the heads of the hooks paid more, so Mike had a try but threw up his hands after two weeks. He was better fishing with the hooks. Besides, fishing saved more grocery money than making the hooks produced.

One year they ate chicken and catfish—catfish fillets, catfish sandwiches, catfish soup—catfish every way from Sunday, or so it seemed, although Ginger took pride in her inventiveness.

Most people turned their noses up at drum, considering it a greasy trash fish, but Ginger steamed it with tomatoes, peppers, and onions and served it over rice. Quite palatable.

The lake provided more exotic food. One summer evening Casey and Cody splashed in the shallow water at the edge of the lake near their house while Mike fished from a wooden boat in deep water. Ginger had hitched up her skirt to wade near the boys.

"Ginger!" Mike yelled. "Get the boys out of the water. Now, dang it. You, too. Hurry!"

Ginger hurried the boys onto the shore. Mike was sitting very still in the boat, paddle raised, staring at something in the water near the boat. She could see it—bumpy, like a small log. Mike slowly paddled back to shore. He'd spotted a four-foot alligator in the boys' swimming hole.

Later that night and for the next two nights, he stood on the bank and shined a flashlight on the water. Red eyes at water level told him the alligator had taken up residence. The next night he eased the boat into the water and paddled quietly away from shore. His rifle lay at his feet. He sat motionless, waiting, until he saw the now familiar red eyes.

The shots reverberated through the woods. Ginger heard them from the house. Had she not known Mike's plan, she'd hardly have noticed. Someone was always shooting a rifle somewhere close by.

Mike hauled the dead gator from the water using a rope. With a hatchet, he hacked off the tail. Ginger helped him dig a deep hole to bury the carcass. Neither of them knew the penalty for killing an alligator, but they knew they couldn't afford to get caught. The tail they kept, and its meat became steaks.

At last, the sun burst through the clouds. Mike found construction work in Sedalia, Missouri, as a gas plumber, installing stoves, furnaces, and gas appliances.

Ginger was left to cope with a leaky refrigerator that gave the house a foul odor, a faulty carburetor, and the $10 per month back child support to Mike's first wife. But the hardship separation brightened once Mike's good wages rolled in. Some weeks he topped $2,000.

Ginger and the children locked up the Hackleberg house and joined him. Ginger splurged on an antique sofa at an estate sale and found a good deal on a new washer, dryer, and refrigerator. With financial stress lifted at last, times were good.

Or at least there were fewer mines in the field, fewer places where a misstep might trigger an outburst. She had become very skilled at tiptoeing around Mike's moods, so much so she hardly gave it a thought.

Within six months, winter shut down the job.

In January, they packed their transportable goods, including the sofa and appliances, onto the oil-soaked heavy-duty trailer Mike used in his work. With it hitched to the car, they set out on the fifteen-hour drive back to Texas.

Midnight shrouded the house they'd toiled over so long near Hackleberg. The grass was overgrown and the leaves were deep. Fire ants had built mounds all over.

Mike maneuvered the trailer up under the porch roof and unhooked it from the car.

When they opened the house, they discovered the pipes had frozen and burst. They had no water. Mike built a fire for heat and went out to unload.

"I'm going to pour some gasoline on these fire ants," he called out.

WHOOSH! Flames leapt higher than his head. The fumes had reached through the open door to the fire inside the house and ignited. Next the leaves over the yard flamed up.

Mike grabbed a coat to beat out the fire, but the leaves under the trailer caught up fast. He crawled under it, but the coat was no good. Carpet scraps on the trailer glowed orange and let loose smelly smoke.

He jumped into the car to hitch the trailer and pull it away from the house.

"Everything we own's on the trailer!" Ginger shouted.

"We got to sacrifice the trailer to save the house."

Ginger stood in the burning leaves and shouted directions to guide him until the car lined up with the trailer.

Mike grabbed a chain and pulled it around the trailer hitch tongue, then fastened it tight and floorboarded the car.

The tongue started burying, even with the motor in low, digging into the ground, because of the weight of the trailer. Mike tugged it as far as he could get it, about forty feet from the house, before the flames licked through the tarps and he had to bail out. The trailer lit up like a bonfire, directly under the power line that fed the house.

In a couple of minutes, the coating insulation burned off the wires coming to the house, 220 volts. When the wires touched each other, they produced a light show that lit up Texas. The power went out in the house, but they had light from the arcs dancing in the sky.

Bright light to watch everything they owned burn to ash and blow away in the January wind.

Someone called the fire department, but it was too late.

They bunked at the Salvation Army that night. The next day the Red Cross gave them $600 for toothbrushes and clothes.

"That's about all we got but the house," Mike told Ginger. "I figure we lost more than $15,000 dollars."

As if that weren't enough, they had no way to prove for insurance pur-
poses what had burned. Nor could they substantiate the extent of the loss
the year they faced their highest taxes because of Mike's good pay.

"The IRS is beating us with a pencil." Mike paced back and forth for
days, waving their tax forms with his hand, and ranting at the government.
"They think we're crooks. We'll spend years paying what they say we owe. It
isn't right."

It was a bleak winter.

Mike had always bucked at authority and rules, other than his own.

"I don't color between the lines, and nobody tells me what to do," he
always said.

Consequently, he found much that rankled him, especially in organized
religion and the government. The sword crossing with the IRS cemented his
distrust and resentment of the government's power.

What he saw as the country's downward path also disturbed him: foul-
mouthed teenagers, alternative lifestyles, schools teaching little girls to put
condoms on bananas.

*Where are we headed? What would happen if the government collapses?
What would happen if we had a nuclear explosion?* Drugstores didn't keep
potassium iodide in stock, the chemical to counter radiation sickness. He
had already checked them out.

Ginger's job at H&R Block sustained them into the spring when they all
moved back to Missouri. There they remained for two good years, until that
job played out the winter of 1993.

The storm clouds began to gather with their return from Missouri.

Ginger went back to tax preparations in January, anticipating $2,500 at
the end of tax season in April. Mike had no prospects, but they knew he

could go back to Missouri in April. They'd become friends with a couple who held prayer meetings in their kitchen, so Ginger and Mike tried printing a Christian newspaper at home, a shopper. But the paper sponged up their investment and died in debt. Their bank balance sank lower each month.

Ginger suspected that Mike worked harder at avoiding employment than finding it. He just didn't seem particularly concerned that he had no job. And when it came to money, Mike was a sieve—he spent money they didn't have, $1,800 for a generator or $600 for a Hobart mixer, always buying on credit. He didn't maintain appliances, so there were always repair bills. He'd buy firewood when they had plenty of wood on their property that he could chop. Often money just disappeared without anyone knowing where it had gone. The less money they had, the harder Ginger had to stretch what was left to feed them and cover essential expenses. She'd already learned to suture small wounds to save money on doctor's visits. Any work she could find, any way she could supplement or save she did.

Being poor was just a temporary phase, she told herself. They would get past these hard times. But she felt stained by poverty, as if it were something that wouldn't wash off. It set her apart, made her less than other people.

She prayed they could just make it to April.

One day, when the shelves held just two jars of beans, all the meat gone, Ginger knew starvation lurked around the next curve. In despair, she walked with Mike out into the sunlight.

"Look, look," she shouted.

Two piney woods rooters, wild pigs with tusks, were strolling down their driveway.

"Hush or you'll scare them off." Mike rushed inside for his gun.

He shot both of them. They dressed them, iced them in Casey's red wagon, and ate pork and beans for supper that night.

The pigs weren't the only animals that came to their rescue. Mike was in the yard with a machete when Ginger spied a six-foot rattler coiled on the septic tank cover. Mike looked at his machete and opted for his gun. The snake had thirteen buttons. Its meat was in two long muscles the size of Ginger's little finger, white like pork and firmer than chicken. Really very tasty, Ginger thought.

Her parents hit a squirrel with their car just up the road from Ginger's house one day and brought it back to her. They ate squirrel with dumplings. Ginger teased about eating roadkill. They never ate possum or armadillo, though. Armadillos carry leprosy, Ginger had heard. They'd had everything else. They didn't need leprosy.

Mike turned down the job in Missouri.

Leprosy would have been no less a shock.

"How can you refuse to work?" Ginger said. "We need—"

"I went up there and earned an armload of money, and what good did it do? Just came home and burned it up," Mike said.

He refused. Period. He'd been without work for five months and had no intention of taking another job.

No amount of cajoling, pleading, arguing would budge him.

Ginger felt a social stigma because her husband was able to work but didn't. Anger fueled resentment.

"I'm tired of the game," Mike said. He offered no other explanation.

One afternoon, in late April of 1993, Mike stopped by the office where Ginger worked. "I signed the papers for a disability check this morning."

"Disability? What disability? You're as healthy as a horse."

He reminded her that when they walked on the beach so long ago, he'd told her about facing a bout of depression.

"When I was in the hospital," he told her now, "they misdiagnosed me. I've always had a sleep disorder, that's all, and that's what the doctors came back to, a sleep disorder dating back to childhood."

The doctors stopped all medicine. But somewhere along the way he'd been qualified for a disability check. "I never filed for it before, but if the government wants to pay me, I'm going to take up the offer. After all, it's my money, money I've paid in all these years."

Twelve thousand dollars would be coming every year. But Ginger wasn't to tell anyone.

She was knocked off kilter, confused, mad, and guilty over being mad. Was Mike sick, lying, or lazy? How could he collect money for being disabled when she knew he was fully able to work? That didn't sit well with her despite the financial cushion it provided.

The disability check became their deepest secret and sole income. Mike couldn't take a job without jeopardizing the check, even though it left them $5,000 below the government poverty threshold for a family of four. Their family totaled six at times, with Mickey often living with them and Trent there on occasion. The money Ginger earned helped, but it was never enough to close the gap. The few ups they'd had couldn't offset the downs. Now they'd dug themselves so deep into a hole, so far below the official poverty level, they would need a step ladder to climb out.

Like chopping off a dog's tail a little at a time, that's the way we've sunk lower into poverty.

Long before Mike filed for disability, he had buried himself in the Bible. Rather, three different versions of the Bible plus a concordance, all piled on the bed with him. He reckoned he spent eighteen hours a day studying for what seemed like a good two years. He literally wore out one Bible, thumbing through its pages until they were dog-eared and torn. Daniel and Revelation just flew apart.

Ginger scrimped and stretched. Mike laid in bed and read about John the Baptist and locusts.

chapter eight

The following September, Mike slouched at the dining room table, lingering over a cigarette and a cup of coffee, watching Casey and Cody playing chase outside. Ginger folded into a chair opposite him and pillowed her head atop her arms on the bare table. She wore jeans and a t-shirt, and her feet were bare. She rested them on the stretcher between the chair's front legs.

"You know my check that'll come next week?" Mike said, tapping his ash atop a layer of butts.

"Umhmmm. Your disability check."

"Well, don't count on it because it's already gone."

Ginger snapped her head up.

"What do you mean it's gone?"

"It's gone. Over. Finished." He flicked the cigarette with his finger.

"How could it be gone when it hasn't come yet?"

He leaned forward and looked her in the eye. "I spent it on things we're already using, that's how."

"The power bill's due next week, Mike. How're we going to pay the bill without your check? Tell me that." She planted both palms flat against the table and glared at him.

"Santa Claus is coming to town," he sang.

"Mike, this isn't funny. Your family's going to be in the dark if we don't pay the power bill. Why can't you be serious?"

Her eyes narrowed and her words charged through clenched teeth. "What have you spent the money on this time?"

"That's for me to know and you to find out," he said in a singsong.

"Mike! Where did the money go?"

"If you want to get hot about it," he said, "this'll help." He reached his cup across the table and sloshed coffee at her face.

It caught her as she rose from the table, a warm splash against her chin. Most of it soaked her shirt. She pulled the wet cotton away from her skin, her hands shaking.

"Why did you do that? I can't believe you threw coffee at me!"

Mike grinned. "You going to a wet t-shirt contest?"

She huffed off to the bedroom to change shirts. When she returned to the living room, she wore a blue gingham blouse that buttoned down the front. Its shirttail hung loose.

Mike still sat at the table. She had to edge past him.

He grabbed her shirttail into a wad and yanked. The blouse ripped. Two buttonholes tore open, and their buttons popped off.

She shrieked.

He let go and threw both hands up.

She dashed to the sofa, well out of his reach. "Look what you've done."

She fumbled with the buttons, trying to close the shirt over her breasts. "You've ruined my blouse."

Mike stalked across the living room from her and leaned against the wall's bare yellow sheetrock. He took a long draw from his cigarette and exhaled.

"If you don't rein yourself in, I'm going to slap you." The smoke curled around his words.

"I'm sure you will," she said, chin out.

He narrowed his eyes, focusing on Ginger as if he were sighting a rifle. Five steps it took to cross the room, fast, heavy steps. When he reached Ginger, he swung his arm down and smacked her jaw with the full force of his open hand. A man-blow that rocked her jaw.

She staggered backward against the couch, her skull reverberating. Tears washed down her cheeks, but she was too shocked to notice them. He'd never hit her before. No one had ever hit her. This pain was new. It took her breath.

Mike headed for the kitchen. Most likely, his anger was over. Like a bubble, it had burst, at least for a while. Ginger slipped back into the bedroom to change clothes again.

Her mirror reflected the white print of his hand on her cheek. She touched her fingers to her jaw. It was really sore and already swelling. *This is what Mike felt as a child when his father hit him.*

She had to think, to make a decision.

It was a conversation she'd had many times in her head. Every time something happened, the same choices flashed on the screen. Every time she had to ask, is this enough to leave over?

Crazy, but she still loved him. He wrote her poems. He was good to the boys. That's what always stopped her. That's why she'd swallowed the little things, even though they weren't really little, they just weren't big enough to make her leave. Like when he slung the TV out into the yard. Or threatened to hit her after Casey was born. When he insisted on sex whenever she ran a fever. Or the times he squeezed her arms and pushed her. Each time was either as bad as the last or a little worse, escalating a notch at a time.

When she tried to remember the starting gate, it was lost. Instead of looking back to the beginning, now she only looked at the latest incident. That became the starting gate. So, is slapping me that much worse than throwing coffee or pushing me?

Yes. He'd crossed the line. Next time the slap might be a fist.

She stared at the mirror again. The white handprint reddened as blood returned to the skin.

The bedroom window slid open. If she could get to her boys, she could scoop them up and they could run away down the road to safety.

She swung through the window, dropped to the ground, and crouched against the house. The sun hung like a fireball at the tree line. Deep shadows collected around the base of the trees to the west, while angled sun rays tipped everything else in soft gold.

Casey and Cody weren't in sight. She scurried up the driveway to peer down the road but didn't see or hear them.

She sensed Mike's presence and heard his steps heavy at her heels. She ran.

He was too fast. He tackled her.

She pitched forward. Her knees buckled onto the manicured grass around Roy McNeil's oak tree. Mike's knee hit between her shoulders and drove her to the ground. He grasped her by the collar and ripped the shirt away from her back. She felt a sting at her neck. The gold necklace Mike gave her, the unbreakable gold necklace, broke in two. His fingers wrapped around her bra from the back, then jerked it until its hooks broke loose.

He stood over her as if he'd just roped a calf.

"Now get in the house."

He turned his back, plodding toward their house.

Ginger quickly ran her fingers through the grass, feeling for the necklace. *We have so little, especially after the fire. This necklace matters, now where is it?*

She patted the cool blades of grass, but it was gone.

She knelt on the ground like a rabbit and waited for the distance to widen between her and Mike. When he was almost back to their house, she bolted.

The closest house belonged to the Old Goat. Years had passed since she'd entered it or even spoken to either of Mike's parents. Bad years. But she was more afraid of Mike than of Roy right now. She fled to his house.

She pounded at the back door until Thelma cracked it just enough to peep out, just enough for Ginger to shove it open and shoot past her into the laundry room.

Thelma bounced against the paneling before recovering her balance. She stuttered while Roy pushed past her.

Ginger balled into a corner beside the washer, shuddering. She clutched at her torn blouse and bra, then drew her knees to her chest and wrapped her arms around her legs. She buried her face against her knees. Her back and shoulders were bare, as were her feet.

"What the hell?" Roy said. "What in holy hell?"

Thelma pulled one of Roy's shirts from the clothes hamper and spread it over Ginger's shoulders.

Ginger looked up, and Thelma gasped when she saw the handprint on Ginger's face. Roy leaned close to see better.

"That piece of…" he said.

He marched into the kitchen.

"You goddamned bastard," he yelled at Mike over the phone. "You never saw me do anything like this to your mother. Now you get yourself over here and take this woman home."

"No!" Ginger screamed. "No!"

She brushed past Thelma and out their door.

The last orange in the western sky faded to purple as Ginger ran, her bare feet slapping the asphalt. She held tight to Roy's shirt as the night air chilled. Scrub pines behind sandy shoulders lined most of the narrow road. There were only a few houses, and she didn't know where to go. A dog yapped at her ankles when she passed.

She ran without destination for two miles, until the subdivision intersected with the highway to Hackleberg. The town lay eight miles to the left. She stopped. Too far. She couldn't run that far. She tried to think while she sucked deep breaths.

Her friend Janey would come get her, if she called. Janey and her husband Donald had friends who lived on the road to Hackleberg. She'd met them once. They'd let her use their phone. Mike had met them too. She hoped he wouldn't think of them now.

Theirs was the last house before miles of woods, a bungalow with no cars in its carport.

Ginger knocked at the back door. She panted for breath. Waited. When no one answered, she tried the door. It opened. She ducked into the dark house. She didn't dare turn on lights, so she felt for a telephone. Her fingers ran over the kitchen countertops, then the end tables in the den. Something moved. A shadow. Startled, she stumbled backward against the paneling onto the wall-mounted phone. She dialed Janey's number, watching a cat skitter down a hall.

Janey and her husband Donald sheltered her overnight. The next morning, the redness from her face had faded to dull purple. Her jaw remained sore to the touch. Gently she dabbed on Janey's make-up to make the mark less noticeable.

I'm not going back. Which meant she had to get her boys. And her car. And some clothes and money. *Why didn't I think?* She needed so much.

Donald agreed to negotiate with Mike for the car and the boys. The men were friends; nevertheless, Donald steeled himself for a confrontation. Janey went along to get some clothes for them.

In the meantime, Ginger sought out the preacher and his wife from the kitchen prayer meetings in nearby Remlap. The man had boxed before Vietnam took one hand. Now he hosted a talk-radio show and preached part-time. His wife was round and solid as a tree trunk. Ginger sat with them in their kitchen around an oak table where they had all held hands and prayed for other people in need.

"I'm the one needing help now." She began to cry.

The preacher took her hands in his hand and his wife scooted her chair close and put her arm around Ginger. She told them everything, what had happened the night before and how afraid she was of Mike's moods.

"What scares me most is how violent he's become. I'm afraid of what he'll do next."

"Excuse me," the preacher said. He patted her arm before he tiptoed out of the kitchen. Ginger continued to pour her heart out to his wife.

When the preacher returned to his place at the table, he took Ginger's hands again.

"Ginger, we'll pray for Mike. We'll pray for both of you. But you have to go back to him."

"Yes, you must," said his wife.

"I can't. I'm—"

"It's your duty, Ginger. Don't you know, the Bible says…." and he quoted verses about women submitting to their husbands, squeezing Ginger's hands.

"But he hit me. Didn't you hear me? I'm afraid."

"Surely it wasn't all that bad. It's not a big bruise." He released her hands to run his finger across her cheek.

"It's covered with makeup." Ginger sat back, away from this preacher.

"Ginger, I called Mike and told him you were here. He'll come get you—"

"NOOOOO!"

She shot up and darted for the door.

The preacher lunged toward her. He grabbed her by the arm.

She twisted loose from his grip and bolted out the door.

Mike surrendered Casey and Cody and the car to James while Janey packed clothes.

"When I saw her running," he told Donald, "I chased after her and I fell down. I ripped a muscle in my calf, so I was barely able to catch her. I reached for her. I'd bought her this unbreakable gold chain, and I limped up behind her and grabbed her collar and got the necklace. She was screaming. When I saw the cherry red mark the necklace cut into her neck, I let her go. She ran on to my dad's house."

He was hobbling, unable to tend to two small boys. He sent the necklace with the boys; he had pocketed it when it broke. In fact, he'd told the preacher he was sending someone for Ginger because he couldn't come himself.

Ginger drove her sons to a remote cabin Mileah and her husband owned, a place Mike wasn't likely to think about.

In less than a week, she went back to Mike.

She couldn't say why she went back. She just did. She drove into Hackleberg to go to the bank and there was Mike, standing on the street where she parked. Cody leaned out the window to call to him and both boys started crying and begging to go home. And she did. She didn't want to think about it.

Ginger knows now that women leave and go back an average of eight times before leaving for good. Maybe the known demon is less scary than the unknown. Not so for her.

"I'd left one marriage. I knew the hard road ahead, the sense of failure, the guilt. Call it commitment, minimizing, hope, fear, it really doesn't matter," she says of why she went back, "it's all mixed together. I didn't stop to analyze what I felt."

Two months later, Ginger sat at the kitchen table with the boys coloring Thanksgiving turkeys on paper plates. A warm November breeze drifted through the open windows and with it the sound of Mike's car on the driveway. She heard the door slam.

Mike joined them at the table. He was folding a wad of bills into his wallet.

"Where'd that come from?" Ginger asked. Mike's next disability check was ten days away.

"The Andersons gave it to me," Mike said, taking a chair. He put Cody's paper plate turkey to his face like a mask, playing with Casey.

"Why did the Andersons give you money? They don't owe us anything."

The Andersons were an elderly couple, long-time family acquaintances from Ginger's church in Baycross who had moved to Hackleberg.

"Mr. Anderson cashed a check for me."

Her ears perked up.

"Why Mr. Anderson? Why didn't you go to the bank?"

"Because we don't have any money in the bank and I needed some money, that's why." He struck a match to light a cigarette.

"No money? We had $1,500 three days ago." Ginger stood up, shoving her chair away from the table. "How could there be none now? Where did it go?"

"We had bills and expenses and things we needed," Mike said, twiddling the turkey plate in one hand, not looking at her.

"You spent all our money and gave Mr. Anderson a bad check?" She stood feet apart and arms akimbo. Her face reddened and her voice rose. "We're flat broke and you're sticking him with a bad check. What's more, you did it on purpose!"

"Quit your harping," Mike said. "My government check'll be deposited before he gets around to cashing this one."

"That's wrong."

"Ginger, if you see two stripes painted on a parking lot, you're going to park between them. Me, I'll straddle the stripes, if I want to. No line is going to stop me from nothing."

Their argument simmered and flared throughout the day.

Money and principles. Right and wrong. The one topic Ginger could expound upon. In nearly everything, she bowed to Mike's lead, the way she'd been taught. But she couldn't hold back her moral indignation when he did something clearly wrong. Wrong before God. It was her duty to speak up, her duty to her husband and to God.

"Writing a check you can't cover is bad enough," she said after supper. She was squatting on the bare floor, pinning a sewing pattern to fabric. "But shorting old people like the Andersons—"

Mike sprang at her. He knocked her backward, smacking her head against the floor. With one knee to her chest, he pinned her with his weight. She flailed, reaching for a handhold, gasping for breath. He grabbed both arms and squeezed hard. With his face over hers, he spoke in a growl.

"You shut your mouth, or I'll knock your teeth to your toes."

She lay motionless, the sting of his slap fresh in her memory.

"What's going on in there?" called Casey, now seven. He bounded out of his room.

"Why're you on the floor?"

Mike crawled off Ginger and stood up. He offered his hand to help her up.

"It's okay," Ginger said. "Come on, Casey. Let's go back to bed."

She hugged him against her legs all the way back to his room.

"Here, I'll crawl in with you." And she did.

With her arms wrapped around Casey, she watched shadows play on the ceiling until he fell asleep.

Mike tiptoed to the bed and put his hand on her shoulder.

"Come here," he whispered.

He led her upstairs, to their bed. She complied. She always complied.

Expectant, tense, she faced the wall beside the bed. There nail heads in the wallboard formed a familiar path and she danced barefoot in its cool grass. She caught snowflakes on her tongue and felt them melt away. She sang *Jesus Loves Me*.

Mike rolled away.

She felt the sting of chafing. Her tears wet the pillow. Underneath it she balled her fist.

The next day, the bruises ringed her arms like bracelets.

For Mike, the sun rose on a new day. He made no mention of what had happened and chatted in his usual affable manner. When Ginger showed him her bruises, he refused to talk about it, as if it hadn't happened at all. Not that he didn't remember or was in a trance, he just declined to discuss it. It was his way.

Two weeks later, Mike flared up again. This time they were in the upstairs bedroom talking about the butane gas tank on the camper. He bumped against the bed table and the telephone fell to the floor. An accident, but something about it ticked him off.

He ripped the phone from the wall, pushed open the door and marched onto the roof over the porch. He held the phone high in one hand, like a football and threw it into a pine tree. It knocked against the tree trunk, bounced through several limbs, and stuck. The receiver continued to fall until it bobbed up and down as if it were on a bungee cord.

Mike did an about face and stomped back inside.

"One day, we're going to move so far out in the woods—"

He didn't need to finish his sentence. He had begun to talk about living somewhere more remote than where they now lived. Maps from the Army Corps of Engineers cluttered his desk.

He clomped down the stairs. Ginger followed on cat feet, well behind. Her purse sat open on the dining room table. He snatched up the purse with her billfold, keys, and driver's license, strode out to his car and locked her things inside his trunk. Before he drove off, he shouted, "You're not going anywhere unless I say so."

Throughout his tantrum, Ginger had stayed out of his path and said nothing. She walked into the yard where the car had been parked. Back inside again. At the table, she reached out for the purse, which wasn't there. A shiver ran up her back and she pulled on a sweater to warm up.

*Whatever was going on with Mike...*the thought faltered and she shivered again.

"Casey," she said a few days later, "Let's play a game. I'm going to tell you a secret word, and that word's a signal. Do you know what a signal is?"

Casey nodded. He was seven.

"If I ever say 'cottage cheese,' then you get on your bike and take Cody on his tricycle and ride as fast as you can in the road all the way to the house with the blue shutters."

She described a house more than a half mile away, a long ride for two little boys, but she wanted them to get far away. They rehearsed the plan, their secret, until she was certain he was prepared.

It wasn't long until she and Mike crossed again, this time over Christmas shopping. Mike fisted a handful of Ginger's hair and pulled her neck over the arm of the sofa.

"Please, please. You're hurting my neck."

"Someday I'm going to move you out in the woods so far there won't be any shopping, won't be anything I don't say." He yanked her hair, then let go.

Cody darted from the kitchen doorway and hid under the table.

Later that afternoon, when the children were playing in the leaves in the yard, Mike nudged Ginger toward their bed.

She'd given in to him the last time. But it left her feeling dirty and used, like a whore. So, like a whore, she stripped and lay spread-eagled across the bed.

"Go ahead. Take it. Do whatever you want."

He scrunched his eyebrows together and his face reddened.

"Hmmmmph."

He walked away.

Ginger jumped up and pulled her clothes on. She'd shamed him. How he would handle shame she didn't know, but she feared it would build like steam in a pressure cooker.

She heard him banging around in the kitchen, drawers pulling out and slamming shut, cabinets opening and closing. Something hit the floor and broke. He exploded. She heard him dial the telephone.

"Come get this bitch!" he shouted into the phone. "Yes, you, come get this bitch."

Helen Mitchell, Ginger's mother, held the phone away from her ear, aghast at what she heard. She repeated Mike's words to Claude, who became livid. They didn't use that kind of language, and no one talked to his wife like that. What was this about?

It was their first inkling of trouble between Ginger and Mike. They'd been painfully aware of how scarce money was for them, how they struggled in that half-finished house. But they didn't know there was trouble within the marriage.

"All we can do is pray for them," Helen said.

Mike slammed the receiver on the phone so hard it fell to the floor. He kicked at it and stormed out the door.

Ginger crept into the kitchen. She hung the phone back on its hook and it rang, startling her. It was her friend Terri.

Mike heard the phone ring and swung open the kitchen door. From the stoop he shouted and raged at Ginger.

She cupped her hands around the phone. She knew Terri could hear Mike in the background.

"Please ask Ben to come get me," she said. Ben was Terri's husband. "Please come, I'm afraid."

Ben wasn't at home. Terri called the police.

Mike was still stomping, red-faced, thrusting his arms back and forth when the squad car drove up, nor had Ginger quieted down. When the policemen tried to ask questions, she blurted out her story. The policemen looked for marks, but there were none to show.

Mike mouthed off about letting the policemen put their boys in custody of DHR rather than let Ginger have them.

"Boys?" one of the policemen asked. "Two little boys?"

They had passed two little boys peddling up the road as they drove into the subdivision.

While one stayed with Ginger and Mike, the other policeman backtracked. He retrieved Casey and Cody, one on his bike, the other on his tricycle.

He quizzed first Cody, then Casey, in the squad car.

"Have you ever seen your momma and daddy have a fight?" he asked each one.

"Daddy pulled her hair," Cody said.

"Daddy sat on Mama on the floor, and that was after she crawled out the window. And one time he threw a television out the window." Casey said.

"That's enough," the policeman said. He handcuffed Mike.

Mike shook his handcuffed wrists at the boys. "See what you've done."

One policeman took Ginger aside.

"Whatever you're going to do, you better get started," he said. "We can only hold him four to six hours."

After the police car drove away with Mike in its back seat, Casey tugged on his mother's arm.

"Mama, you forgot to say 'cottage cheese.'"

The sky sealed over with black clouds and the bottom dropped out with torrential rain before Ginger could collect their clothes. Bags packed, they dashed through the rain for the car.

The car doors were locked.

Back in the shelter of the house, she searched for her keys. Then she remembered that Mike had stuffed them into his pocket.

She phoned the jail, but he refused to relinquish them. The clock was ticking away.

The locksmith charged extra for hurrying out in the country in the rain, but Ginger had no options. She had $50, barely enough to pay him and buy gas for the four-hour trip ahead.

She called her mother. "We're on our way."

Her car passed within a block of the Hackleberg jail minutes before Mike walked out its door.

"I got to pay $65 for the privilege of cooling off," Mike told me. He still burned with the injustice. "In Texas it's always the man that gets thrown in the cooler. They let the woman stay with the kids. I was in a room with coffee and a Coke machine, and I could smoke. I couldn't leave, but it wasn't a cell. I wasn't in jail."

"Once you're gone, you're gone. You're not coming home."

Her father's words. They were imprinted on Ginger's mind as clearly as the yellow line painted down the center of the highway. Yet she was going home. Her daddy would protect her. He wouldn't let anyone hurt her.

They talked, Ginger, her mother, and her father. She told them everything, the TV, the telephone, the threats, the shoves, the hair-pulling, the coffee, the slap, the disability check, the bad checks, everything.

"If I'd known he harmed my daughter, the state of Texas, the whole U.S. isn't big enough—I'll hunt him down, I'll, I'll—," Claude ranted while he stalked from one side of his den to the other.

When he calmed down, he asked Ginger why she didn't come home.

"But you said we couldn't come home once we left."

"I didn't mean that," he said. "You know I didn't mean it."

"You were mighty convincing," she said. "Besides, I didn't want to burden you. I wanted to stand on my own feet."

"Well, you're home now and safe," her mother said.

"Yes, and close to Trent. I worried about his spending Christmas with us this year."

The FedEx delivery man brought a letter from Mike. One every day. Letters saying how sorry he was and that he'd been under such stress he didn't realize what he was doing. Love letters. Poems. He telephoned, then hung up if Helen or Claude answered. When Ginger answered, he begged her to let him see Casey and Cody. It was Christmas, and he was so alone without her and his boys.

"This is my castle, and I'll shoot him if he comes here," Claude said.

Ginger agreed to meet Mike at a school yard so he could visit with Casey and Cody.

Later she determined Casey and Cody were just tools to gain entry. Mike spent a few minutes with them and sent them off to play. He and Ginger sat in the car, and he talked all sweetness and romance. He gave her a gift, a lovely sweater.

"I'm so lonely. I feel empty without you." He stroked her arm, back and forth, lightly brushing against her breast.

He's trying to arouse me, and he's doing it. Foreplay was not a part of their lovemaking, so she responded to his touch. But it ended right there.

After supper on New Year's Eve, Ginger pulled an ottoman up to the chair where her father sat in the den, watching bowl games on TV.

"Dad, I'm going back to Mike."

Claude grimaced.

"Hear me out, Dad. I've wrestled with this decision. I've tossed until the bed sheets twisted loose every night, but now my mind is made up.

"Mike's really sorry for the things he did, and he promises things will be good between us. Even if they aren't perfect. I know he loves me and the boys to the depth of his heart. Without us, he has no one, no family."

Her father tried to talk her out of it. "The Bible says one man, one woman, one marriage."

"Yes, and I've messed up already. I've torn one family apart and I can't undo that."

"You're going against God and the church."

"God and the church may not bless this marriage, but I don't want it to fail. I have to go back. We can make it work."

Her father reasoned, argued, pleaded, but she would not be swayed.

"He's my husband and he's the father of these boys. I have to give him another chance."

"Then it will cost you your relationship with me," Claude said.

Ginger let his words sink in.

"That breaks my heart, but it's your choice." She wrapped her arms around him and hugged him.

Claude stiffened. His jaw set. His arms hung at his sides.

An hour passed. Claude sat molded to his chair, his lips tight together. The roar of the football game filled the den. Helen watched the screen from the kitchen sink where she washed black-eyed peas.

Ginger phoned Mike, speaking above the television.

"I'm coming home, but there's something you need to know, and I'm saying this in the presence of Mom and Dad: If you ever hit me again, I'm going to shoot you. You can't watch me every minute. You have to fall asleep sometime. And I will shoot if you hit me again."

She and the boys left early the next morning, before her father was awake. She would wait several months to call him and, when she did, the phone lines iced over. She didn't call back.

She smiled as she drove toward Hackleberg, thinking about her threat to shoot Mike. *I'd never shoot anything other than a target. Guns scare me, but I'm capable of shooting a gun and he knows it. After all, I am a Texan. I want him to have a little something to think about, that's all.*

They returned to an empty house. She hadn't told Mike when to expect them, and he wasn't at home.

They were unpacked, almost settled in, when she noticed the collage hanging in the hall.

She'd made it from a yard sale frame she couldn't afford and filled it with family snapshots: Trent at age eight standing over the first deer he killed, Cody with a "thumbs up" for his fish, Mike with his arm around her, Casey with his dog. She treasured the memories it evoked, so she paused to gaze at it when she passed by.

The frame was splintered, its glass removed. Her picture had been slashed and her head cut off.

chapter nine

U nable to act on the mutilated picture, Ginger locked onto the broken frame as Mike's offense. It hurt that he damaged something so precious to her, but she never mentioned it to him. She'd come home to start anew, and she didn't want to begin with a fight. Besides, she was sure Mike would pretend to know nothing about how the frame broke.

They finished the house. They nailed railings on the stairs, hung a door on the bathroom, and painted the walls. Three months later, they moved to a faraway part of Tennessee.

The telephone receiver still bounced on its cord from a pine tree in the back yard.

Mike honeymooned Ginger. She didn't know that term at the time.

In retrospect, the pattern of isolation and need were apparent, but Ginger didn't see them. Nor did she recognize the pattern of physical abuse followed by "honeymoons," a period marked with romance, gifts, happiness—and rekindled hope—a time when the batterer begs forgiveness and promises the abuse will never happen again. Honeymoons draw the battered spouse deeper into the relationship and make leaving all the more difficult.

Even more entangled is the woman who's been trained as a nurturing caregiver, like Ginger, who feels she's the sole source of her abuser's emotional support, especially if he suffered abuse or neglect, which Mike did.

Ginger was determined this marriage would succeed.

"I trusted him. I had a traumatic attachment, a complete dedication to oneness," she tried to explain to me.

"Traumatic bonding" was the term Ginger would later learn to describe the attachment abused spouses feel toward batterers.

She could have left. She had a phone and a car. Leaving would be as easy as unplugging life support for each of them.

The move to Tennessee came during the honeymoon period.

Friends from Hackleberg had moved with their six stair-step children to Wayne County, Tennessee, and Ginger, Mike, and the boys visited them there.

That part of Tennessee, so Mike had determined, held the best land with good water and timber and the fewest people—even better than Montana, where the government owns so much of the land. The fewer people, the less crime, the fewer laws to worry about.

"We had planned—kinda. Ginger didn't participate much in the conversations—," Mike told me. He had studied population densities and water resources. He wanted a secluded place to live where his boys wouldn't learn about alternative lifestyles. "You've got to have good water. If you find water with periwinkles, then it's good water."

Their friends lived in a white farmhouse with a stone chimney rising from the center of a tin roof, two rooms on each side of the chimney. The house tucked against a hill where a spring flowed into a rivulet full of periwinkles. It provided their drinking water.

In front of the house, a grassy meadow with yellow flowers fanned down to a shallow creek. Their children, the girls in pigtails and pinafores, ran barefoot through the grass to wade in the creek and chase crawdads into Mason jars. It could have been *Little House on the Prairie*. Ginger felt a window had opened to a quaint new world of peace and calm.

So different from the house in Hackleberg they'd labored over so long, where they lived in the shadow of the Old Goat, where they'd been banned from the church, where fire had destroyed everything they owned on the trailer. Where so many bad things happened—nightmare things she wanted to get as far away from as possible.

"How could we not be happy in a place like this?" she told Mike when she agreed to move to Tennessee.

She never went back. Mike returned to Texas to hammer a For Sale sign into the yard of the house they built. All their belongings he loaded onto a truck bound for Tennessee, including the collage.

The plan was to rent a place while he searched for secluded land with good water, where they could live as they chose. He found a house to rent in Lutts, Tennessee.

Lutts is a stretch of countryside between two highway signs that proclaim its existence. At its one intersection, in a blue and white stucco building across from the post office, Kathy's Country Store fixes tires and sells bologna, fishing bait, and hunting licenses when it's open. The only store in Lutts, it serves the hundred or so people whose homes speckle the hills and back roads.

Everybody knew the house Mike rented for them. Mrs. Snead lived there until a few years back, and it had been empty since she was laid to rest. But her clothes and all her possessions remained just where she left them, and that was the condition of the rental: her things were to stay in place.

Nothing was to be moved. The McNeils could move in, but around and on top of what was there.

The first time Ginger saw the house, Mike turned their car off the two-lane blacktop just past the Lutts sign and onto a narrow gravel road. For more than a mile, the road tunneled between tight walls of trees, their green limbs interlacing overhead. Their car and the cloud of red dust it threw up were all that stirred. They passed no houses, no people. Ginger's skin crawled with the uneasy sense of passing through a dark corridor whose end she couldn't glimpse.

As the road climbed a gentle slope, the forest gave way to meadows fenced with barbed wire. Then one house. Across from it, on the right side of the road, a double reinforced wire fence rose six feet above the ground, marking the back boundary of a fox farm where hunters came to run their dogs. The fence followed the road to the crest of the ridge where, on the left, under three spreading oaks, Mrs. Snead's' house rested on cinderblocks.

Except where some had blown away, wine-colored asphalt shingles clung to its walls. The house had a concrete porch wide enough for a swing on the front and a narrow open porch across the back. Its rusty tin roof curled over the front porch.

The road curved downward for a mile until it ended at another county road beside a large strawberry farm, Ginger learned. No houses interrupted the expanse of either road. In bad weather, neither road was passable. Nothing but woods lay between Mrs. Snead's house and a settlement of Mennonites a few miles away.

Mrs. Snead's house would be home for the next two years.

"We already live apart," Ginger wrote to Trent when they moved to Tennessee. "This is just a little further."

They had fallen into letter-writing years back. Every card, Valentine, every word Trent wrote, she saved and reread when she needed to hug her firstborn and he wasn't there. The letters fell far short of the everyday contact she had with Casey and Cody, and that she regretted, but they bridged the gaps between Trent's visits.

He had spent Christmas and summers with them since he was out of diapers. Some milestones he had passed with them and some stories they retold.

He'd learned to swim as a tot when they lived in an apartment complex with a hot tub. Mike put pennies at the bottom and Trent would retrieve them. Soon he was swimming.

That was the summer she noticed his fundamental sense of orderliness. Trent appointed himself the "shoe straightener," spending long stretches of time lining up their shoes in the closet, matching pairs in perfectly straight lines.

When they bought gas for the car, Trent took the money inside to pay the cashier, always holding the bills with his arm outstretched.

The next summer, he told Ginger to kick the shit out of a ball. Where did he learn that word? She and Mike laughed about it. They didn't talk that way—Mike abhorred strong language.

Trent had awaited Cody's birth with his brothers in the camper and he had bathed in the lake when the Old Goat shut off the water. He'd hammered and hauled alongside them as they built the house.

His stepmother, Erika, excelled at creating conflicts, both on the calendar and between people. Erika would schedule something special either during Trent's visit time or overlapping it. Usually, he opted to visit his mom. Once, though, Erika phoned him at Ginger's house. "We're slipping off to Disney World next Friday. Don't you want to join us?"

He did. He packed up and left two weeks early.

Ginger couldn't blame him. Nor could she compete with such an offer. She'd already had words with Turner about her letters to Trent being intercepted. Now she was being outmaneuvered, and there was little she could do.

During Trent's last visit, when Ginger stumbled over converting her summer sausage recipe to bulk quantities, he chalked an equation on the blackboard and found all the answers.

"Just trust me, Mom," he'd said. "Here's what you need."

Algebra. He was growing up and had apparently inherited his father's knack for math and guns. He was a good shot. Both he and Turner spent hours oiling guns and reloading bullets.

"It's just us and the critters out here in the woods," she continued with her letter to Trent, knowing the outdoors would appeal to him. "At night we hear dogs running the foxes across the road, while off in the distance coyotes howl. A big tree limb reaches out over the swimming hole at the creek, and we need you to shimmy up to hang a rope swing."

She enticed him with what fun he'd have exploring this new countryside. And she said how eager she was to see him. Six months was a long time to be apart.

He didn't come their first summer in Tennessee. He'd found a girlfriend.

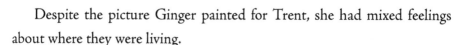

Despite the picture Ginger painted for Trent, she had mixed feelings about where they were living.

The sense of isolation on this lonely road engulfed her. No cars ever passed. Only one other house shared the road, and it sat a distance away. Her closest neighbors were the penned up foxes across the road.

They had a phone, but she knew no one to call. She'd left her family hundreds of miles behind, and she knew hardly anyone in Lutts. They occasionally saw their friends who had moved from Hackleberg, but something didn't seem right there. She and Mike both noticed it, although they couldn't say what it was. Then one day the family was gone. No good-byes, just gone. Vanished.

She wasn't likely to ever fit into this community where most of the people had been born in houses where their grandparents were born.

She was different, but strangely, this time being different felt good. She felt free, without the constraints of family, community, traditions, and other people's expectations. In the woods, at the top of her ridge, she could let loose. And she did.

Kathy at the country store gave her a homemade tape of Yanni, and Casey cobbled together a cassette player. She played it outdoors and pretended. If she were an eagle on the edge of a bluff, she would soar into the clouds. Or she would dance like a dervish under the clothesline, whirl around the sheets and sing to the treetops.

Some days she tossed a bucket to each of the boys and they tromped off in the woods to pick blueberries or up the road to the strawberry patch. Back home, she measured the ingredients for pie dough. "Here, let me show you how to cut the shortening into the flour," she said as she drew two knives past each other.

Flour fell over the kitchen like snow when the boys took their turn, and Ginger laughed, remembering her early efforts. While the berries cooked, she rolled out the dough. "Did you know Noah's ark was in my back yard when I was a little girl?"

Cody became her pie assistant. Casey chose another chore, but always in hearing distance of his mother's stories.

Mike had reached his goal, Ginger concluded. He had her and his boys to himself, totally isolated, totally dependent on him. He seemed content, at least as content as he ever was. And why not? She knew her role, as did Casey and Cody. Mike ruled and they obeyed.

If he wanted to do something, he did it. If he wanted the family to be a part of it, they were. He gave his permission as to when and where they went, who went into a store, and who sat in the car.

"I need some thread," Ginger might say as Mike pulled into Kathy's Country Store on a humid summer afternoon. Both boys in the back seat would move toward the doors, ready to hop out of the car.

"Stay put," Mike would say when he left the car.

"Why can't we go in?" one of the boys would say. "It's hot out here. The store's air conditioned."

"Because your father said for us to stay in the car," Ginger knew how unreasonable Mike was being, but she also knew it was her duty to uphold him as head of the family. So, they'd sit in the hot car until it pleased Mike to return.

"Where's my thread?" Ginger would ask as Mike put the key in the ignition.

"I didn't say I'd buy you thread."

Ginger knew to wait for another day to request the thread, even if she needed to sew something for Mike.

Or, at other times, Mike would hurry back with a whole box of thread in assorted colors for Ginger and popsicles for the boys.

Infuriating, the extent and senselessness of the control he exerted over her.

Yet she chose this role, she chose to live with him in this manner, and having the choice allowed her to feel free.

Or so she tried to convince herself.

As always, money was scarce. At least for Ginger and the boys.

Casey broke his arm, a bad break that had to be treated by a doctor.

"It hurts, ohhhh, it hurts!" he cried. "What's it going to cost to get it fixed?"

He was only eight, and he knew money was tight at their house. That his dad had taught him well.

He remembered going as a family to the dollar cinema. He was five and they saw Jean Claude van Damme in *Timecop*. At some point during the movie, his dad had said, "We're just burning money."

He held up a wrinkled dollar bill and lit it with his Bic. He held it by the corner, and it flamed up in the dark of the theatre.

Casey jumped to his feet, shocked and scared.

Mike raised the bill higher, above Casey's reach.

"Hey, buddy!" a man behind them called out.

Mike held the dollar until it burned to the corner he held. He let it drop to the floor between the seats, and it glowed orange, then black.

Casey never knew what point his dad had tried to make with his mom. What imprinted on his mind was an intense fear of being poor.

Ginger wrote checks to pay the bills and buy groceries. If she wanted something for herself, she asked Mike's permission. Mike also wrote checks, for whatever caught his fancy.

"How much do those things cost?" He was pointing to the new box of sanitary napkins under the cabinet. "All they are's a wad of cotton that you throw away."

Whatever he intended, Ginger heard a rebuke. She bought three flannel baby blankets at a yard sale and stripped them into sanitary pads. They became a point of pride as a symbol of self-sufficiency. The homemade pads said her family had so little money she couldn't afford sanitary pads, yet she had overcome this adversity.

The next week, Mike bought a Jet Ski, a used 1993 blue Kawasaki model you stood up on to ride. It cost $300.

Ginger read the notes posted on the message board at Kathy's store. Once a month, a flyer announced a meeting of the Ladies Home Demonstration Club.

"Why don't you come?" a woman said one day.

"Oh, I couldn't," Ginger said.

"It's at my house and I'm inviting you," the woman said. She spoke to Ginger but faced Mike.

He nodded. She had his permission. *It was just some ladies' thing once a month*, he told Ginger later. *Why not?*

Through the club, Ginger met a woman who worked part-time as assistant to the veterinarian, a woman who hired Ginger to babysit one afternoon a week, two Mennonite women who shared their Sunday school lessons for children, and other women in the area. At their bake sale, Ginger launched a small business baking bread, not much income but every bit helped. Mike even allowed her to deliver the loaves to elderly customers.

The club helped Ginger save as well as earn money.

Not long after she became friends with Barb, the veterinarian's assistant, Cody fell off a fence onto the hacked end of a young sapling and gouged his thigh. Ginger rushed him to Barb, who sewed the wound with sutures from the veterinary clinic.

The McNeils were the poorest Jet Ski owners in Lutts.

"Why aren't your boys in school?" a man asked Mike one day at the country store.

"We homeschool them," Mike said.

"Is that so?" The man furrowed his brow as if he were thinking hard on Mike's words.

Ginger had homeschooled the boys in Texas. They'd learned to read from *An Acorn in My Hand* by Edith Bolden. For all other subjects, they had one dictionary, a *Book of Knowledge*, and a 1935 set of *Compton's Encyclopedias*, which they went through one page at a time.

Tennessee, she learned, had a required state curriculum with designated textbooks. Homeschooling was allowed, but only under the auspices of some recognized authority such as a church.

Mike hit the ceiling. They'd moved here to get away from folks telling them what they could and couldn't do, and nobody was going to start now. They'd dang well do as they pleased, and the state of Tennessee need never know.

On another visit to the store, Ginger spotted one of her Home Demonstration Club acquaintances by the canned goods, talking to eight-year-old Cody while pointing at a can. She practically hurdled a crate of motor oil to reach them.

"Cody's reading the labels for me," the woman said. "I walked off today without my glasses."

With Cody in tow, Ginger eased their way out of the conversation and out of the store.

"Did you know the words?" she whispered.

"Most of them."

"What else did the lady ask you?"

"She asked me what grade I was in."

Back home, Ginger pulled an assortment of household products into a basket for a reading lesson from the labels.

"If people question you about school or want you to subtract or divide for them or read hard words, you come find me," she told the boys.

That evening she pleaded with Mike. "All we have to do is register or sign up somewhere. I'm scared the state will come in and take the boys away from us."

"You're always scared of something," Mike said. "Nobody's dragging my kids out of my door. Period."

His assurances stirred her stomach with all the old fears about rules, laws, and doing what was right. They had moved, but they hadn't escaped the old conflicts.

Every day, Ginger wrestled the rebellion that flared up inside, until she shouted down its voice in her head, then she would see the Mennonite women coming and going. They seemed so at peace with themselves. *That's what I want: peace in my heart.*

She turned to the Bible for guidance. Paul's letter to the Corinthians said the head of a woman is her husband. Head, hair, glory to God. She seized Bible verses, vague fragments from old sermons, Mennonite lessons, and kitchen church theology to stew together over the fire boiling up in her soul.

She knew what she had to do. Mike didn't object.

She cut white fabric into a square and hand-stitched a handkerchief hem around its edges. Even so she set it aside to prolong its completion while she waged the internal battle. At last, she sewed ties on two corners. Tears wet her cheeks when she tied the head covering in place and stood before the mirror.

The scarf lay tight against her forehead while the back flared out to the top of her collar and tied underneath her hair. It covered her hair yet gave a sense of hair.

"A head covering is an outward sign that the husband is head of the wife," she explained to her boys. It was exactly what she needed to do. She did it with all her heart and in all sincerity. It was her last-ditch effort to quell her individuality and assertiveness in her marriage —and it worked.

Mike told her she'd become meek, docile, and kind.

"That's what the head covering brings out," he told her.

She made one for each day and wore them everywhere except to bed. From her upbringing she knew that what you put on the outside conveys who you are. As a Christian, as a member of the Church of Christ, you stand apart.

It became easy for her. The head covering said "I'm a gentle woman, I have a head, I defer to his authority, and I have no authority of my own." She put it on, and it quelled that thing that rose up in her.

"Except you yank it off if we get in an argument," Mike said.

"That's true," Ginger said. "I feel so conflicted. If we're arguing, I'm striving against your authority, so I rip it off my head. I'll try harder to defer to you."

But her anger still boiled over on occasion. She threw her head covering at Mike one morning.

"Rebellion. That's what this is!" Mike yelled. "Judgmental rebellion."

He stomped through the house, gathering up all the head coverings. When he had a fist full, he threw them into the wood stove and burned them up.

After Ginger calmed down and repented for the fight, she wanted her head coverings back. "I feel naked without them."

Remorseful, she curled up on the couch. She ran her hands under the cushion, hugging it to her chest. Her fingers brushed against something soft. She lifted the cushion to see.

"What? Oh, oh!" she squealed. She'd discovered a head covering that escaped the oven. "Look, it's the first one I made."

Quickly she tied it on her head.

That night she lay in bed staring at the dark ceiling. *Why did I feel so bereft? Why is it so important to me, to me more than Mike, that my head be covered?*

She listened to the familiar call of an owl and the answer of its mate. Suddenly it became clear—*I've made a religious belief of submission and I wrap myself in it to get through each day."*

Late one Sunday morning in January 1995, when snow covered the ground and *nothing* passed down the road, Mike answered a knock on the front door.

A man wearing a quilted parka and a plaid hat with ear flaps stood in the yard. His pants tucked into heavy work boots, he stomped snow from one foot, then the other.

"See this rock?" he asked, holding up a jagged rock bigger than his fist.

Mike braced himself. *My God, did the boys break out this man's window?* He wondered how the man had driven his truck up the hill in the snow, but this wasn't the time to ask.

Instead, the man said, "You get me a semi-truck of these rocks, and I'll pay you $10,000."

What sounded like a fairy tale turned out to be a legitimate offer. The rocks were conglomerates, sedimentary rocks cemented together. When polished, they looked like peanut brittle with marshmallows.

Suddenly the McNeils were in the rock business. They sorted through the rocks the road scraper piled on the edge of dirt roads, picked out the conglomerates, and tossed the rest back. Sometimes they'd offer to clear a farmer's land of rocks.

They did three loads. First, they put them in nylon corn sacks, which rotted in the sunlight. After a week or two, they bought a cotton scale to weigh them in buckets. Mike got where he could estimate the weight and be right on the mark.

Ginger wrote Trent, "We collected two and a half tons of rocks yesterday and my hands are scratched and bruised and so dry in places they're starting to crack. My pinky on my left hand got smashed between two big rocks and it burst open like a grape. I usually wear my gloves, but I didn't yesterday. The good news is we have only two and a half tons to go and we'll be finished. We'll have to bag them, but that won't take but a couple of hours. You should see the sea of bags in the field!"

All in all, they picked up rocks for three years. When they'd gathered a load, an eighteen-wheeler hauled the rocks to Minnesota, where the man lived almost on the Canadian border. Driving in snow was second nature to him. He sent cashier's checks made out to Ginger. Being disabled and drawing Social Security, Mike didn't want a paper trail leading to him.

"People around Lutts cussed those rocks for years," he told Ginger, chuckling after she endorsed a check, "and we come and sold them for good money. Now they're cussing us."

Rock money smoldered in Mike's pocket in late spring of 1997. He needed $8,000, but the $3,000 in his pocket would make a down payment. He'd found 45 acres of land that suited him.

Trent came for two months the summer of 1996.

Hot June air whished through the open windows of the '79 Chevy Caprice and the torn headliner flapped in his face. He reached overhead for a thumbtack and tacked it back in place.

"When was air-conditioning invented?" he asked his mom, pushing a lock of sandy hair off his forehead.

Ginger laughed.

"Hey, be glad the radio works and the wheels turn. This car's older than you are."

"It's bigger than a barge." He twisted the radio dial to a country music station.

"You're right. I call it our redneck-white-trash-mobile," Ginger said. She gave the car a quick look over and chuckled.

A crack ran down the right side of the windshield. Stains splotched the cloth seat covers, even across the splits and snags. A spring peeped through a hole in the back seat. Thumbtacks held the headliner in place. And the air-conditioner didn't work. But it was spacious, and it got them around. So far.

She turned north onto the Natchez Trace, its two lanes a macadam stripe through green hardwoods, homebound to Lutts from a supply run across the state line in Alabama. Trent's guitar rested on a croker sack of potatoes and fifty pounds of chicken feed in the backseat. His straw cowboy hat sat on the front seat beside him.

"Hey, listen. That's a new song." He strummed an imaginary guitar with his right hand, careful not to drop the black marble he always held. He joined Garth Brooks in singing the chorus.

He's improving. He was practically tone deaf, but he'd been taking singing lessons. They'd sung with the radio much of the way on the first leg of the trip. Ginger chimed in on the next song, and they sang together for several miles.

"Watch out. There's the law." Trent pointed to a highway patrol car up ahead. "We're riding so low with all that stuff in the trunk, he'll think we're bootlegging."

"Bootlegging? Now just what would you know about bootlegging?"

Trent started to laugh.

"What's funny?" Ginger asked.

"Oh, nothing." Trent forced a deadpan expression. Then he cracked out laughing again.

"Tell me," Ginger said.

"What if that trooper pulled you over, thinking he'd nabbed a bootlegger, then saw you with that, that thing tied over your head. I'm sorry. I shouldn't have—" He laughed again.

"I wondered when you were going to ask me about my head covering," Ginger said. "What do you think of it?"

"Wierrrrrd, to be honest, but if you want to wear it, it doesn't matter to me." He picked up his hat and twirled it around one hand. "I want a black hat."

"You want to wear a black hat?" Ginger asked.

"To go with my marble." He held up his hand with the marble for her to see.

"Back up to bootlegging. What do you know about that?" She grinned at Trent. He was sixteen. The question was part teasing and part a mom's probing. Trent wasn't one to volunteer much information.

"More than you do, Mom." He grinned back, his chin down and eyes cut toward her, just like his dad.

"Oh, don't be so sure."

"Granddad says the Baptists and the bootleggers keep Texas afloat." He looked her in the eye. "I don't go to bootleggers if that's what you're fishing for. I truck my booze up from Mexico in eighteen wheelers every weekend, just for me."

"Okay, you're teasing me. I'll back off."

"Becky's brother sneaked their dad's car and went to a bootlegger. Cops drove up and busted him and the bootlegger. Coach kicked him off the team." He bounced his hat on his hand twice and put it back on the seat. "That was dumb. He can have all the beer he wants right out of the fridge."

Becky was his steady girlfriend, the reason he didn't visit the previous summer.

"Her dad tells me to help myself anytime, but I'm not going to drink his beer. He's just trying to set me up to get in trouble." He rolled the marble through his fingers.

"I drank a couple of cans with him one day when we were watching the Cowboys. So did Becky."

Ginger said nothing. She knew he was waiting for her reaction.

Trent went on. "He kept popping them, and she kept drinking them and later on she barfed in my car."

Ginger laughed. She remembered the Armour-Alled car of many years back when she was dating Trent's father. "In your car? I'll bet you did some fancy scrubbing before you went home."

"Dad didn't know. He's off working somewhere. But you know who smelled it and threw a hissy." He referred to Erika. Erika's hissy fits had become a staple in his stories.

Ginger held her tongue.

"I don't like Becky drinking. I don't like her drinking with him. And I don't want her dirtying my car again." He rolled the marble through his fingers. "I told her to choose: Bud or me, 'cause there wasn't going to be a second time."

"But Becky didn't mean to be sick."

"Well, that's what I told her."

"Trent, listen to what you're saying, son." Ginger's hands tightened on the steering wheel.

"I don't want a girl who tastes like alcohol." Trent looked at his mother when he spoke.

"One sip of beer, a whole can even, or a case, isn't going to change Becky from who she is." Ginger looked back at the road winding under leafy trees. "What I'm saying, son, is that Becky's going to do some things you don't like. That's human. You're going to do things I don't like."

"I don't drink."

"Good. I'm proud. I'm not encouraging you to drink. But you may at some point. Or you'll do something else." Ginger's wrist waved back and forth, reaching for an example. "Get a speeding ticket. Fail a test. Something. That's part of growing up. It's normal. What I want you to know is, you'll make mistakes and it's okay. You'll mean the same to me no matter what you do."

Trent folded his hands in his lap and stared at the road. "Hey, did you see that buck in those trees?"

Ginger looked. "No, missed him."

She said, "When I was growing up, I felt like my parents didn't love me when I wasn't perfect, and I knew deep inside I was never perfect. Nobody is. So, I never felt loved. That's why it's so important to me that you understand what I'm saying."

Trent didn't reply.

They rode in silence. Ginger hoped Trent was mulling over her words. She couldn't tell. He held his thoughts so close, like his dad.

"Would you love me if I drank a beer right now?" Ginger said as she turned onto the county road leading to their house.

He smiled big. "I want a picture of that. You holding a can of Bud up to a prayer cap."

"I had a life before I put on a head covering." Ginger laughed with him. "You didn't answer. Would you love me still?"

"Sure, you're my mom. I've always loved you. You know I'd keep on."

Ginger twisted a thought through her head a minute, one she'd gnawed on for years. She wanted to know, needed to know, yet feared its answer.

"Trent, what have you been told about me? What has your dad or anybody said about why I left?"

Ginger let go the breath she'd been holding.

"You're old enough to know and you need to know. It's going to come out, and I want you to hear it from me."

She slowed the car onto the packed red earth near their house and switched off the ignition. She turned toward Trent and pulled her knees onto the car seat. Her mouth felt dry.

"I'm not perfect, son. I never have been. It's hard to…I cheated on your dad, and I hurt him." She said it, but she looked down at the car seat the whole time. She couldn't face Trent while she told him what she'd done.

She could see Trent's hands in his lap. He rolled the marble through his fingers, back and forth. Then he fisted it. Rolled it again, faster. Looking up, she saw tears moistening his face, but he didn't interrupt her. When she stopped talking, he sat motionless, staring out the window at the reinforced fence that penned in the foxes.

What is he thinking? Why doesn't he say something? Have I lost him again?

Suddenly he flung open the car door and hopped out. He walked around the car, opened his mother's door, and took her hand to help her out.

"I'm sorry, I'm so, so sorry," she cried. She buried her face against his shoulder. "I'm not a bad person. I wasn't doing something to your dad. I was doing it for me—bursting loose from a straitjacket before it suffocated me. And you were the casualty of it all."

He hugged her tight.

"It's okay, Mom, it's okay. There's nothing to forgive."

"We don't live together. I've done a horrible wrong and because of that you weren't raised by your mother, and I *hate* that."

"But, Mom, that's just the way it is. I live with Dad. That's my life. I've never known anything else." He squeezed her again. "You don't need to apologize. I'm okay. It's been okay."

They began to walk, hand in hand, to the house.

"I don't think Mike and the boys are here." Ginger motioned toward the swing on the front porch. "Come sit here with me."

They sat close, Trent's arm around his mother's shoulder. She traced her fingers up and down cracks in the brown paint while they swung to the soft creak of the rusty chains.

"I remember when you left," Trent said.

"Oh, baby, you couldn't remember. You were too young," Ginger said.

"No," he said. "I remember it. I was standing in the door. You hugged me and told me goodbye, and I watched you leave. I remember."

Ginger bit her lips. It wasn't possible, he was only two. But she didn't dispute him. Tears flooded her eyes again and she looked at her lap.

"I never wanted to leave you, Trent, never. I always loved you. But I didn't have the option of keeping you."

She squeezed her hands together, squeezed again. Shame held her head down.

"Your dad threatened to bring out everything, the cheating, everything if I tried to take you. It would have hurt me, but it would have hurt my family even more. I'd done this thing, and I was bad. Besides, I didn't have money for a lawyer." She shuddered and began to cry again. "I didn't even fight."

Trent patted her shoulder and pulled her closer to him.

"My parents considered me bad. I'd tried to be a good mother, but your grandmothers could always do for you better than I could, and I was convinced that I wasn't good for you and that they and your dad were better than me. I thought you'd be better off with them and without me. Oh, I had this horrible sense of worthlessness."

"Mom, that's so sad," Trent said through his tears.

Ginger cried so hard she heaved.

"Mom, it's okay."

"Can you forgive me? Can you ever forgive me?"

"Mom, I forgive you. I love you." He rocked her against him while the swing went back and forth.

He held her hand in his, fingers entwined. She turned his hand and opened it to look at it. It was big and pale like his dad's. He was taller than his dad, but he had his dad's funny hunch to his shoulders. *This is the man he's going to be, and it's okay.*

"Tell me about Becky," she said.

"She's pretty, Mom, but you know what I don't understand…"

They talked in the swing until the setting sun brought Mike and the boys home with a string of crappie.

Long after Trent returned home, Ginger remembered the feel of his arm around her in the swing. *He had a sense of manliness about him, and he was nurturing me. I feel such sweet comfort that somehow I haven't failed Trent as a mother and he's going to be able to relate to a woman. I feel a sunrise with his forgiveness, a laying to rest. It's going to be okay.*

chapter ten

Mike's 45 acres hugged the eastern end of Wayne County, close to the Natchez Trace. It came with a spring, a rock pit and Mrs. Dunn.

Mrs. Dunn was a retired teacher who had inherited land and money, an 89-year-old widow who clipped her hair into a pixie cut, dressed in her dead husband's work clothes, and owned a small fleet of red vehicles. She had taken a liking to the McNeils or else the acreage would not have been available. While no expectations were even whispered, Ginger and Mike understood she was part of the package. Or rather, they were part of her package for minor repairs and occasional help with heavy chores.

They weren't the only ones. She had a pattern of sequential attachments. For some time, she'd befriended the Fowler "boys," two grown sons of a neighboring family, who helped mend the fences and load cows off to market. With Mrs. Dunn as the linchpin, the Fowlers and McNeils became friendly.

Ginger and Mike built the cabin in thirty days. They used a bucket of sawdust for a toilet, but they moved in.

They didn't anticipate such a rush.

Mike had studied. He knew how he wanted to live and what he needed to do. First priority was a good supply of water and a gravity flow water system. With the cash from rock sales, he bought solar panels to power a pump that would force the spring water uphill to a cistern. From there, it could flow downhill to their house. Once they had water, they would build their home.

But Mike had hardly installed the pump, much less laid the pipes or built the cistern, when their landlord doubled the rent on the house in Lutts.

"Bull corn. Thirty days' notice, you say? You got thirty days notice back. We'll be out by then." And the whole family set about hammering together a shelter in the woods in the heat of late summer. The water system had to wait.

Racing against the calendar, they chain-sawed trees and bush-hogged underbrush, all the while wiping sweat and clawing at chiggers. They cleared only enough space to build a 500 square foot cabin, which left a thicket to hide it from the road. Mike sawed rough lumber and Ginger pounded it together as board-and-batten siding. The boys, nine and ten, toted boards and fetched nails, tools, and water. Through summer rain and broiling sun until dark and fatigue chased them home each night.

Mike bought a dilapidated mini-school bus that had been refitted as a camper and stripped its cabinets and sink to use in the cabin. The hull they kept for storage. They splurged on a King wood stove, a black iron behemoth that took over half of one room. When the last nail anchored the corrugated tin roof, they filled a bucket with sawdust and moved in.

Like the house in Hackleberg, much work lay ahead. They had no plumbing, power or telephone. The plumbing they would add. But not electricity or a phone.

Fed up with nudity, dirty talk, and disrespectful kids—what he called garbage—Mike wanted to separate his family from society, to make a break with everything that he found objectionable. Besides, he sensed the tremors of an economic earthquake ahead, an upheaval that would bring about a total collapse of government and society. He intended that his family be prepared.

They would live off the land, much as the original settlers had lived.

Mike's lifelong abhorrence of authority fed his distrust of the government.

"I saw my dad wiggle out of things and it rubbed off," he said. "I question authority. I don't follow and I don't trust the government worth a dang."

As soon as the dust had settled in Waco, Texas, back in 1993, he drove out to see for himself how government agents blew away the peace-loving, God-fearing Branch Davidians.

"That didn't influence me, really, except to substantiate what I already believed," he said.

"We knew a few militia people when we published the Christian tabloid in Texas. They usually line up with religion. But I was never, never involved."

"It scares me how close we tiptoed to all that," Ginger says. "Mike doesn't have a political bone in his body. All he wanted was to be left alone to do as he pleased."

Since he expected the government to topple, he began to study *Foxfire* books and survival manuals.

"I read up on water power and how to store food without refrigeration. If you dip eggs in fat, then layer them in a bucket of salt, they'll keep up to a year. I already knew how to butcher a deer from hunting, so a cow or pig couldn't be much different, just bigger."

It wasn't until 1996 or 1997, after they had moved to Tennessee and already committed to a *Foxfire* lifestyle, that Mike heard about Y2K, the worldwide computer problem anticipated when the clock ticked past midnight on December 31, 1999. The concern was that critical industries such as electricity, finance, and transportation, along with governments, would cease to function at that minute because their computers were not programmed to change to the year 2000.

Y2K put a date on the collapse Mike predicted and there were people all over the world who shared his concerns. It underscored the need to be prepared.

Thus, the McNeils opted to do without electricity or a phone in 1997.

Ginger went along. Her head covering declared that she bowed to the authority of her husband. Submission was her new religion. All the ardor, devotion, and loyalty she once felt for the church she invested in Mike. If this was the lifestyle he chose, she would embrace it with all her strength. If it meant they had less, she would stretch more.

Drop a frog into a pot of boiling water, so goes an old tale, and he'll jump out. Drop him into cold water, then gradually turn up the heat. He'll stay until the water boils, and he dies.

"I was the frog in cold water except that by now the water was steaming, and I just kicked harder," Ginger said.

"Ginger was a chameleon," Mike said. "She blended in. She was compliant, just as her church had taught her."

Mike anchored a metal gate between two posts and fastened it shut with a padlock. Unless he unlocked the gate, no vehicle could enter. Or leave.

Then he strapped a .38 to his belt. He told Ginger he'd heard talk of drugs. And he wanted to make his point.

"Here comes that man with the gun," little children yelled as they hid behind store counters.

"Trespass on my land and I'll shoot you," he said more than once in public places.

When two policemen asked if they could hunt deer on his land, Mike told them, "You come on my land, and I'll be pulling you out by the legs."

There would be no mailbox, no 911 address, nothing to indicate that a family lived a little way up the dirt road.

"It's the law," Ginger pled.

"Not my law."

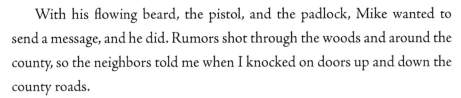

With his flowing beard, the pistol, and the padlock, Mike wanted to send a message, and he did. Rumors shot through the woods and around the county, so the neighbors told me when I knocked on doors up and down the county roads.

There were miles between neighbors, but the McNeils were known and discussed. Mike, I learned, attracted one thing he didn't want: speculation.

"If they weren't in the Witness Protection Program," one neighbor said, "then they were either running from something or running to it. That's what most folks thought."

"They lived off the land without any visible means of income, and that tells you right there something's going on."

"Mike scared people. He never smiled or acted friendly, and he wore that gun everywhere, even to Wal-Mart."

"Those boys should have been in school."

"Mike was lazy. He wouldn't turn his hand, even to clear the thorns from under the clothesline. He thought a woman should walk behind a man, never beside him."

Wayne Fowler said Mrs. Dunn and the Fowlers discussed the padlocked gate. They didn't think it was meant for them, but still it was unsettling. They blew their car horn and hollered from the gate until someone let them in.

Court Street Café, 2007

I had hardly introduced myself to Wayne at the Court Street Café, a steak and burger spot, when he was off and running. Two hours later he wound down, having royally entertained me with his stories and turn of phrase.

Had he not had a class at the community college, he might have talked longer or until his fiancée called him home.

"Everybody in the county was either related or had some connection," Wayne said.

"These strange, weird people came out of nowhere. With that beard Mike looked like Moses and was holier than the pope, sitting in the swing all day reading his Bible with a pistol on his belt. I was standoffish around him. He kept the gate locked all the time and carried on this nutty talk. They had no clocks or watches because time made no difference.

"Ginger had stringy hair and always wore dresses. He wouldn't let her wear pants. She always upheld him though. And she went two hundred percent into that way of life."

I asked him about Casey and Cody. He was twenty-three then, single, and had time for them.

"I was drawn to the boys," Wayne said. "They were outgoing and fearless, and they hung on to me like puppy dogs. I used to stop by to see them when I came home from work, or I'd take them places. They never worried about whether they were dirty or clean or what was proper. They begged to do yard work for me so they could watch TV at my house.

"But I thought Mike was some radical militia nut. He said he'd erased his whole family and I never understood what he meant."

Living without electricity and a phone took some getting used to. Some things, such as cooking on a wood stove, required a new set of skills.

Ginger stood at the wood stove, poking a meat fork into pieces of chicken in a cast iron skillet full of oil. "They're oozing red. They've cooked plenty long and they're still not done."

"Cook 'em longer," Mike said from the couch.

"Something's wrong. Chicken never takes this long to cook." She turned the pieces with the fork. The oil bubbled but didn't boil or spatter.

"Just because some recipe says one thing doesn't mean it's always going to be right. Here you go again, bumping headfirst into the lines on the parking lot," Mike said."Everything's new here. If the recipe doesn't fit, then adapt it."

"I've fried enough chicken to know what I'm doing. And I say something's wrong."

"Dang, woman, you've got a right mind. Figure it out. Don't make me have to stay on you."

She figured it out. And she could have earned a merit badge in forestry.

To fry chicken, she needed red cedar to get the fire hot enough, then some oak, hickory, or pecan hardwood to toss in for sustainable heat. No sweet gum. It wouldn't give heat. To bake bread, she used oak and no cedar and turned the draft down to keep an even temperature. Coals meant a *really hot oven.* New wood would absorb the heat and cool the oven. *There's a rhythm*, she discovered. She had to learn how much and what kind of wood to use for what purpose, which meant learning to identify trees. Then she cut the firewood.

Baking was easier than cooking on top of the stove. On top, she controlled heat by moving the pot close to or away from the firebox. She burned the tops of baked goods and stuck rice to the pan until she caught on.

Canning was even trickier. And noisy. She used a clacker that made a noise four times a minute to show the pressure was sustaining. She would bring the pot to a boil, then move it to the side to keep it clacking, an hour for meat, 95 minutes for corn. Canning meant washing tons of jars, washing until her knuckles were red and chapped.

They bought a cow for milk and raised pigs and mail-order chickens. Mike would pick up 200 baby chicks at a time at the post office and in ten weeks they'd fatten enough to butcher and sell. Ginger learned to pull the skin off the feet and right on up, just like pulling a sweater over her head. Then she put them up in jars, all without refrigeration.

She made lye soap and grated it to use as laundry detergent. Milked the cow and churned butter, which she kept in a jar of water for two weeks at a time. Planted a vegetable garden. Sewed their clothes. Smoked meat. Home schooled the boys. And wrote to Trent:

Men who trophy hunt deer give us the venison, and I've put up 75 jars of meat already. Made half of one doe into jerky. I'm reading The Lord of the Rings *to the boys and* War and Peace *for me. Timely topic, war. The store closed where we used the pay phone, so the closest phone now is twelve miles away.*

In hindsight, Ginger regretted most not having a telephone so Trent could call her.

The little house in Hackleberg finally sold, four months after they moved into the cabin. It netted Mike and Ginger $13,000 and retired the sawdust bucket. They added a bathroom to the cabin, built a shed for laundry, and dug a root cellar sixteen feet deep into the side of a hill.

Ginger thought they gave the little house away, but it had been vacant for two years and this was their first offer. Nobody wanted the Old Goat as a neighbor.

What appeared to be a windfall blew away like dead leaves in winter. The buying-spending-debt pattern didn't change.

Until the house sold, rocks had paid many of the bills. But the rock money dribbled in a little at a time. Sometimes Mike phoned the buyer and arranged for advances, which were spent by the time Ginger learned about them.

They had bought $1,000 worth of barrels for the rocks and paid $1,500 for an old blue flatbed truck for hauling them. And a solar-powered golf cart.

The golf cart turned out to be a work horse for gathering rocks, despite Ginger's initial misgivings about its usefulness. All in all, the rocks brought in about $8,000. Like water poured through a sieve, it seeped out and trickled off. After its third year, the rock business came to an end.

Building materials for the cabin had cost $5,000.

"That was bare bones," Ginger said, "just enough that we could move in. The beginning. Later on, there was the septic tank and field line, renting the ditch witch, buying the blocks for the root cellar and cistern. Five hundred for this and eight hundred for that and it would vanish."

Solar panels, batteries, pumps, chain saws, metal for a shed, a stove, gravel for the road, a gas tank for gas, and a $1,500 gas refrigerator. School books. The list seemed endless. While money came in, it disappeared in a flash. And Ginger would be back to selling chickens or bread, and canning catfish for them to eat.

Resentment flared when Mike spent foolishly, but she tamped it down, or tried to.

Mike hired a man with a backhoe to build the root cellar. He dug into the side of a red clay bank sixteen feet deep and eight feet wide about one hundred yards from the cabin. Mike shored it up with beams and walled it with concrete blocks. When it held up after two drenching rains, he declared it safe to use.

Ginger rejoiced. She could unload the pickled cucumbers and canned corn from under the bed. They toted for two days, back and forth from the cabin to the root cellar, arms loaded with glass Mason jars. They emptied jars from under the couch and over the rafters until they had shelved 1,000 jars of canned food. Ginger plopped onto the bed, exhausted, when they had finished, no longer worried about breaking the jars underneath.

The way they lived was hard work, but there were good times. Ginger thought Mike was a good father. All the abuse he saved for her.

They caught crawdads in the creek or played with the 200 baby chicks. They stretched out on blankets spread across the car late on a moonless November night watching the Leonid meteor showers. After a deep snow, they went sledding in the moonlight. They panned for gold in the Talladega National Forest.

Casey loved the space. He could walk for a day without coming to a road or a fence. He discovered a law of physics on a tire swing. Years later he was miffed when a textbook credited *The Law of Conservation of Angular Momentum* to Johannes Kepler. Kepler had bested him by four hundred years.

Casey and Cody made a clay slide at the rock pit with a small ramp at its end. They wet the clay to make it faster, stripped naked, and slid. The ramp tossed them eight or ten feet into the air before they landed in a mud pile.

Cody had a beautiful singing voice, and Ginger and Mike enjoyed listening to him. He carved small funny faces on trees, so that the other family members discovered little surprises throughout the woods.

Ginger made yogurt in a compost pile. She scalded fresh milk from the cow, stirred in a cup of store-bought yogurt, sealed it in a five-gallon can, and buried the can in the compost pile. In eight hours, the heat of the compost pile produced yogurt. She mixed in some blueberries and invited the Fowlers and Mrs. Dunn to share.

A leg injury left Mrs. Dunn homebound. Ginger and Mike rose to her expectations, albeit with much consternation. For five months, Mrs. Dunn kept her herd bull locked in the barn. She might forget sometimes to feed or water him herself. Yet she insisted he get a measure of hay each day rather than simply put out a whole bale to eat at will, which meant Mike, Ginger or the boys had to pitch hay every day. Mike hooked up an automatic float-type waterer so the bull wouldn't be without water, but Mrs. Dunn kept unhooking it. Not to mention that the bull hadn't serviced the cows in five months.

The leg wasn't Mrs. Dunn's only problem, Ginger discovered when she began sorting mail and came upon unpaid bills. Which led first to Ginger's paying the woman's bills, then counting out her pills, and finding her keys, glasses or whatever she'd misplaced.

Mrs. Dunn asked them to pasture her two Jersey cows that were about to calve to get them out of the herd. Nurse cows, they didn't object to any baby that wanted to suck. Consequently, they'd been pulled down and over until they looked haggard. They needed to fatten up before their calves came.

Maybelline, the cow Cody named because she looked like she wore eye makeup, didn't show up the second morning at the cabin.

"Dadblasted cow. I'll go hunt for her," Mike said. He downed his coffee and tromped into the trees. An hour later he came back, shouting as he approached. "Come on, everybody. Grab some shovels. She's in the ravine and we need to hurry."

The boys took off running. Mike grabbed two shovels, tossed Ginger a coil of rope, and they rushed down an old logging trail to an abandoned rock pit. One side of the red clay pit opened into a ravine that ran about fifty yards along the side of a hill. It sloped to about twelve feet deep in places and ranged from three to ten feet wide. Pine trees grew at its edge, their roots jutting out from the red dirt.

Maybelline was buried up to her backbone. She'd caved in the sides in her struggle to get out and her head was turned at a hard angle against her body.

"Start digging," Mike said. Cody took one shovel and Casey the other. "Ginger, you work that rope under her front legs. When we get them dug out enough, I'm going after the tractor."

"Let's get her some room around her head first," Ginger said.

For an hour they dug and pulled and tugged until Mike returned riding Mrs. Dunn's tractor.

"Here Cody, grab the rope."

Ginger lay on the ground, one arm over Maybelline's neck and the other reaching under her legs with the rope. Cody took hold of the other end and tied it to the tractor.

Mike pulled her up and back, rocking, trying to free her. The fifth try pulled her free and onto the pine straw and dirt beside the ravine. Her legs were useless until the circulation was restored.

"Roll her," Mike said, and they all pushed until they forced the cow first on one side for a while and then the other.

She just lay on the ground—alive, breathing, but she wouldn't budge on her own.

"Casey, go get the dogs," Mike said.

The dogs would bark and nip until she stood up. Otherwise, Maybelline would stay down until she died.

From autumn into December, Ginger described the cabin to Trent, told him about the big wood stove, the sawdust bucket and, later, the new bathroom, all from the nearest pay phone, twelve miles away on the outside wall of a Dairy Queen.

Just wait till Christmas, she had told him. He'd fit right in, she knew he would. He camped and hunted and loved the outdoors. He always picked up where he left off, one visit to another, as though he'd been gone only a day or so.

Christmas came and so did Trent, decked out in his usual cowboy garb, a grin as big as Texas across his face. Casey and Cody glued themselves to him. Six years their senior, he stood tall as a giant to them. They told him about the farmer who found the newborn calf frozen solid. He put it in his barn until he could bury it but found it the next day thawed out and bleating for its mother.

"Is this Christmas vacation or a labor camp?" Trent teased early one day while he buckled on a tool belt before joining Mike in carpentry chores.

Later Ginger looked out at him through the window of the cabin. He stood on a ladder, white cowboy hat on his head, nailing the trim boards over the window. A pine tree leaned close to the cabin by the front window, but he was thin enough to squeeze behind it and secure the trim, even bundled against the bitter cold. She studied his face, the concentration in his eyes, the set of his jaw. *Look how strong and solid he is, what a man he's become.*

Cody piled into the Chevy Caprice with Trent and Ginger for the return trip to the Nashville airport.

"Tell me the heater works," Trent said, "Or should I grab the blanket off the bed?" He stashed his bag in the back seat beside his Christmas gift, a black felt cowboy hat.

"Come on, it's a summer day," Ginger said. She laughed. The near-zero temperature of the past two days had surrendered to today's bright sun.

She considered which road to take, the interstate or the Trace, while the car eased down their road to the blacktop. Two hours either way. The Trace ran north ninety-nine miles, almost to the airport, and there'd be less traffic. Besides, it would be woodsy and scenic. She'd felt a heaviness when Trent left in the summer and she'd cried at the airport. Braced against sadness at his leaving again, she welcomed a pretty drive. She turned left onto the Trace.

The black pavement, wet with run-off water, glistened in the sunlight as did melting ice on the tree limbs. Rustic markers notched off each mile—historic markers interspersed with nature trail signs.

"Hey, Dogwood Mudhole," Cody shouted, reading aloud a marker. "Did you see that one?"

And later, "Napier Mine. What kind of mine? Gold, do you think?"

Ginger slowed so he could read the marker. The mine had produced saltpeter for ammunition during the War Between the States.

"Move on," Cody said. "No gold."

"Hey, Mom," Trent said a few minutes later, "Swan Valley Falls. I'd like to see the falls. Let's stop. Can we?"

Ginger saw the sign up ahead that marked the trailhead to the falls. Mike never wanted to stop or take side trips, nor had her dad. *Wait a minute. Who's driving this car? Who's in charge?* She pressed her lips tight, shutting back the automatic responses, and slowed the car to a stop. Silently she promised Mike they'd be quick.

"Okay but make it fast. I'll wait in the car."

"Come on, Mom," Trent said, "Come with us. We could spend an hour here and still have time to spare for the plane."

She checked her watch.

"On my way." She hurried to join them. *I'm in charge; I'm making the rules.*

From the rise the trail circled down under dripping hardwoods to a log bridge across a ravine, then up steep steps cut into a hill. Where it wasn't soggy, it was slick, and the boys held out their arms for Ginger. She didn't require such deference. After all, she lived in the woods. But she reveled in their attention, proud of their manners.

They stopped at two small spills tucked deep in shade where water trickled over sheets of jagged ice into a widening creek. Here the trail swept far wide of the creek and down more steps, icy in places, and they grabbed hold of tree trunks for balance. Finally, it emptied onto an outcropping of shale. They had rounded back to the creek, coming to the pool below its waterfall.

"Beautiful!" Ginger cried. "How beautiful!"

From the banks of the pool, they gazed at the sight before them. Immense icicles, some as round as a man's thigh, hung from a horseshoe-shaped ledge forty feet overhead. They reached almost to the pool where Ginger stood with Trent and Cody.

"A giant ice sculpture," Ginger said.

Trent reached for a rock and hurled it at the top of an icicle.

"What are you doing?" Ginger shouted. She grasped at his arm, too late to stop him. The rock fell short of the icicle and splashed into the pool.

"Trying to hit the top of that icicle," Trent said. He bent toward another rock.

"But why? You could break it off."

"That's what I had in mind."

He tossed the second rock. It hit and bounced off the icicle.

"Just to see if I could do it," Trent said.

Cody threw two rocks, one right after the other. Both fell back into the water.

"Why break them?" Ginger said. "Why ruin some-thing so beautiful?"

"It's not like they're permanent," Trent said.

"That's not the point."

"They're melting right now, Mom," Cody said.

"Soon as the weather warms, the sun hits them a few days, they're toast, gone, nothing left," Trent said. "Today they're Goliath and I'm David."

The Biblical reference silenced Ginger. She stepped back two steps. Put her hand to her forehead to shade her eyes while she stared at the icicles. Yes, she could understand. The icicles challenged Trent.

What was going on in his head?

"Pressure, just lots of pressure," he'd told her on occasion.

And being seventeen, he responded with rocks.

Her boys were playing, and she was in charge. Let it be. The icicles were going to melt anyway.

He and Cody tossed more rocks, breaking off small icicles with some throws, but not a big one. The rocks just bounced off.

Trent trounced back into the trees and emerged with a broken tree limb the size of a baseball bat. He flung it, his jaw locked in determination, eyes narrowed, and his expression took on an intensity that troubled Ginger.

The log flew high, circling horizontally, until it crashed against two forty-foot icicles. They cracked with a POP, an explosion that reverberated through the woods. Ice shattered into sparkling slivers that crashed into the pool. Its calm cold water splashed high and sent Ginger and her boys dashing out of its way. Even then a silvery mist hung in the air.

"Wow!" Trent shouted. "Whoooooowoweeeee!"

"You did it! You did it!" Cody yelled.

"What a show!" Ginger said even while she shivered in the damp chill of the woods.

The boys jabbered about the icicles the rest of the ride to the airport.

"Did you hear that crack?" Trent said more than once.

"Like a sonic boom," Cody said.

Trent hugged Ginger goodbye at the gate and turned away. He adjusted his new black hat on his head.

Ginger didn't wait to see his plane off the ground as she usually did. She didn't think about it until later. What she couldn't get out of her head for several days was the image of Trent destroying the icicles.

She phoned him a couple of times over the next month. He had said he'd be back during spring holidays in March, but she couldn't pin him to any plans. He was busy. He didn't have time to talk.

The wash house was no more than a shed with a roof overhead and a wash tub on the cement floor, but it allowed Ginger shelter from the winter wind while she hand scrubbed the laundry and hung it to dry on wooden racks. Like everything else, she and Mike hammered the shed together themselves. They had finished shortly before Christmas.

In late January Ginger was kneeling on the hard floor, wringing out blue jeans when Mike ambled in with Samson, a hound dog that had taken up with the McNeils. Mike turned a metal folding chair backward, straddled it, and lit a cigarette.

Samson nosed up to Ginger, then sniffed at a pan filled with damp white laundry waiting to be hung out to dry. Ginger waved him away from the clothes. Muddy paw prints already dotted the floor. She didn't want him—too late. He stepped onto the white clothes, leaving a dirty print on the clean wash.

"No, Samson! Come on, out of here." Ginger jumped up from the floor and shooed Samson outside. She turned back to the wash tub just as Mike grabbed her left breast. With his thumb on top and his fingers underneath, he pinched until Ginger yelped with pain.

"Let go, let go!"

He dropped his hand, picked up his burning cigarette from the seat of the metal chair, and stomped outside.

Ginger returned to the washing. After a time, the pain in her breast subsided.

That night she slipped into the bathroom and examined it by the light of a kerosene lamp. A reddish-blue thumbprint marked her white skin, and the entire breast was sore to the touch. Mike refused to look.

"You bruise at nothing," he said.

For two weeks she watched Mike's thumbprint turn first purple, then yellow and finally a sick green before it went away. She never looked at the underside of her breast to see if there was a handprint there.

They'd just learned about a woman who had breast cancer. Ginger had heard about trauma to the breast being a precursor to cancer. *Why did he do that to me? Why? What lies ahead for me?*

Mike had pushed and shoved but he hadn't hit her since she ran home to her parents. Did her threat to shoot him hover in his mind? Was she so compliant that she gave him no cause? or had she just learned to steer clear of his edge? She didn't know. He'd never hurt her breasts before. Somehow a pinch on the breast seemed different. It puzzled her.

Like the sting of Mike's slap on her face, the bruise on her breast faded, but not its imprint on her memory. An occasional push or shove would refresh the memory, as intended.

chapter eleven

O n a bleak Sunday late in February after Trent went home, when cold rain beat a staccato rhythm on the cabin's tin roof, the family hovered around the toasty warmth of the woodstove.

Ginger had slipped on a black challis jumper with a tiny pink flower pattern, gathered under the yoke and long to the ankles. It had been a sample dress in the Wal-Mart fabric department. She had coveted that dress for a full year until they finally sold it to her for five dollars. Underneath the jumper she wore a black sweater.

"You look funereal," said Casey, who'd just turned twelve.

"Funereal?" Ginger laughed at his choice of words all the way to the shed where she milked the cow and fed the pigs.

By noon, Mike had clouded the cabin with cigarette smoke. He paced like a caged animal until he could stand the confinement no longer. He grabbed his rain gear and splashed across the clearing. An hour later, he burst through the front door and shook like a wet dog. In one hand he held a new carton of Winston Golds. Rain drops from his coat spattered the boys, who lay on the floor reading. They flinched, so Mike shook again, playing with them, before he crossed to the stove to warm up.

"What's cooking?"

"Chicken stew in the pot and cornbread in the skillet," Ginger said. "Rainy day food, just waiting for you to come back."

After the lunch dishes were washed, she attacked the mound of mending in her sewing basket. Casey had left the seat of his britches high in a pine tree. She fished through the basket for a scrap of denim to patch the hole and stopped to look at her watch. It was 2:50.

Why notice the time? Nothing's in the oven. She shrugged and returned to mending Casey's jeans.

The rain slackened to a gray drizzle and soon after, the dark of day slid into an early night. Ginger reheated the chicken stew for supper. Afterward Mike drilled the boys one more time in the steps in building a smokehouse. He had laid the foundation. Their task, a test akin to an exam in applied science and math, was to calculate what supplies were needed, then build the smokehouse. He'd oversee and advise, but it was their project. By nine p.m., everybody climbed into bed.

An hour later, all four awakened to the noise of a car engine outside the window. Before they could get their feet out from under the covers, someone rapped loudly at the front door. Casey lay there a moment, fascinated with the yellow zebra stripes of headlights across his arm and the top bunk. Then he scrambled out of bed to join the others racing to the front door.

It was Mrs. Dunn, bundled against the weather, a clear plastic rain bonnet tied under her chin. Behind her idled her red Polaris four-wheeler.

"Ginger, hurry, you've got to come now," she said. "Your family's trying to reach you. There's been a death."

Ginger dialed her parents in Baycross from Mrs. Dunn's house. When her mother answered, she let out half a sigh of relief, but stopped herself.

"Mom, who is it? Is it Dad?"

"Dad's right here beside me. Who have you talked to?"

"Nobody. Who, Mama, who is it?"

"I don't know how to tell you this, honey." Ginger heard her take a breath and let it out. "It's Trent. He shot himself just before three this afternoon."

Ginger's knees buckled. She fell to the floor by Mrs. Dunn's table. The phone dangled by its cord from the wall.

She watched as Mike snatched up the phone to hear from Helen himself. Minutes later he lashed out at her mother.

"Why does she need to fly out there?" he yelled.

Ginger pulled herself up from the floor and grabbed the phone away from him to protect her mother from his outburst.

She told Casey and Cody about Trent when she and Mike returned from Mrs. Dunn's.

Casey stared at her as if he'd never laid eyes on her before.

"Are we going to the funeral?" Cody asked.

Mike walked up and stood next to Ginger.

"Costs too much for all of us, son. Your mother's going to go."

Mike left to borrow money from someone. When he returned, he said, "I've known Trent all his life except when he was a baby. All his life," He shook his head fast, as if to push this bad news out of his brain

"We should've insisted he come live with us. I told you we should have. I didn't know he was depressed, but teens and trouble find each other." He tossed some wood into the stove to warm the cabin more.

Ginger sat on the couch in a knot. She'd hardly moved since he got back.

"Last summer he hung up the phone down at the Dairy Queen and slammed his fist against the wall. I didn't say anything. We just should have insisted." He sat down beside her, and he buried his face in his hands.

Ginger made no reply.

A minute passed.

He looked up at Ginger. "I got the money. We got to get up early to get to the plane."

"We're going to fly?"

"You are. Just you."

"Aren't you coming?" Her expression changed and her voice rose in pitch. "Mike, please, I need you."

"I don't go to funerals. You know that."

"Please, Mike."

After a while he went to sleep.

Ginger burrowed into a chair close to the heat of the woodstove, knees tucked under her chin. She shivered, her teeth chattering despite the two blankets wrapped around her. *No, no, no, no, no* somebody screamed, somewhere deep inside, over and over, yet she felt . . . what? Flat, numb, hollow, an observer floating outside herself. *It can't be. I'll wake up and it will all be a bad dream.* And for a minute it would be a dream. It hadn't happened, until she again heard her mother's words, "No, honey, it's Trent. He shot himself just before three this afternoon."

He and Becky had broken up, her mother said. He told Becky and he told other friends he was going to kill himself, but no one believed him. Then today he had phoned Becky. While they talked, he put a pistol to his head and pulled the trigger. At 2:50. Ginger knew the exact minute.

She sat there all night, cold, flat, hollow—alone.

When the first light of day showed through the front window, she looked out. There stood Trent on a ladder, his white cowboy hat on his head. It had been a bad dream. He'd squeezed between the pine tree and the cabin to hammer the trim above the window. Look what a man he's become.

She sprang to the window, arms outstretched.

Mike opened the bedroom door.

"Time to go," he said.

They set out to the Nashville airport before sunrise for a 7:30 flight. Ginger didn't wear her head covering, not back to Baycross, not to Trent's funeral.

At a Shell station just outside the city, Mike pumped gas while Ginger went inside to the telephone.

Nell, her friend in Texas from the time of Trent's birth, answered.

"Oh, Ginger, I was waiting for you to call. What can I do?"

"Meet me at the airport."

She still had forty miles to travel from the Houston airport to Baycross, where her baby lay dead—where? She didn't know where he was or whose hands were now touching the body she'd once rocked in her arms.

Nell would be there, she knew. And would drive her to Baycross.

When she pushed open the glass door of the service station to return to the car, a little boy in jeans, about three years old, with sandy hair falling over his forehead, brushed past her with his arm held out. He marched toward the cashier, waving a fistful of dollar bills.

He took her breath. He looked like Trent at that age, his hair, the way he walked. Exactly how Trent looked when she lost him the first time. He was taking the money to pay for his family's gas, just like Trent back then.

When she reached the car, Mike had seen him, too. He thought he was Trent all over again. He held her tight, and they both cried.

That little boy is my angel, and that encounter was meant to be.

The closer to Baycross they came, the less Ginger and Nell spoke until a hush settled inside the car. Ginger gazed out the window, seeing and not seeing, while she twisted a Kleenex to shreds in her lap. She let her mind drift across the flat fields and train tracks that led to her hometown.

The pecan groves, the "Welcome to Baycross" sign. Then Baycross High, Home of the Wildcats, where "choir," one word, summed up four lonely years. Dull brick buildings spread over dull brown grass. The Dollar Store, then Kroger, and the apartment building where she lived when she left Turner ... and lost Trent.

So far it looked as if nothing had changed.

Three years had flown by since she'd last seen Baycross or her mom and dad. Three full years. Nothing had changed, yet everything had changed.

Nell turned into Ginger's old neighborhood.

Almost home. The trees were greening up. Some had really leafed out. Almost at the end of the street on the left, she saw the yellow shingles on a ranch-style home and three people out front. Her dad, in denim and work boots, wound a garden hose onto a reel by the corner of the house. Her mom wore an apron and her hair was pinned in curls with bobby pins. She was talking with Debbie's mom from next door, where Ginger used to sit on the stoop and watch Debbie practice cheerleading. Debbie's mom held a platter with both hands.

Nell stopped the car in front of the house. Ginger got out, brushed Kleenex shred off her skirt, and started across the grass toward her parents. Nell caught up but yielded the lead to Ginger.

"Hi, Mom, Dad," Ginger said. She looked from one to the other.

Her mother's hello fell under her dad's baritone,

"Well, I thought you'd be getting here about now. Nell, pull the car up in the driveway if you want to."

Both parents looked Ginger's way but neither moved toward her, not a step, not an arm extended, or a wrist raised. Her father continued to reel the hose.

Ginger stopped when she reached her mother.

"Debbie's mom brought—" Helen began.

Debbie's mom shoved the platter to Helen, grabbed Ginger with both arms, and hugged her tight.

"Oh, honey, I'm so sorry, so sorry. I made some chocolate chip cookies for you. I didn't know what else to do."

Once inside the house, after ten minutes of front yard chatter, her mother hugged her, and they cried together. But not her father.

Her mother centered the cookies on the kitchen table and she, Ginger, her dad, and Nell settled onto its ladderback chairs to visit. Stacked at the side of the table were four plates and a platter of ham sandwiches, ready for lunch.

Ginger began to tell about the little boy at the Shell station that morning.

"His hair was silk and sandy, just like Trent's. It was like seeing Trent all over again, like he was an angel meant for me—"

"Hmmmph! You can put a halt to that crap right now." Her father shoved his chair away from the table so fast the dishes rattled in the hutch. "There'll be none of that New Age angel nonsense in this house."

Ginger stood up. "I have to go."

She and Nell started toward the front door.

"No, Ginger, no," Helen said with her arms outstretched toward her daughter. She followed them to the door, "Please don't go, Ginger, don't go."

"Mom, I can't stay here now. I'll come back, but I have to leave now."

"And that was my reunion with my family after three years and the hole ripped in our very being by Trent's death. My dad, even in that moment, had to trounce the smidge of comfort I'd found."

She went back after the funeral. She had to. They were her parents, and their house was home. It was expected of her—and being the obedient daughter, she complied. More than anything, she craved consolation from them. No matter how tenuous or frayed the ties, they were bound together. Besides, her parents were grieving in their own way. They were all she had, next to her husband, and he wasn't there.

"I floated on the surface of that week." She remembers it from afar: the funeral, everything, blurred and cracked apart like a kaleidoscope picture, jagged pieces that didn't fit together. "Other people have to fill in the gaps," she said.

From Monday until after the funeral on Thursday, Ginger stayed with Nell.

She phoned Turner Monday afternoon. They'd had few civil words since she left him, but she had to talk with him now.

"You left him in my keeping. Looks like I did a bad job," Turner said.

"No, not at all. He did this. Not you."

Turner dissolved. They talked and cried for more than an hour.

"I've got to see the bullet," he said, "to see if it's one I loaded."

"What can I do for Trent?" Ginger asked Nell. Turner and Erika were making all the funeral arrangements—Erika's church, her pastor, the cemetery lot. She'd tangled with Erika over Trent ever since Turner remarried. She was Trent's mom, and they were ignoring her.

Had they included her, though, she couldn't have shared in the expense. Ginger had no money. None at all, not even pocket money.

But she wanted desperately to do something.

Nell drove her to a florist who suggested something intimate—a small bouquet to attach inside the casket—white roses, Trent's favorite, for twenty dollars. It appealed to her. Nell loaned her the money.

Ginger opened the car door to leave the florist when she heard someone shouting her name. A young girl sprinted down the sidewalk toward her.

"You look just like my Trent," the girl said, when she caught up with Ginger.

Ginger hesitated, trying to recollect her.

"I'm Becky," she said.

Ginger realized she had never imagined Trent's girlfriend with a face. She reached out her arms and Becky fell into them. They held each other.

"I should have told a grownup," Becky said through her tears. "He told everybody, but nobody believed him. He'd talked about it before. This time he gave me a marble to bury with him. I should have told."

Whatever troubled Trent reached beyond Becky. He had confided in Ginger, but he hadn't revealed much. "A lot going on, just pressure," he would write or say when they talked on the phone, pressure at school, pressure at home. He was too possessive with Becky—Ginger had seen that in her son, and it sent shivers down her spine. He had exploded at Becky last summer because she said hello to a classmate Trent didn't like. Ginger knew Becky held no fault in his death.

"He left you a note," Becky said. "And me. He told me on the phone, just you and me."

"Where—"

"They can't find them."

Turner helped Ginger search. They sifted through every corner of Trent's room, turned though the pages of his books, looked inside drawers, under them and behind them. No notes.

Mike phoned.

"I can't come home yet, Mike. We haven't had the funeral."

He called again the next day.

The local mortuary hosted the viewing in its largest parlor Wednesday evening, after the coroner's office completed the autopsy and released the body that morning.

The parking lot overflowed and cars lined both sides of the street when Nell and Ginger arrived. A line four abreast, mostly teens, friends of Trent's, trailed from the front door out into the parking lot. Nell drove to a back entrance.

Double doors opened into the parlor, where floral sprays lined the walls from ceiling to floor: gold chrysanthemums with Wildcats written in gold glitter on purple satin banners, red carnations, white gladiolas, long-stemmed yellow roses, a blast of sweet scent and color overpowering the soft blues of the room. Hymns played on an organ piped through a sound system. Photos filled a large board on an easel against one wall. At the far end of the long room, a white casket rested under a blanket of white roses. Turner, Erika, and a host of family—aunts, uncles, cousins—already hovered around the open casket.

When Ginger walked in, a hush fell over the room. Everyone stared. Nell knew Ginger felt it because she felt it herself like a burn all over.

Ginger wore the black challis jumper with little pink flowers, gathered under the bodice and falling to her ankles. Men's heavy black work boots, laced above her ankles, covered her feet. Her hair straggled below her shoulder blades, and she wore no makeup.

Nell knew it wasn't just Ginger's appearance. Some people didn't know she was Trent's mother—others knew and wondered where she found the gall to come.

Ginger saw Turner break rank with his family. He came and walked beside her to the casket.

She caught her breath, then shuddered, when she saw her boy, asleep on a cushion of tufted satin. He wore a cowboy shirt, jeans, and a big western belt buckle. On his chest, one hand rested on the black cowboy hat she'd given him. She remembered him settling it to his head at the Nashville airport after Christmas, after he'd crashed the icicles to smithereens. That was the last time she saw him, and she didn't stay to see the plane off. She shook her head to rid it of the memory. Trembling, she grasped the edge of the casket with both hands. *He looks so big, big shoulders, big chest. He's grown into a man, and I missed so much of it.*

Later, the room filled with people. Its buzz overpowered the piped-in music, and the perfume of tube roses and lilies filled the air. On one side, friends bunched around Turner and Erika. Some looked puzzled until they recognized Ginger standing with Nell across the room, then they either embraced her or looked the other way.

The room swarmed with teens, dungareed boys with red eyes, and girls sobbing out loud. As they filed by the casket, many dropped in notes, ribbons, or some other small memento.

Ginger felt Becky pull on her elbow.

"He's not going to like that," Becky said.

Ginger's family came—Sam, Pete, and Mileah with spouses and children, and her mom and dad. They beat a path from Ginger to Turner and back. Sam left early to lead the prayer meeting songs at his church.

"I'm having trouble with this," Claude said. He motioned with his chin toward the casket, then he pressed his fingertips against his eyelids.

Ginger recalled seeing him do the same thing to suppress tears at his father's funeral. "Go ahead, Dad. Let the tears flow. It's okay."

"Tears do no good," he said. He and Helen stayed a little while and went home. They did not pass by the casket.

Ginger stood at the edge of the crowd. A cluster of teachers and school kids talked about the photos: snapshots of Trent hunting, playing his guitar, with friends, with his dad and Erika at Disneyworld, the Grand Canyon, the beach. She listened to good times she hadn't shared. She felt more alone than she'd ever felt in her life.

No one was near the casket, so she went to her son. She leaned over and put her hand on his chest. Turner came up beside her. Without a word, he laid his hand on top of hers. A simple gesture laden with meaning. When Trent was born, when he first lay beside her at the hospital, she'd put her hand on his chest and Turner had laid his hand over hers.

It was a silent letting go of him. Two parents, hearts bleeding at the same moment, connected through grief.

"He broke his big toe, and she didn't even come."

"Only six years old."

"Poor baby."

Ginger overheard several women talking while she was in the ladies' room. She couldn't see them, but she was certain Erika was among them.

"When was she ever there for him?" one asked as the group filed back into the parlor.

Their words boiled up in Ginger's mind until she encountered Erika an hour later in the parking lot. Enough. She'd heard enough. She charged up to Erika.

"No, I didn't go to Trent when he broke his toe." She straightened her shoulders, standing tall to approach Erika's height. "I'd just delivered Casey at home."

Nell drew closer to Ginger. Ginger glanced at Nell and turned back to Erika. "I've been crushed with guilt over what I didn't do for Trent. But I've also forgiven myself, many times over. The good thing is, he never saw it that way. He loved me. He adored me."

She turned to go before more burbled up, then wheeled back around.

"Mom. *Me.* That's my name."

The words blurted out. Turner rushed to his wife's side, so Ginger addressed them both. "I'm speaking to you as Trent's mother. You've had his life, but I'll have him now. I brought him into the world, and I'll usher him out. I'm going to close the casket, and if you interfere, I'll make a scene, that I promise you."

The airport recorded an inch and a half of rain during the night, but the sun shone brightly the next morning, the day of the funeral.

Mileah washed and rolled Ginger's hair at Nell's house. She brought three dresses on approval from Dillard's where she clerked, and Ginger chose the most modest one, a navy blue with a skirt that fell to midcalf.

Her mother gave her a pair of low-heeled pumps.

A white steeple topped the Baptist church, a traditional one-story red brick building. The funeral director shepherded the family to wait in a parlor to one side of the sanctuary.

"The front pews are roped off for family," he said. "I'll let you know when it's time to enter, and the parents go first, followed by other family members."

Ginger stood, sat, stood again. Nell squeezed her hand. *Thank you, God, for Nell.* Turner's family had grabbed nearly every chair. She didn't expect him to seek her out today.

At the funeral director's signal, Turner and Erika took the lead and entered the sanctuary. Parents first, he'd said, but their family closed in behind them, leaving one parent and Nell to bring up the rear.

A thousand people packed into the church. They pressed three-deep against the walls, stood in the aisles, and overflowed into a fellowship hall with a closed circuit television. Most were kids, since school had let out for the service.

When the family entered, all stood.

Turner's family seized the front row center, closest to the open casket. Ginger and Nell squeezed onto the end of the row, with Ginger next to Becky.

"I feel so alienated," Ginger whispered to Nell, "so pushed aside."

"A brilliant mathematician with a promising future," the preacher began his eulogy. The service ended with a recording of a Vince Gill song.

When the sanctuary emptied, Ginger motioned to Becky to join her beside the casket.

"Oh, God, wouldn't he have a fit," Becky said. The casket was filled almost to its brim with mementoes from his friends, total disorder for someone as meticulously neat as Trent.

Ginger agreed. They rearranged, tucked and straightened, best they could. Becky placed the white marble in his hand that he'd given to her a few days before he died with his request that she bury him with it. She'd written his name on it with black ink.

"You need to go now," the funeral director said. "We have to load the casket and the flowers to go to the cemetery."

Ginger needed more time. She felt rushed. She replaced Trent's hand on his hat, kissed his cheek, and closed the casket.

Her isolation was complete.

Black and white. Black marble, white marble, white hat, black hat. He couldn't make his life work. What could I have done? What? What?

She rode in Nell's car to the cemetery. They didn't talk.

At the graveside, a white tent whipped in the wind. Underneath it, four rows of metal folding chairs rested on a carpet of artificial grass. They overlooked the casket and an ocean of flowers. Friends closed in around the tent, waiting for the family to be seated. They stood on rain-soaked grass, the women's high heels miring into the mud.

Ginger noticed some shuffling, but she took a second-row seat, Nell beside her. At the end of the service, the preacher shook each person's hand, but he kissed Ginger. *He singled me out for a kiss, and he said, "God bless you." He included me, and it means the world to me. I feel so left out and angry.*

Her family had come to the funeral, she knew. She didn't know where her siblings sat. Her mom and dad sat on the back row at the church. They didn't go to the cemetery.

Shattered, alone, but still afloat, adrenaline atop sorrow, Ginger moved back to her parents' house that evening. They had prepared a supper for the family and some close friends.

Mike telephoned. "When are you coming home? It's over now. When are you coming home?"

I'm coming home, Mike. Why you didn't come with me, you and the boys? Did you think if I had Casey and Cody here, I wouldn't go back to the cabin with you?

Ginger returned home on Saturday, the sixth day after Trent's death.

Baycross, April 2006

Ginger told me she remembered her brother Pete's big arms around her soon after she arrived in Baycross for the funeral. He was curled over his car when Nell drove up with Ginger, and he gave Ginger a bear hug inside the garage of his house.

He had sided with Turner when Turner and Ginger divorced, even to the point of moving in with Turner.

"I have great feelings for Turner," he told me when we talked in Baycross. "After all, it was my sister who left him. He had all our family's support." As for Trent's funeral, Pete said Ginger was treated like an outcast, as if she had no part in her son's life. "She didn't even sit with the family. It was embarrassing."

"Then why didn't you sit with her? Why didn't somebody in her family reach out to her?"

He gave no answer. I don't think it had occurred to him.

Turner told me he wasn't spared Claude's sting a few weeks later. Turner said Claude was reflecting on his own life. He concluded that all in all, he had done well and would be admitted to heaven.

"The only black mark on my slate," he said, "is the one your son put there when he committed suicide."

chapter twelve

Ginger went to the funeral alone, and she grieved alone back home. *Had I not moved so far from Trent, if we had a phone, if he could have reached out to me*—all these thoughts tore at her, and she wasn't allowed to voice them.

"It's over," Mike told her. "He's in the ground, so let it go."

Do the canning, milk the cow, make a hoop of cheese, butcher a hog, render the fat, grind up what's left for sausage, season it with tears when no one's looking.

"Please hold me, Mike." He didn't have time.

"Mike, I need to tell you—" He clamped her off.

"Mike, if I don't need you for this, then what do I need you for?" She stood at the wood stove scrambling eggs in a cast iron skillet, but she faced Mike when she said it. Her voice held no defiance. She spoke from deep inside, a sincere question put to her husband.

"Your mistake was caving in to Turner when Trent was little. You put all your stock in having him when he grew up. You gambled," Mike said, "and you lost."

Mike, oh, Mike, please. Why do you stuff my grief back down my throat? Why didn't you go with me to the funeral? Why didn't we all go? You've shoved me off on Casey and Cody in my grief. She tossed her head coverings to the back of the closet shelf and never wore them again.

The emptiness she felt with no husband to share her grief turned Trent's death into a new beginning. It became the wedge that separated her from Mike. It forged some independence in her.

~~~~~~

"Her airfare alone came to $700 and I had to borrow that," Mike said. "She never forgave me for not going with her. She was in the boiling point of her soul."

He mashed one cigarette out with his thumb in a glass ashtray already heaped with butts and lit another. Remembering the weeks following Trent's death was painful.

"That whole Trent deal was like pouring gas on a fire. She harbored a lot of resentment, both towards me and circumstances. That's what Trent's suicide did to her and, as a result, to us."

~~~~~~

There was nothing of Trent's, nothing of him, at the cabin. He came with a suitcase and left with a suitcase. No one in the area other than family had known him. It was as if he'd never existed, except in their minds and hearts.

Ginger needed a memorial, something tangible and fitting. When she saw a flowering cherry tree bursting into pink blossoms in a yard near the store, she said, "That's it! That's what I want as Trent's memorial."

She priced a flowering cherry tree. Seventy dollars.

Mike was setting out apple trees, so she opted for the winesap, at seven dollars. *Second best, this symbol of the life of my first-born.*

Mike dug the hole and patted it down with wet soil.

Had she asked, Mike would have bought the cherry tree, she knew. But she'd have to stretch to make it up because Mike wouldn't work to earn money. So, she didn't ask and blamed Mike.

At the base of the apple tree, she placed an artificial rock with the word "Remember," a $10 purchase. She did it alone. No one else attached any significance to the rock. *Silly. How could I forget?*

May 10 marked Mother's Day, ten weeks since that Sunday in February. Ginger pulled the bedcovers around her neck and drew into a ball, her heart too heavy to lift her head. Mike had got out of bed early, as he always did. His .38 lay on the bedside table. She heard him and the boys stirring in the next room. Sunlight trailing through the window fell on the far wall. Her gaze focused on a knot in the wood, a small misshapen brown circle with a ragged gouge in its center.

Mike yelled her name from the other room. He'd told her to get up when Casey and Cody raced in with Mother's Day cards. He told her once more after that.

He trounced into the room.

Mike says he told her to get herself up out of bed, that they had two more boys to finish so stop wallowing in sorrow about the one who was dead and buried.

Ginger remembers a tongue-lashing about being an unfit mother who'd already buried one son.

They agree he was angry, and his words were harsh.

Mike's tirade, however it was worded, didn't jolt loose the weight on Ginger's heart. It only made the weight heavier. She searched the wall, seeking the brown knot.

Later, maybe an hour, she raised up on one elbow, her face within inches of Mike's pistol. She had seen his pistol every day now for two, almost three years. A .38 standard issue, with a thumb latch. She studied it. Trent's gun was a 9 millimeter.

She swung her feet onto the floor and picked up the gun.

Mike looked up when she entered the room, the gun in her hand. He lunged across the room and knocked the gun away, screaming at her. He yanked her by the arm, slung her onto the floor. She scrambled up on her knees. He grabbed her arm again and dragged her along the floor. She twisted, planted one foot beneath her, tried to stand. He leaned back against a chair arm and pulled her over his knees. All the while his free hand worked at unbuckling his belt and pulling it loose from his pants. With the belt doubled in his fist, he lashed down, cracking the belt against her buttocks.

She screamed. He brought the belt down again. She screamed again, tried to wriggle away but there was no escape. He towered over her, the belt whipping up and down her legs, on her buttocks and her back. She dodged, twisted, and writhed at the stinging pain.

"If somebody had done this to Trent, he might still be with us," he yelled.

Suddenly he stopped. He looped his belt back through his pants, stepped past Ginger, and walked outside where the boys were playing in the woods.

She thrashed about on the floor, nerves afire with pain, until at last the burn tapered into an ache. As the pain subsided, humiliation washed in. She crawled back to the bed.

~~~~~~

"I was terrified when I saw Ginger with that gun," Mike told me over and over. "The next day when I saw the purple bruises, I put my face in my hands and cried."

Ginger remembered it differently.

"He refused to look at my bloody knees or the bruises," she said. "He snapped at me when I tried to tell him how deep and sore the bruises were.

"The only emotion Mike ever taps into is anger. I frightened him, and he whipped me in anger. When he snapped to the fact he was out of control, he stopped.

"I had to hold a gun like Trent, to contemplate how that felt. I wasn't going to kill myself, certainly not with a gun. Guns scare me. But my son had shot himself. I had to go there. All I wanted was to be by myself and hold the gun, in the woods, under a tree, and think about the gun, Trent, death, and suicide. It was something I needed to do. I wasn't going to shoot anything. I had two boys to raise.

"I can see how it frightened Mike. But he beat me with the belt, and he beat me with his accusations about being a bad mother. The words hurt worst."

Early in June Ginger discovered an ant bed at the base of Trent's tree. Mrs. Dunn said boric acid powder would kill the ants.

It did. It also killed the tree.

A sycamore had sprouted out of the compost pile. For two months, Ginger watched it grow. When she was certain it would thrive, and without telling anyone, she moved the rock to the sycamore.

She chose a morning when the sun broke through white clouds and she could see its rays reaching down, a quiet time when she was alone. Kneeling beside the sycamore, she said, "It isn't right, baby, but it's all I have. Life isn't what things should be but what you settle for."

And I've settled for a sycamore tree in a compost pile for Trent.

Ginger's house. July 2007

Ginger had pulled the box full of letters and mementoes from under the bed again. She was sorting through them, passing some on to me, when I saw her stiffen. She held a large manila envelope with both hands.

"Do you want this? It's the autopsy report."

"No."

The word jumped off my tongue. No. I've never read an autopsy report. I hope I never have reason to read one. I don't look at autopsies on CSI. No.

I said nothing else, nor did she.

She dropped her hands to her lap, still grasping the closed envelope, and her eyes filled with tears.

"Five months after Trent died, I thought I was ready."

~~~~~~

She had sat in the swing under the hickory tree near the cabin and opened the envelope containing the autopsy report. It had cost her $10, but she had to see it. Turner thought Trent had been drinking. She needed to know. She needed to know everything.

She took a deep breath and emptied the envelope. The toe label fell onto her lap.

"There was this name I'd chosen out of all the names in the world, and it had been hanging on a label on his toe. I remembered kissing those baby toes. They'd measured him and they gave his height and weight—I didn't even know how tall he was.

"I spent a lot of time over the bullet wound, like an elephant. Elephants are morbid creatures, standing over their dead, poking at them with their trunks. I pictured myself as an elephant wanting to understand that bullet wound. I read it over and over, the size and diameter of it. I wanted to understand that wound where the soul of my baby flew away. I needed to know."

I sat quietly while Ginger cried. I didn't know what else to do. There was no solace I could offer her other than my presence and silence. She soon collected herself, dried her eyes and told me more about what the envelope disclosed.

The bullet was new, not one Turner had reloaded. From the markings on it, they speculated it had been put in and out of the chamber many times, leaving Ginger to wonder how many times did he start—and stop? What made him squeeze the trigger?

There was no exit wound. The investigator said it looked like the work of a professional executioner, a 9 mm bullet so strategically placed that it didn't even exit the head.

"That was so like Trent. The mathematician in him. He was so concerned with making a mess he calculated it to the nth degree."

He had not been drinking.

Ginger laid the manila envelope on the bottom of the box. With her foot, she pushed the box back under the bed.

From late August until Trent's birthday on September 10th, Ginger felt a giant wave building, tugging at her, its threat to crash down on her and pull her under more fierce each day. Her skin prickled with tension and her neck ached with the weight of her head.

"Mike, I feel strange all over. You know Trent's birthday's coming up on the tenth?" She wrapped her arm in his to pull him toward her. They stood in the yard by the swing.

"Do dead people have birthdays?" He shook her arm loose.

She yearned for him to wrap his arms around her and hold her tight, for the intimacy of touch, but Mike wasn't a hugger.

"Mike, I feel like a giant wave's about to crash on my head."

"So, what do you expect me to do?" He flipped his cigarette butt into the yard and lit another from the pack in his shirt pocket.

Asthma rolled in on his birthday. Ginger wheezed, struggling for her every breath, often heaving with dry sobs.

A manila envelope arrived from Turner the following week. He'd found Trent's suicide notes. They'd been on his desk at the bottom of his stack of computer paper, edges neatly aligned. Two poems and a note for Becky.

The bottom of my heart, the way it will feel,
The back of my mind, how it would think,
The base of my soul, where it is:
Who am I, where I go;
The real me, who it was;
The frame of my life, who made it;
JUST WHO WILL EVER KNOW?

The next poem was entitled "Mom," with the word *Mom* underlined and *Ginger* in parentheses, to be certain who he meant.

There once was a day,
Oh can I recall,
What it was I thought I'd say
Was it last winter,
I can't remember,
It was only your absence that kept me together.
What was the date,
It seems to fail me,
That your presence could bring my fate
SPRING BREAK OF '98,
I found it,
Would bring my wish and cultivate.

I wish to die,

I now know it,

I just can't wait. GOODBYE.

Ginger clutched the paper to her chest, holding it tight with both fists. He acknowledged her as mom, and she was one of the two people he told goodbye. Some comfort, but not enough to settle the fear in her stomach. *If needing to see me kept him together, could I have changed his mind? If he could have reached me, if we had a phone, if I could have gone to him, if…*

The wave rolled in and crashed, churning the pain.

In October, eight months after Trent's death, Mike beckoned to Ginger to sit with him in the swing in the quiet of late afternoon. The sun hovered over the treetops in the western sky, ready to sink into twilight, and the boys had not yet returned from some adventure in the woods.

"Cody's faces always make me smile," Ginger said, relaxing in the swing. The tree beside the swing was populated with funny faces Cody had carved.

"I hate to tell you this," Mike began, flicking his cigarette to scatter the ash, "but I'm not well. I'm going to die."

"What do you mean, Mike? What are you saying?" Ginger spun to face him. She planted her hand on his leg beside her.

"I'm dying. That's what I'm telling you." He spoke slowly, not looking her in the eye until he finished.

"Mike, what's wrong? What makes you think you're sick?" She avoided the word "dying."

"There's something in my lungs."

"How do you know? Have you seen a doctor?" she asked, eyes wide, still leaning toward her husband.

"I haven't seen a doctor. God told me."

He jutted his head forward toward Ginger, brow furrowed, and stared at her. Then he said, "God told me I'm dying, and I have inside of two years to live."

"Mike, are you saying God talks to you?"

"Are you listening? Do I have to say it again?" Mike twisted his cigarette under his foot in the dirt, then toed it to a mound of cigarette butts in the grass beside the swing.

"Then please see a doctor." Tears brimmed in her eyes.

"I don't need to hear from a doctor what I already know."

When she pressed him then and again over the next few days, he was adamant.

"This is about me, not you, me and God. I don't want to talk about it, so don't bring it up again. If I want to talk to you, I'll let you know. And don't tell anybody else. No one."

She could feel small lumps under the skin of Mike's chest when they lay close in bed at night. Sometimes the lumps went away, but they'd come back.

God was angry, it seemed to Ginger. Deadly hurricanes smacked shorelines, and something called La Niña changed ocean temperatures. Strange things were happening all over, and everything seemed out of kilter. So, if Mike said God spoke to him, then God spoke to him. And if God declared him to be terminally ill, that was the gospel truth.

Here I am, pining over Trent, and these are the last two years of my husband's life. She vowed to make them his best years.

Despite Mike's illness, he showed no symptoms, and nothing changed about the way they lived. He slept little and lit one cigarette off another. Ginger cooked, canned, and scrimped. At one time, all four of them picked blueberries, gathering 225 gallons of blueberries to sell at $5 a gallon. She watched the sycamore grow.

Mike ran across an insulation blower at a fire sale price. He'd worked at installing insulation in Texas for a short while, so he bought the blower and insulated the cabin. Soon he was blowing insulation for hire, assisted by Casey and Cody.

He added a third room to the cabin, a separate bedroom for himself and Ginger. With the boys sprouting into long-legged teenagers, space was tight in the one bedroom they'd all shared. The boys were sound sleepers, or pretended to be, and sex was infrequent—nevertheless, it was time he and Ginger gained some privacy.

He built a window box outside the new bedroom windows, and Ginger planted red geraniums.

"There, after I'm in the ground, don't say I didn't do anything for you," he said in jest.

"Mike, how do you know it's God talking to you? Does he talk out loud?"

"I just know."

"I don't hear him," Ginger said.

"That's because he doesn't talk to you. Just me," Mike said. "I'll tell you what you need to know. And anything you want to say to God, you tell me, and I'll pass it on."

As the year 2000 approached, Mike grew increasingly concerned about Y2K, as did much of the world. No one, scientists, world leaders, or Mike, knew what to expect. He might be approaching death anyway, Mike told Ginger, but he intended that he and his family be prepared for any crisis Y2K might unloose.

He stockpiled matches, candles, batteries, and survival gear in the back of the root cellar, well past Ginger's rows of Mason jars. At the end of a top shelf, he placed a Colt .45. Later he added an SKS assault rifle, then a second one, hunting rifles, another pistol, and 400 rounds of ammunition. Ginger saw the guns and gear but didn't venture beyond her canned goods. The back of the cellar belonged to Mike.

He hired a man to bulldoze dirt to obscure the entrance.

"These walls are thick like a prison," the man said. "Somebody could get shut up in here and never be heard of again."

Ginger heard what the man said from where she stood beside Mike, just outside the root cellar. His words stayed with her all afternoon.

When she entered the root cellar before suppertime, she studied the concrete block walls and how they were cemented in place. Suddenly she felt a cold breath on the back of her neck. She shook the feeling off.

She filed the man's words away, along with the mutilated collage from the house in Texas.

Any time Mike cracked the door by mentioning his illness, Ginger jumped at the opportunity to talk. She pled with him each time to see a doctor.

"I don't want to pay a doctor to tell me what I already know," Mike would say.

"But, Mike, there may be a treatment and you could get well."

"God says I'm going to die, and that's his will."

"Then if you're determined to die, what happens next? What about us?" she'd ask. "What if you're away somewhere in the car when it happens? What if that old Caprice breaks down and we're stuck out here with no way to leave? That car's twenty years old, and it wouldn't run now if you weren't always under the hood tinkering with it. We can't phone for help. What would we do with you?" She hammered away; fear bundled in frustration and sarcasm.

"Tell the boys to dig a hole and bury me under that hickory tree," Mike said. "God'll see to you."

"God hasn't told me how I'm to raise two boys."

"I told you God doesn't talk to you. He talks to me. I'm the head of this family. He talks to me, and that's the end of this conversation."

She wouldn't push. Pushing might hasten his death. Countering God's will, even questioning it, might upset God. At the least, it upset Mike, and that wasn't good for a sick man. She would wait until Mike gave her another opportunity to talk. Her concerns about what would happen to her and the boys were valid. She hoped she was planting seeds in Mike's mind

One day in the fall of 1999, Ginger accompanied Mrs. Dunn to have her glasses checked. En route to the doctor's office, Ginger noticed a '93 Honda Accord with grass growing around its tires parked in the side yard of a house. On the return trip, they stopped to ask about the car.

Once home, she sidled up to the topic with Mike. The Honda had been wrecked, but the owner had assured her it was in top repair. When she told Mike that Mrs. Dunn had offered to lend them the $1700 to buy the car, he acquiesced.

Ginger owned a car. She could drive anywhere, so long as Mike granted permission. And unlocked the gate.

The closer the calendar flipped to the end of the year, the more Mike paced and smoked. He checked and rechecked the supplies stored in the root cellar.

"I bought some gold coins," he told Ginger in mid-December.

"Gold? You bought gold? Mike, where did you ever get the money—" It was no use to ask.

"I wanted you to know where I hid it, in case I die," Mike said.

The night of December 31, 1999, many families filled bathtubs with water and placed flashlights with new batteries by their beds. The McNeils had no need for such preparations. Their water came from a spring, pumped by a solar-powered pump. Kerosene lit their lamps. They weren't dependent on electricity. They fell asleep before midnight rolled into the new year, confident that they were prepared for whatever the morning would bring.

Mike arose before the sun came up the next day and turned on his radio for the news. Nothing disastrous had happened. Internal clocks in computers flipped from 1999 to 2000.

"Not yet," he said to the family.

By nightfall, when it was apparent that Y2K had fizzled away like the sparklers celebrating the new millennium, Mike turned off his radio.

"It didn't matter," he said later. "We slipped by the midnight hour, but even the radio said there could be problems months ahead. Whatever comes, we're as ready as possible. Even if nothing happens, we got a long supply of food stored away."

~~~~~~

"From what I'd heard, I thought their way of living was cool," their friend Terri told me. She and her husband James had dropped in on them in the spring of 2000. "But they weren't doing it right. It was if they were running away, and Mike was keeping Ginger."

~~~~~~

Mike discovered a telephone for a car at a warehouse sale. The more he thought about it, the more he wanted a phone in his car. He'd owned a Thunderbird with a phone once, back in Texas when he first met Ginger. Not many people had car phones then, and his was a law enforcement model, just like the sheriff's. He'd kept it in a Kleenex box on the floorboard by the driver's seat.

"That auction warehouse up at Waynesboro's got a car telephone for sale," he mentioned over supper one night, "and I think I'm going back up there to buy it."

Ginger was thrilled to have some means of communication with her family. What if something happened to her mom or dad? What haunted her even more were thoughts that Trent might have reached out to her if he'd had a way to connect.

"Good," she told Mike. "Buy the phone."

He did. A Motorola bag phone with a handset attached to a transceiver and battery pack in a case. In the county where they lived in Tennessee, service was spotty at best, and especially in the woods at the cabin. But he accepted that limitation and installed the telephone in the Honda, the car Ginger considered hers.

Ginger and Mike both knew the phone belonged to him. He made calls, and he checked the bill. On the few occasions Ginger made a call, Mike sat right beside her during the entire conversation. When she climbed into the car, she often noticed the message signal flashing with messages from Mike to her.

Having that black bag with the Motorola phone in the car seemed just like having Mike with her wherever she went.

Ginger helped Mike set out tomato plants in the garden in April, after the last frost. "You bought too many plants," she said after she counted the flats spread out on the ground.

"I know what I'm doing."

"Setting them out's only the beginning. I'm thinking about who'll do the weeding." She rested her trowel on the ground and looked up at him from where she was crouched.

"I said don't worry. I'll see to the tomatoes."

Within two weeks, grass poked up between the plants and, two weeks after that, the grass threatened to overtake the tomatoes. Disgusted, Ginger grabbed a hoe and began to chop at the grass. She knew the chore would fall to her anyway.

"Come on," she called to Casey, who was untangling fishing line near the pond. "Give me some help."

"Drop that hoe!" Mike yelled from the porch. "You'll ruin my plants."

Ginger dropped the hoe. Casey stopped in his tracks. The fishing line dangled from one hand.

"The weeds are going to overrun the plants if you don't get them out!" Ginger called back.

"You can get that grass out without digging up my tomatoes," Mike said from the porch.

"Me?" Ginger chuckled. "I thought you said you'd see to the tomatoes."

"I'm seeing to it," Mike said. "Get some scissors."

"Scissors?" Ginger laughed. Casey laughed too. Cody emerged from the cabin and Mike waved him toward the garden.

"You heard me. I said scissors."

"Oh, Mike, you're not serious," Ginger said.

He was serious.

At first, she teased. Casey turned his back and coiled the fishing line. Cody tried to escape back into the cabin. Mike grew adamant. Both boys protested, but to no avail.

In the end, Ginger and the two boys each cut grass with scissors. Mike watched from the swing for a while, then went inside the cabin.

Absolutely insane. Ginger squeezed the kitchen scissors against the tough blades of Johnson grass, the scissors growing duller with each cut. The boys' quiet snickers gave way to grunts.

Ginger cut for an hour until the scissors rubbed blisters on the inside of her thumb and index finger. Suddenly she threw the scissors to the ground and marched straight into the cabin, ready to say "Enough, I quit."

But Mike was asleep on the couch.

"That's the craziest thing I've ever heard of," she said when he woke up.

"Then why'd you do it?" he asked.

She asked herself the same question that night when she lay in bed, looking out through the window at the sky. Cutting the grass with scissors was so ridiculous it was funny, yet it scared her to the core.

This is the man I live with, sleep with, make love with, and he's crazy. I know he's crazy. Look at all the crazy things he does. And look at the crazy things he has me doing. He seemed so steady, so sane when I fell in love with him.

Mike had reminisced with James, Terri's husband, about their trip to Waco to see the remains of the Branch Davidians' compound. The Davidians thought they had the right to do whatever God told them to do, and God told them to die. That conversation, the grass-cutting, God talking to Mike, all this and more boiled up in Ginger's head:

We've danced so close to that way of life. Everything said about David Koresh except the incestuous relationships, all the elements are here in how we live—self-subsistence, the belief system, all of it.

Like David Koresh, Mike thinks God whispers only to him. He's the head of this family. And God has told him he will die.

She shivered and pulled the bedcovers under her chin. Through the window, she looked out into the black night for the moon, a bright star, anything with light to focus on. *It's insane. So, am I insane for staying with Mike?*

"We don't need this golf cart any longer," Mike said. "Let's sell it."

"Rick," Ginger said.

Rick was her sister Mileah's husband. His job required him to inspect an area of land, yet he had an injury to one leg that made walking any distance very painful. The golf car would be a godsend for him.

Ginger and Mike phoned him on the car phone, and he jumped at their offer to sell him the cart for $300. Ginger jumped at the chance to chat with Mileah.

Rick and his brother drove a flat bed truck from Texas to Tennessee to pick up the golf cart. They turned off the Trace onto the blacktop, as Mike had told them to do, but drove past the dirt road leading to the cabin.

"Nothing to mark it, you just didn't know it was there," he said. "Once we found the road and turned in, I saw an old woman—an old hag really—way up ahead waving her arm like she was motioning us toward her. We stopped when we got next to her. She jumped up on the running board of the truck and stuck her head in the window and that's when I realized she was Ginger. I'd never have known her. She was skinnier than a rail, sick-looking skinny, and her hair was long and tangled. She had hollows around her eyes and, when she smiled, her teeth looked long against her gums. I couldn't say anything, I was so shocked. She'd always been pretty."

He and his brother spent two days at the cabin before they returned to Texas with the golf cart strapped on their truck. They slept in a camper Mike had hauled onto the property a few months earlier.

"I was worried about Ginger, scared for her, really," Rick said. "The entire two days there I tried to get her off by herself to talk. I wanted to know if she was safe, but Mike never let me be alone with her. He kept slipping between us. He never did anything to her that I saw, but he was abusive in how he talked to her. He frightened me."

He tugged at the stump of his leg as he faced Mileah. "When we got home, I told Mileah I was afraid Mike would kill Ginger."

"I was afraid," Ginger said. "I understood the power of mind control, and Mike was doing that to me, and I knew it. Yet I wasn't able to stop it and I couldn't get away from it. I was powerless to change, and I don't know why.

"People think women who stay in that stuff don't have a clue—they have a clue about what's going on—they just don't have a clue how to get out. They're lacking something. I was."

One sunny day in June, Ginger hung Mike's jeans on the clothesline to dry. She clipped the second clothes pin to the waist of the jeans and a thought hit her. These jeans were years old, she didn't know how old, and they still fit Mike. He'd neither gained nor lost any weight. Remarkable for a man who was terminally ill.

It was in October of 1998 when Mike first told her he was dying the two-year mark was approaching. His beard had grayed, but otherwise his appearance, his weight, his stamina, all remained the same. He wasn't getting worse, it seemed. She wondered if he had recovered or if he had misunderstood what God told him. Or if he'd never been sick in the first place.

What she couldn't do was ask him about it. She couldn't tell anyone about his illness, not even his sons could know.

She stirred up biscuits that night for dinner. "Have another one," she said, pushing the plate toward Mike.

"How's your appetite?" she asked him.

"Like a horse," Mike said, spreading butter and honey on the biscuit.

Ginger could count on headaches and allergies arriving with July each year. Her nasal passages closed, and she wheezed with asthma.

Despite feeling so bad, she picked corn with Mike and the boys from Wayne's field one scorching day. Wayne said to take all they could carry, and they filled the Caprice from floorboard to ceiling with ears of Hickory King corn.

Early next morning, before the heat set in, all four found a place in the yard to sit and shuck corn.

"Twenty ears each, who's the fastest?" Cody's challenge made a game of the chore.

Yellow-green shucks dropped to the ground with each race. Before noon the temperature hit ninety-five, about even with the humidity. The men had shucked their shirts along with the corn, and sweat left trails down their bodies. Ginger fanned and wheezed. By the time the corn was shucked and cut off the cob, the corn filled two wash tubs and it was suppertime.

Wayne came driving up.

"The gate was open," he said. "Looks like you got enough corn. Hey, Casey, you remember me telling you about that guy selling the diving equipment? I'm on my way to see him right now down at Lake Wilson. Want to go with me? You, too, Cody?"

Each boy looked to Mike and then to Ginger.

"Wash up," Mike said.

"Would you bring me the Mason jars from the root cellar?" Ginger turned away from Mike, hoping he didn't notice how often she avoided going to the root cellar.

They brought her the jars before leaving with Wayne.

Ginger unpacked the Mason jars beside the sink. She heard Mike's car start.

"Where're you headed?" she called to him from the front door.

"To get some cigarettes. Don't know what else."

"Mike, we're not finished here. I need your help."

"You're not going to put that corn up tonight, are you?"

"There's no choice," she said. "We don't have a refrigerator. It'll go bad."

"Then throw it out."

With the tension, heat, and wheezing, Ginger was on her last nerve. She lashed out, but her angry words died in the dust of Mike's car driving away.

When his car swerved back into his parking spot at nine p.m, one batch of jars sat on the table cooling. Ginger mopped her brow and tightened the lid on the pressure cooker for the last of the corn. After the cooker built up enough heat to start clacking, she stepped out onto the porch.

Night brought little relief from the day's heat. Fireflies flashed in the dark. Mike lay lengthwise in the swing, his head propped on one arm and his feet against the other arm.

Ginger approached an overturned barrel, facing the swing. Her bare feet peeked out from under her long denim skirt, feet and skirt dirty from the long day's work. Sweat beads ringed her neck. She stood perfectly still— except for the wheezing, eyes fixed on Mike, churning with everything she'd fumed about while putting up the corn. All at once the words in her head spilled out from her mouth.

"You said you were dying, that you had two years to live."

"That's right," Mike said, "and I told you if I wanted to talk about it, I'd tell you." He flicked his cigarette and orange sparks fell with the ash.

"Mike, it's July, and the two years are almost up. Yet you don't look like a dying man."

"God's been good to me." With one foot, he pushed against the ground to make the swing move faster.

"You haven't changed at all, Mike. You're not weak or frail. Nothing hurts."

"You don't know what's inside me."

"The truth is, Mike, you're not even sick." Ginger swallowed a breath. "All that's wrong with your lungs is they're full of smoke. I can't breathe, and you're smoking right now."

She paused to suck in another deep breath.

"You've let me put my life on hold, thinking you were going to drop dead. I've grieved over you in advance, knowing what sorrow lay ahead. And now you're not going to die and it's not ever going to—"

She hushed.

Her outburst crystallized her feelings, put in solid form what she'd failed to acknowledge until now: she dreaded the pain of losing Mike, but after it happened, after he was dead, she'd be free. Angry with Mike that he wasn't going to die and horrified that she'd verbalized her innermost thoughts, she gasped for breath.

Mike pulled on his cigarette and exhaled rings of smoke, barely visible in the light coming through the cabin window.

Ginger stared at her feet. With the toes of her right foot, she scratched the left foot. *For two years, I've held my breath and now fate has robbed me of my release right on its cusp.*

She planted her right foot firmly by the left and glared at Mike. *What's more, I put my mourning for Trent on hold to give you all my attention. I sat my son aside for you. Were you jealous of my grief? Is that why you told me you were dying?*

She watched the red glow of the cigarette when he inhaled and smelled smoke when he exhaled. *Killing himself with smoke, but not now. He's not going to die, and I'm trapped here for the rest of my life.*

The more she dwelled on these thoughts, the angrier she became. He'd orchestrated it all. God hadn't talked with him. He'd duped her with her faith and her trust.

Anger boiled in her stomach and rose in her throat until she threw her arms skyward to scream to heaven for relief. But no sound escaped. Only the clacking of the pressure cooker on the woodstove broke the silence.

What does it matter? There's no one to hear, no one but Mike, and he's lying in the swing, blowing smoke rings.

She returned to the cabin to finish canning the corn.

In the days following, anger chewed its way into frustration. Ginger stood at the sink, suds up to her elbows. She washed every dish, pot, and pan, and cleaned every tool she could find. She weeded the garden, using a hoe. She toted buckets of water to the sycamore tree.

At last exhaustion overcame her, and she took to her bed.

Mike had rigged a window air-conditioning unit in the camper and hooked it to the solar-powered generator, and that's where he spent nights and most of each day.

Ginger slept with the windows wide open to welcome any breeze. But bird songs at daybreak no longer signaled a time to wake up. If she heard them, she rolled over, pulled the covers over her face, and fell back asleep.

"Mom's still sawing logs," Casey said two weeks after Ginger's outburst about Mike's not dying.

"Again?"

Cody looked up from a comic book he'd bought when he rode to town with Wayne. Casey checked the water-proof Timex on his wrist.

"Yeah, and it's nearly eight o'clock this time."

"We better wake her up before Dad gets back from buying cigarettes," Cody said.

"I'll flip you to see who milks the cow." Casey pulled a quarter from his pocket.

When Ginger finally pulled herself out of bed, she zombied through her chores. After she washed the lunch dishes, she succumbed to the humidity and napped through the afternoon. It was the same every day.

"I sank into a deep depression," Ginger recalled five years later. "I knew what it was—I'd been there before, after Trent was born—a black pit with no ladder out. I don't know if there was a light overhead or not because I never looked up. Looking up meant hope, and I had no hope. No feelings. I was suspended in thick black nothingness. Pills could make it go away, but I didn't want it to go away. I embraced it. I wanted to join Trent.

Mike did all he knew to help Ginger.

"Get in the car," he said one afternoon. "We're going for a ride."

He and Ginger drove to an old cemetery in a grove of hickory trees twenty miles north in Tennessee. A rusty iron fence stood knee-high around the graves. Weeds grew up through the fence, and the tombstones that weren't tipped over leaned to one side.

"Come on, but watch out for copperheads." Mike stepped over the fence and beckoned to Ginger.

They picked their way through the graves, trying to read dates on mossy stones.

"Here, look here." Mike pointed a few feet ahead. "Look at all those little graves. Six of them."

He drew closer. "This one's a baby, not much bigger than a shoe box. Ummm, died in 1898. Only six weeks old. That one was eight."

He read the names and ages of each of the children, then the age of the mother. "That's what I wanted to show you. That's why I brought you out here."

He paused for Ginger to look at these tombstones.

"Think about that woman for a minute. She lost six children. What do you think it was like for her? And she lived to be sixty-two. Do you think she spent her whole life crying over these babies? Or did she get over it?"

One sultry Friday the last of July, the boys begged to go to Florence, so Ginger drove them there. She sat in a wooden chair, her arms propped on a long table at the public library, her head cradled in her palms. Casey stood in line with four books nestled against his chest. Cody paced through the stacks, still trying to decide which books he wanted. *Take your time. All the time in the world.*

A pale blue book lay atop the table. Something about co-dependency. Ginger picked it up, and without thinking about it, started reading. The words began to register, and she read until both boys coaxed her toward the car. She drove them home, the book on the seat beside her.

She didn't put the book down until she reached the last page two days later. She knew she was in deep trouble with depression. The book said if you see yourself here, get to an Al-Anon group. *I fit that shoe, even though I don't know a single alcoholic.*

On Monday she gained Mike's permission to return books to the library. She went to the health center and rattled nonstop to the receptionist.

"I found this book last Friday, and it talks about Al-Anon, and where can I find out about the meetings?"

"Right here, see the list?" The receptionist pointed to a green memo pinned to a bulletin board.

Ginger scanned the list. Al-Anon would meet next at six that very evening. She glanced at the round clock on the wall. Two p.m. Thirty miles to the cabin to report in to Mike and then double back thirty miles to the meeting. There was time. She could do it.

Back at the cabin, Ginger rapped on the window of the camper. Mike rolled the window down and a blast of cold air smacked her in the face.

She hadn't planned what she would say.

"I have to go."

"Go where?" His face nearly filled the small opening.

"I've got to do something," she said. "I've got to come out of this depression."

"That's what I've been telling you, haven't I? Just do it. Shake it off. Shake like a dog." Mike grinned, trying to tease her into action.

Ginger didn't reply.

"You thinking about going to a doctor?" he asked, serious now.

"I'm not going to a doctor and I'm not going to give out my social security number. I don't know what, but I've got to get some help."

"I'd get you help if we had the thousands of dollars it'd take. We don't have insurance, you know."

"I'm going to an Al-Anon meeting in Florence tonight. I don't know how long it'll last but I'll come straight home after it's over. I'm leaving now."

She turned her back to Mike and hurried to the Honda. With a quick glance at the sycamore tree, she drove away.

Once on the road, she reflected on what she'd just done. She couldn't remember another time in seventeen years when she had informed Mike rather than asked his permission. She should be afraid, but she felt no fear. Yet, new-found courage wasn't the impetus for what she did.

No, just the opposite—to someone wallowing at the bottom of a black pit, it didn't matter how Mike reacted.

She had glimpsed her shadow on the floor of the pit and, if there was a shadow, there must be a light above. That was what mattered.

Ginger parked her car in the lot of a strip shopping center and waited. Shoppers wheeled grocery carts to their cars, and two boys on skateboards circled the far end of the parking lot. She spotted the small storefront Al-Anon shared with Alcoholics Anonymous, noticed the beige draperies over its windows and an AA sign by the door. A young man on crutches entered first, then others dribbled in. Ginger switched on the ignition and drove away.

She stopped for the red light at the first intersection, not long but long enough to change her mind. Three right turns circled her back to the strip center. This time she parked close to the door. With quick steps, before she could change her mind again, she entered the Al-Anon meeting.

Ginger went to five meetings in all. Mike never forbade her. He doubted her, so he followed her several times, checked to make sure the car was there. Then he left it alone.

Al-Anon meetings, like those of Alcoholics Anonymous, insist on confidentiality, so Ginger doesn't tell what happened at the meetings.

"What I learned is that the skills used in dealing with an alcoholic also fit anyone dealing with neurotic behavior. Neurotic behavior, they said, is any behavior which defies logic, and that shoe fit Mike," Ginger said.

"As for me, I learned I didn't take care of *me*, and I blamed other people. I'd have needs or expectations of others I never told them. Then I got mad or hurt when they didn't do what I needed. That was an epiphany. I rounded a bend in Al-Anon.

"Then I became very repentant."

A bird chirped into the early morning silence to announce the first day of September. Mike sat in the swing, his finger moving down the page as he read his Bible by the dawn light filtering through the trees. Inside the cabin, Ginger poured a cup of coffee to take to him.

"I want to apologize to you," she said, handing him the coffee.

"Apologize? For what?" Mike looked up at her, his finger marking where he had been reading. He shifted in the swing and furrowed his brow. "What have you done?"

She steadied the barrel before sitting on it so she faced Mike.

"For the times I've been mad when you didn't do what I thought you should, and I didn't even tell you what I wanted you to do."

"Say that again?" Mike said.

She tried to explain what she'd learned about herself.

"You're telling me that meeting's opening your eyes? Praise be!" Mike said. "That's what I've been telling you for what? Seventeen years? However many years I've known you. You tell me to do something, to make a decision, then come along six months or a year later and you tell me it wasn't right."

He wasn't really getting the point, but that wasn't the point.

"And I apologize."

"Get me another cup of coffee," Mike said, holding out his cup. After she took the cup, he lit a cigarette and took a long draw.

When she returned with the coffee, she said, "And I've had my feelings hurt—"

"Oh, here it comes," Mike said.

"It's what I just told you. You got blamed for not doing something you didn't even know about, and I got my feelings hurt." She sat back down on the barrel. "And I apologize."

"Well, bullcorn." Mike leaned forward in the swing and rested his elbows on his thighs. "Bullcorn and praise God."

"Now I need to tell you something else."

Ginger folded her hands in her lap and looked Mike straight in the eye.

"If you ever hit me again, I'm going to leave you."

"Sounds like a threat to me," Mike said. He frowned. "Did you learn that in Al-Anon?"

"It's not a threat."

"Sounds like a threat."

Ginger had shed her head covering after Trent died. In September she gave up homeschooling duties.

"I can't be the teacher any longer," she told Mike. "Algebra was the end of the road for me. Either you take over, or we put them in school."

"They're not going to public school."

They often passed an old house across the state line in Alabama with a sign out front about some church and a school. Mike checked it out.

"They teach God and the Bible. Real small. We'll give it a try."

One morning after Ginger left to drive the boys to school, Mike walked down to the black top and stood at the edge of the trees on a nearby rise. He smoked one Winston Gold and, when he finished it, lit another.

He saw Ginger driving back up the road, coming home. She stopped the car, backed up a little, pulled forward. *She's trying to pick up a signal on the car phone. Trying to call somebody. She doesn't know it, but I'm on to her. I figure I know who she's trying to call.*

Except for the nip of fall in the air, Friday, September 29, 2000, began as an ordinary day. Mike walked down in the woods that morning to read his Bible. Close to lunch time, just as the day heated up, he sat down in the swing with a cup of coffee. Samson snored near Mike's feet. Ginger came out from the cabin and joined him in the swing where they talked for a few minutes. Until something Ginger said ticked Mike off.

Ginger stomped back into the cabin. He followed her.

That danged rifle pad's spread out where she's been sewing it. I've had enough of that crap. He yanked open the screen door and threw the pad out in the yard.

Later on, Ginger slipped out to pick it up. *Just like I don't see her and hadn't said anything. I've got to go after her.*

He told her to get back in the house.

"I don't want to come back in the house," Ginger said.

She's intentionally provoking me. She knows what she's doing.

He pulled and shoved until he got Ginger back inside.

She lay across the couch at first. Then she crossed to the sink and started scrubbing up the dishes. *Like she always does. She's washing her hands, wringing them, grimacing, focusing on something like she's real distressed-like.*

He walked up behind her and poured his coffee on her head.

There she goes, charging out to the car. Well, I'll go see her off.

He stood where the driveway sloped and circled, by a rocky path that needed to be cleared out of honeysuckle and bushes, where he watched Ginger open the car door. *She's got that look on her face. I need this right now to be over.*

He picked up a rock not quite the size of his fist and threw it right at her. It sailed skee-dab over the top of the car. *I can't hit the side of a barn. Must have scared her though. She's starting off.*

When Ginger reached the big cedars by the sycamore sapling, she slowed down again.

"Drive! Go fast! Go!" Mike yelled. "And take that rifle pad with you!"

If I throw rocks, she won't come back, and I don't want her back. He threw one rock, then another, heard them bam-bam against the car. The car kicked up dust as it sped away.

Once the car was out of sight, Mike walked back to the swing and sat down.

"I remember I was already teared up and crying by then, knowing my world had the potential of changing real quick, and I wasn't ready because I was dependent on her," he said. "My whole every breath, everything was about her and the boys."

Samson sidled over and licked Mike's hands.

"Get out of here, Samson. You always try to fix whatever's going on."

He waited in the swing until time for the boys to return from school. He'd watched Ginger leave before, and she always came back. Despite his earlier moment of panic, he expected her to drive up with the boys any minute. *Where else could she go? She doesn't have a dime.*

Time ticked by. No Ginger. Mike tromped down to the road, marched back to the swing, tromped back to the road again. He pulled on his beard. Lit one cigarette off another. When the boys were an hour overdue, he set off for the school.

A crumpled piece of notebook paper blew across the sandy school yard. Nothing else stirred. Mike opened the front door of the old house which served as the school. He heard his footsteps echo when he walked down the empty hall. No children, no teachers. No one in the principal's office. He called out and no one answered.

"Who's minding this store?" he bellowed, his hands cupped at his mouth.

Still, no one answered.

He stormed down the hall, throwing open classroom doors, circling in one and out to the next. He clamped his teeth together and blew his breath out his nose.

"Mr. McNeil? Mr. McNeil?"

He wheeled around.

The principal, a stout woman with bobbed gray hair, walked toward him, her heels clicking against the wooden floor. Mike met her halfway up the hall.

"Where're my boys?"

"Your boys aren't here," she said. "They took off without signing out—"

"Then where are they if they're not here?"

Mike scrunched his forehead until his eyebrows met in one line.

"Don't you know? Mrs. McNeil drove up to the curb, and they got in her car and left. They're new students, but you should all know the rules—"

Mike was out the door. The tires on the Caprice squealed for half a block.

Wayne was changing a tire on a tractor at his dad's house that Friday afternoon. He was unscrewing the last lug nut when his brother's black pickup spun onto the driveway of the house, slinging a rooster tail of loose gravel. Butch hopped out of his truck.

"Do you know where Casey and Cody are?" he asked Wayne.

"Haven't seen them." Wayne said. "Why?"

"Ginger's gone and taken the boys. Mike's got a shotgun and he's stomping a rut in the road past his gate."

"I was boiling," Mike said. "Like throwing leaves on a bed of coals. I felt a burning in my chest and knew my heart was on fire. I don't have words to say how I felt.

"I didn't dare leave the cabin, in case they came back. But I drove up and down highways, trying to spot Ginger's Honda. I don't know what I did. I panicked."

chapter thirteen

Thirty miles away, inside the locked gates of the shelter, Ginger emptied three grocery sacks of used clothing from an agency onto a bed in the room she would share with her sons. "Pick a drawer, fold what's yours, and put it away," she said while she hung two cotton dresses on a hanger in the closet.

"How long are we going to stay?" Cody's voice was whiny. He made no move toward the clothes on the bed. "This looks like we're moving in."

"It means you have clean clothes to wear tomorrow and the next day," Ginger stretched into a smile, the corners of her mouth began to quiver. Quickly she ducked her head. She folded her new t-shirts and placed them in a drawer.

"Are we going to tell Dad where we are?" Casey asked.

"Absolutely not. We can't tell."

"Then are we going to let him know we're okay? I mean, it's not right just to disappear." Casey had shot up as tall as his mother, and now he looked straight into her face, his chocolate brown eyes level with hers.

"I gave you your choice back at the school yard. Come with me or stay with your dad. You know why I'm leaving—cottage cheese, remember?" She knew they remembered their signal to go to safety—that and a lot more.

"It's not what you're doing, it's how," Casey said. "It's not fair."

"Not fair but safe. Safe is what matters. We'll tell him when it's safe to tell him. Now, put these clothes away." Ginger pointed to the clothes on the bed until Casey gathered what belonged to him and began putting it in a drawer.

"Finished." Casey banged shut the bureau drawer he'd chosen. "Can I go watch TV now?"

"Sure," Ginger said.

"Hang on, I'm coming," Cody said. He stuffed the last of his clothes in a drawer.

Ginger stood at the small closet, which looked cavernous, holding only her dresses. She'd chosen a navy blue dress with long sleeves and colored buttons down the bodice and a yellow cotton print with little capped sleeves. She ran her hand under one of the sleeves, feeling its tiny tucks, just like her grandmother used to sew for her when she was a little girl back in Texas. She shook that memory away. *How long will we be here? What have I done?* She thought about what all happened that day, and she began to tremble.

She was terrified Mike would kill her rather than lose control of her. It frightened her now, here, just thinking about it again.

Casey found the remote control and staked out a place on the couch in the empty rec room just as Cody raced in.

"Go to *Star Trek*," Cody said.

"I'm looking for *The Twilight Zone*," Casey said, flipping through the channels. Whenever they could escape to Wayne's house, they devoured television, so each had favorite programs.

Within minutes, the boy they'd seen earlier in the rec room sauntered back in. He was chunky, solid like a fireplug and not as tall as Casey.

"Hey, I had it on *M*A*S*H*," he said.

"TV wasn't on when we came in," Casey said.

The boy glared at Casey. He looked at the television screen and back at the control in Casey's lap.

"But I'll put *M*A*S*H* on if you want." Casey changed the channel. The newcomer acknowledged the territorial rights of the shelter resident. It was the polite thing to do, and Casey had been taught good manners.

The boy flipped a wooden chair backwards to straddle it, facing the television. "You're new," he said, looking at both boys.

"Yeah," Casey said, his gaze fixed on the television. Cody nodded.

"This is my third time," the boy said. "Food's good."

All three watched *M*A*S*H* until the commercials in silence.

"You can have seconds," the boy said.

"You can?" Casey said.

"The best part about coming here's the police car," the boy said.

"Yeah," Cody popped in. "There're no door handles in the back seat."

"Yeah," the boy said.

"I wanted them to cut on the siren," Cody said.

"Yeah, me too," the boy said. "But they don't do that. One time, though…"
He and Cody began to talk, both of them still staring at the screen.

When the program ended, Casey dashed away to the kitchen. He poured a glass of milk from the refrigerator Laine, the counselor, had said was for their use. On the way back to the rec room, he skirted past Laine in the hallway.

"Whoops, hold up a minute," she said, looking over the top of her glasses.

"Who poured that milk for you?"

"Nobody. I poured it," Casey said.

"You mean you walked into the kitchen by yourself?"

"Sure."

"Maybe I forgot to tell you," Laine said. "Children aren't allowed in the kitchen without an adult."

"What?" Casey nearly dropped his milk. "I can't go into the *kitchen?*"

"You can go to the threshold and ask your mother or another adult to get something for you. Sorry, that's the rule." Laine went on down the hall. Casey went back to the rec room.

"I could have told you," said the boy by the television set. "There's lots of rules."

The boy was right about the food. It was good, and they could have seconds. Everyone in the shelter ate supper together, passing food family style down a long table. Back in their room by eight o'clock, Ginger, Cody and Casey dressed for bed. There was nothing else to do. Besides, the day lay heavy on each of them.

"I've roamed in the woods all day long without hitting a boundary and now somebody says I can't step inside the kitchen." Casey had ranted like a broken record since he learned the kitchen rule. "This place was enormous when we got here, but it's shrinking fast."

"Who's your friend?" Ginger asked Cody, changing the subject.

"Don't know his name." Cody brushed off his jeans so they would be ready to wear again.

"You talked with him all through supper. You never asked?" Ginger said.

"Didn't think about it," Cody said. "Mom, they've got a Nintendo in the rec room."

~~~~~~

Long after the boys were deep in dreams, Ginger stared at the ceiling above her bed. A loaf of bread costs a dollar, a pound of coffee $3.50, what does peanut butter cost? Squeezing her eyes shut, she did a mental inventory of the pantry. A hundred dollars at least, just in the pantry. And then the refrigerator: a gallon of milk at about $2.75 and eggs at $1.80, that price was on the carton. She tried to itemize the food, put a value in dollars to all someone had provided for her use. Then she thought about the refrigerator itself, the stove, the beds, linens, everything the shelter had ready. She couldn't sleep. The total was wrong. It had to be. *Nobody would value me that much.* She buried her face in the pillow and cried.

She's not coming back, Mike realized. *She took the boys. She's not coming back.* The more he rehashed what happened the morning she left, the more he determined it was a premeditated plan. *She instigated it from word one. She picked that fight. She knew just how to push my buttons.*

He stomped his feet walking up and down the dirt road, kicking up red dust. Hoisting a clay pot of Ginger's geraniums over his shoulder, he smashed it against a tree. He threw rocks at the washhouse. *Where is she? Where?*

Suddenly he thought of the phone in Ginger's car. He shot off to find a pay phone so he could call her.

Twelve miles to the Dairy Queen. The phone hung upside down, its wires cut. Mike drove ten miles west to the country store at Lutts. *No dial tone. Dang!* The tires spun in the gravel parking lot as he sped toward Savannah.

The CITGO station. Finally. Fifteen more miles but the phone worked. He stood in a booth with a gashed window and dialed Ginger's number.

No answer. He kicked the wall of the booth. Started toward his car. Went back and dialed again. He left Ginger a message. "You can go to the devil, but first you floorboard it home with my boys. Now."

He lit a cigarette in his car by the empty service station and tried to think. Given a chance, he figured, the boys would call Wayne. He raced to Wayne's.

"Ginger's gone crazy and run off with the boys." Mike paced up and down Wayne's front porch. "I don't want them to get hurt."

"Hurt?" Wayne stepped onto the porch in a tee shirt and plaid boxers. "What makes you think—"

"She's crazy, man. I don't know what she'd do." Mike's eyes were wild.

"Crazy? Oh, you don't really mean that." Wayne shifted his weight from one foot to the other.

"Yes, I do. I'm scared for my boys."

"She's been real down with the blues, but she's not…I mean, I can't believe she left you." Wayne screwed up his face to get hold of what he wanted to say. "Mike, I'll help you find them but it's ten o'clock already. This late at night, all we're going to find are possums. Wait till morning and I'll go with you."

Mike couldn't sleep. He paced through the early hours and set out for Wayne's house right after sun up Saturday morning.

"Take your car," Mike said, and he directed from the passenger's seat while Wayne drove. They checked out every hill and hollow Mike and Ginger had ever crossed in Alabama and parts of Tennessee, searching all day until long after dark. Mike left messages on Ginger's phone all day.

Ginger climbed out of bed Saturday when daylight peeped around the window shades. She dressed in the new yellow dress with the capped sleeves, so short they exposed the farmer's tan on her arms, but long enough to hide most of the bruises where Mike had grabbed hold to shove and drag her into the cabin. Pulling the door shut behind her, she tiptoed down the hall, retracing her steps through the shelter's maze to the kitchen and its pantry. She needed to see the pantry again, to be sure she hadn't dreamed it all.

She wasn't the first to be up and stirring. A girl not much older looking than Casey sat at a table, her back to Ginger, feeding her baby in its chair.

She wore sunglasses, an oversized green t-shirt, and no shoes. The baby had blue eyes but no hair. A white knit undershirt topped its diaper.

"You're up early. Hi, I'm Ginger."

"The baby got me up. She kept me up all night long. I'm Kelly." She pushed a spoonful of cereal at the baby.

"And who are you?" Ginger said to the baby.

"She's Angela and she's four months old today." Kelly talked while a bottle heated in a pan of water on the stove.

Ginger opened the pantry door. It was there, just as she remembered. She took coffee, then pancake mix and syrup to cook a hot breakfast treat for her boys.

"Watch Angela for me for a few minutes?" Kelly asked as she left the room.

Other residents trickled in over the next half hour.

"I see you've met Kelly," said a woman who introduced herself as Lu. An hour even later, after Ginger had cooked breakfast with Angela on her hip, fed her boys, and washed up, she stood alone in the kitchen except for the baby sleeping in her arms.

Kelly wandered back into the kitchen, wearing her sunglasses and yawning. She reached out for Angela. "I'll take her now. I needed that sleep."

Later in the morning, a staff member wheeled a television set with a VCR to Ginger's room. Casey's eyes popped wide. Ginger stammered, ambivalent, wanting her boys to be happy yet not wanting them exposed to the world through television.

Minutes later, channel surfing obliterated Casey's resentment about kitchen rules, at least for a while.

"Come on," Cody said. "Let's get some video games from the rec room."

Ginger insisted she accompany them to select the games and a movie. In the hall, she felt Cody tug on her elbow just as she heard voices.

"Look, Mom, look," he whispered.

Ginger looked. A rail-thin woman towered over Laine, who was show-ing her around the shelter. The woman's face shown ghostly pale except for glossy red lips and waxy black circles at her eyes. Her hair rose in dark spikes from her forehead to the nape of her neck, where black tattoos bled into red flowers. Red and black covered the only arm Ginger could see.

Ginger put a finger to her mouth, shushing the boys, then motioned for them to turn away, not to stare. When they got back to their room, they all broke loose with giggles.

"Casper with lipstick," Casey said.

Annette knocked on their door. "Can you come to my office for an orien-tation meeting, ten minutes?"

And there with Casper, Ginger learned about the regimen of the shelter.

Everybody had cleaning chores. The staff provided meals for the first three days, but after that, residents were on their own to prepare meals for their families.

"You're required to attend group meetings every day. Kids have their own group, once a week," Annette said. "You'll have business to take care of. Since you can't leave your children unattended outside your room, offer to look after someone else's kids if they'll watch yours. After three days here, you're free to come and go."

They had much to do.

"You can't live in the shelter forever," Annette said. Its goal was to help residents find a permanent end to their abuse. That meant learning new skills and taking responsibility. Severing one life and starting another required trips to lawyers, court, jobs, schools, banks, doctors, and agencies to find housing, transportation, food stamps, and income.

Ginger listened with her hands clasped in her lap, her shoulders slumped with the weight of all that lay ahead. When she returned to their room, she melted onto her bed. "The boy was right about the rules."

"Greg," Cody said, staring at the television.

At supper that night families sitting in metal folding chairs clustered up and down a long laminate table. Some families visited with others, some talked among themselves, all of it over the clang of metal pots and the monotone of the TV from the rec room.

"Mama, look!" a little girl shrieked, pointing toward the door.

All conversation stopped as everyone turned to see.

In the threshold stood Casper, a specter in black with crimson lips and coal tar eyes on a pasty mask. A black feather dropped from one ear and the other ear sparkled with silver studs.

Snickers followed muffled gasps as children and mothers glimpsed her and quickly looked down at their plates.

Ginger glared at her sons, a warning to button their lips. From the corner of her eye, she saw the woman step forward and stop, as if considering which empty chair to take.

Like turtles, all the families drew into their shells, heads down and backs turned.

With her head bent toward her plate, Ginger felt the heavy silence. She spied the toes of her boots peeking from under the yellow dress. No one else at the shelter wore heavy boots like hers. She remembered when she wore the head covering, when her appearance differed so from others. Trent's visitation flashed before her eyes, when a roomful of people stared her up and down before they turned away.

"Here's a chair," Ginger called to the woman. "Slide over, Casey."

Wayne and Mike searched again the next day, Sunday, and every afternoon after Wayne finished work for the rest of the week. They burned up two tanks of Wayne's gas and covered every road in Tennessee.

Mike was driving Wayne crazy, calling him at work all day, making himself at home at Wayne's house every night, watching Wayne's TV, programs like the news and *The History Channel*—nothing Wayne liked. He would just go to sleep and leave Mike holding the control.

Ginger's first group meeting convened Sunday morning. Just like Al-Anon, she said to herself. Taking a deep breath, she entered a pale green room with posters covering one wall and a lot of mismatched chairs. She opted for an overstuffed chair against the back wall and settled herself deep into its cushions, hugging a throw pillow to her chest. She spoke only to say her name. By the end of the meeting, she'd dropped the throw pillow to the floor and read the posters. Warning signs, statistics, what to avoid. *Too bad I didn't know all this a long time ago.*

Over the next days, Ginger listened to the other women tell why they sought out the shelter. Often, she recognized herself in what they said.

"We've been talking about different ways one person can control another," Laine said as she began Thursday's group. "What about isolation? Does anybody feel shut off from family and friends?"

Ginger drew her arms closer and sat up in her chair. Laine wasn't looking her way, but Ginger knew the question had her name on it.

"We didn't have a phone," she said. "Or television. We lived out in the woods."

"No TV?" Kelly, the young girl with the baby, held her hand over her mouth when she spoke.

"No electricity," Ginger said.

"What?"

"Did a storm knock it out?"

"How'd you live without power?"

"How'd you see at night?"

Ginger answered every question, but her voice grew softer, and she burrowed deeper into her chair with each one.

"You had a car. Why didn't you leave?" asked Darlene, a fleshy black woman with bleached bangs cut straight across her forehead.

"I left. One time I hid in a cemetery. But I had to go back."

No one spoke, so Ginger filled the silence. "Wasn't anywhere else to go. Until now."

"I left once and went back," Kelly said, "but never again. Nev-er a-gain."

Lu, Greg's mother, began to cry. "What's wrong with me that I keep going back to that man? Why can't I say 'no' and mean it? Why do I drag my boy back and forth through my sewer?"

Other women said they'd left and gone back to abusers.

"See, you've got a lot of company." Laine offered Lu a tissue. "Leaving is hard. Nine times isn't unusual."

"Not for me, baby." Darlene held out a bandaged arm. "He cut me once and he not coming at me again. I seen my mama's scars."

"Good for you," Laine said.

Casper held out her flowered arms. "You can hide scars, but after a while you run out of hiding places."

"Or hiding isn't fooling anybody but you. Like wearing sunglasses in the dark's not going to make people curious." The gray-haired woman exaggerated her words, as if she were on stage.

"Since I'm the only one wearing sunglasses—" Kelly said. She yanked them off and stretched her lips into a too-wide smile. "Okay, look, if you want to see."

A neon-red eyeball glowed between fading yellow-purple bruises around her eye socket. The smile revealed two broken teeth. Moans sounded from the other women in the group.

Lu said, "Put those glasses back on, that eye hurts me to look at it." She winced. "It must hurt you bad."

"Honey, some of us, we been there. We've seen too many black eyes." Darlene threw her arms around Kelly's shoulders. "You don't have to hide it here in this place." Still talking to Kelly, she faced the gray-haired woman. "But you do as you please and not what folks think you ought to."

"Good point," Laine said. "Let's talk again about boundaries, both here in this group and in relationships with others."

When the session ended, everyone filed out except Ginger and Casper. Casper sat on a brown tweed bench opposite Ginger's end of the room. Ginger started toward her and stopped dead. Casper was twisting a silver stud through her tongue. She looked up at Ginger, her tongue stuck out.

Ginger cringed. "Doesn't that hurt?"

"Not anymore."

Taking the chair nearest her, Ginger said, "I felt like you were about to say something more about scars when that woman jumped on Kelly."

Casper shrugged her shoulders.

"Could I see?" Ginger asked.

Casper held out her arms. The roses and black vines disguised slick scars ringing both forearms.

With one finger, Ginger gently traced a scar that ended in a red rosette. "That's a work of art," she said, settling back in her chair. "Tell me about them."

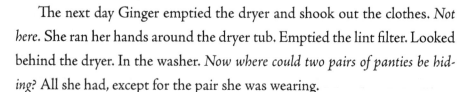

The next day Ginger emptied the dryer and shook out the clothes. *Not here.* She ran her hands around the dryer tub. Emptied the lint filter. Looked behind the dryer. In the washer. *Now where could two pairs of panties be hiding?* All she had, except for the pair she was wearing.

"What're you looking for?" Caspar asked.

Ginger hadn't heard her come into the laundry room. "The washing machine monster that ate my panties."

"Hey, come with me," Casper said. "We wear the same size. I'll fix you up."

Arm in arm they walked to Casper's room, all six feet of Casper in her white make-up, black jersey head-to-toe, Ginger in no make-up, a high-necked shirt under her long denim jumper, her feet laced in ankle-high farm boots.

In her room Casper dug through a drawer. Peering from one side, Ginger saw a tangle of shoelaces. *Wider than the laces in my boots, but....*

Casper thrust a fistful of the laces toward Ginger. "Here, take these. I have more than I need. In here, especially." She chuckled.

"Thanks," Ginger mumbled while she studied what lay across her palm.

"See, thongs." Casper stretched the strings into a V.

"Oh! I thought thongs were shoes." *They won't cover a thing.* She held up the narrow pieces of ribbon and lace and smiled. *They are sort of pretty.*

Then she looked at her long skirt and high-topped boots. *What will I do? The boys can't see me with these. I can't let Casper think I don't appreciate her help. And I can't ask anybody else for help because she may find out.*

She thanked Caspar as she backed into the hall. Quickly she wadded the thongs into a ball in her fist, then she raced for her room. *To think, I've come from a head covering to thongs. And I still don't have any panties.*

She rounded the corner—and collided with Annette and baby Angela. Ginger reached out, an instinct to protect the baby—the thongs dropped to the floor.

Annette stared at them.

Ginger stooped down to the floor and began trying to pile them up, make them disappear. Her face felt hot.

"I never suspected what that long skirt was hiding," Annette said.

Ginger sat back on the floor and laughed.

"Can I trade these in? Do you have something a little larger, with more cloth, in the supply room?"

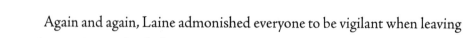

Again and again, Laine admonished everyone to be vigilant when leaving and returning to the shelter.

"Keep your antenna up. Right now is the most dangerous time for you because your abuser lost control when you left and that most likely threatens him to the core. Take care."

Ginger's fear of Mike multiplied. She shivered when she thought about the collage and the possibilities of the root cellar. For so long, she had shoved these threats to the shadows of her mind. Maybe that was where they should stay. Maybe her fears were unwarranted and unfair to Mike. But the more she learned about batterers, the more her fears sneaked out to haunt her.

She clung to the shelter, wrapped in its structure, and terrified of the world outside its gates. Like a wind-up toy, she checked off lists of chores and hurried from one required meeting to another. Nintendo and the television pacified Casey and mesmerized Cody. The three of them settled into the shelter's routine.

The first time Ginger ventured outdoors to her car, which was parked safely inside the walls of the shelter, she found Mike's messages on the car phone—angry, threatening, begging, pleading, crying. Mike had found a way inside the walls. He had breached the protection they offered.

She dashed back inside the shelter and stood with her back pressed against the closed door, trembling.

Unable to comfort her, Annette called for Laine.

"I'm in trouble," Ginger said. She bent forward, hands pressing against her roiling stomach. "I'm in trouble."

"Tell me?" Laine took Ginger's arm and led her to a chair.

"I ran away and he's going to catch me. I feel like a child who's done wrong, and I'm about to be caught. He's wormed through these walls with phone messages, and he'll catch me. I can't get away from him. I can't hide."

Laine wrapped her in a blanket until she stopped trembling.

"Mike's not here, Ginger. You're safe. Only his words reached you and words can't hurt you. They're just words."

Laine talked Ginger's anxiety down, but she couldn't reduce the danger Ginger perceived lurking outside the gates.

Laine had advised the residents to keep a journal. Ginger recorded Mike's messages in a lined notebook with violets on its cover.

At 2:50 a.m. on October 7, he said, "You bottom of the barrel, running scared whore, harlot, infidel…I'm going to find my kids." And at 5:40 a.m. the same morning, "I do love you. You must be ashamed of what you've become." And another: "Trent's dead. You poisoned him with boric acid. You're not going to kill my boys."

On October 7, eight days after they fled, Ginger relented to the boys' badgering and allowed them to call their dad. Besides, she felt heavy with guilt for causing him such worry. He deserved to know they were safe but nothing more. She laid out firm limits as to what the boys could say. They agreed to her conditions.

She dialed Wayne's house from the phone in her car. Casey scrunched between his mom and Cody on the front seat, his legs bent around the phone.

"Ginger? Where are you?" Wayne said when he heard Ginger's voice. "Are you okay? What about the boys?"

"We're fine. Okay. All of us." She did a mental check and smiled at her sons.

"We've been looking all over the country for you. Where are you?"

"We're safe," Ginger said. "When can you get Mike to a phone? The boys want to talk to their dad."

An hour later Casey dialed Wayne's number and Mike answered.

"Hi, Dad," Casey said.

"Hi, Dad," Cody said, leaning over the phone attached to the floorboard.

"Where are you? Are you all right? I've been worried sick."

They all spoke at the same time. The boys told Mike they were safe but would be happier at home at the cabin. They didn't tell him where they were or that they were watching television and playing Nintendo.

"Dad, how's—"

"Put your mother on the phone," Mike said.

"She said she wouldn't talk if we called," Cody said.

"I said for her to pick up the phone."

Cody looked toward his mother, and she shook her head.

"Did you hear me? Tell your mother I said—"

Ginger pressed the disconnect button.

Tears filled both boys' eyes. Cody began to sniffle.

"I wanted to ask about Samson."

At five a.m. the following morning, Mike left a message saying God had talked to him. At noon, Wayne left a message saying Mike was gone. Wayne called later to say Mike had suffered a breakdown and admitted himself to a mental health facility in Florence. "Mike needs you at his side," Wayne said.

Ginger thought about how Mike had fabricated a terminal illness. She didn't respond to Wayne or go to Mike.

She learned the next day that Mike had checked himself out of the hospital and gone home. As she suspected, the breakdown was a ruse.

That afternoon Ginger rolled out dough for biscuits at one end of the blue kitchen table. She'd tied a white bibbed apron over her denim jumper and fastened her hair into a ponytail. Lu sat at the other end, her chin propped on one palm while she balanced her check book. Darla unpacked boxes. Laine and Annette divided new supplies in the pantry.

"Shit!" Lu threw up her hands and tossed the check book over her head. "I can't make it balance."

Laine peered out from the pantry.

"Soon as I get this flour off my hands, I'll help you," Ginger said. "I'm the one who kept our checkbook."

"Ginger, you have a checking account?" Laine asked.

"For paying bills," Ginger said. She cut the dough into rounds for biscuits.

Laine said, "Let's talk when we get finished here."

"Oh, I don't write checks for myself, if that's what you're thinking. And I'll bet Mike hasn't paid the first bill. They'll all be overdue."

"You better take what you can fast before he does think about it," Darla piped in from the pantry.

"That's right," Lu said.

"Wouldn't that be sneaky?" Ginger asked. "Then what would Mike have?"

"Honey, are you looking after Mike?" Darla left the pantry to confront Ginger. "Who's looking after you?"

Laine drew Ginger into her office after supper. "You need to withdraw as much as you can from the account."

"I can't do that," Ginger said. "Not without asking first."

"If it's a joint account, half of it's yours. You better act fast."

At last Ginger promised to learn if there was a balance in the account.

"By the way," Laine said, "I overheard you talking with Sara, that's Casper's real name, about her scars after group the other day. You picked up on her need when I let it slip past."

"Nobody expected that woman to attack Kelly like she did."

"That came as a surprise." Laine leaned back onto her desk.

"Something about Kelly is touching a raw spot in that woman." Concern spread over Ginger's face.

"You're very perceptive." Laine pressed the point of a ballpoint pen in and out. "Have you thought about what you'd like to do?"

Ginger laughed. "I always thought I'd like to study psychology. Right now, I'd like a paycheck."

Annette facilitated group meeting the next morning. She took off her glasses and held them in one hand. "We've talked about control and different means of control. Today let's see if we can pull it all together."

She pinned a picture of a wagon wheel to an easel board and tapped its inner circle with a ruler. "The hub of the wheel represents a batterer's need to have power and control over someone else."

Three women scooted their metal chairs forward for a closer view. All leaned in except Lu. She knew this lecture by heart.

"The outside rim of the wheel represents physical abuse. See, here's beating and throwing down, here's sexual abuse." Annette went around the wheel, reading the words printed on the rim: pushing, shoving, biting, using a weapon, twisting an arm, pulling hair, and more.

"These acts of physical violence can strike fear in anybody, especially in women with a man." Annette slid onto an oak desk and let her feet swing. "Women generally feel vulnerable to men because men usually are larger, stronger, and can overpower women. Right?"

"Right," came back a chorus.

"Some women big," Darla said.

"Yup, and some women are batterers," chimed in Lu.

"The point is that people fear physical abuse," Annette said. "Let's look here next."

She pointed to the sections of the chart between the outer rim and inner circle. "What you see here are ways people can exert their will on others without being physical, such as name-calling, threatening the children, acting jealous. See?"

Ginger saw isolation and economic abuse listed.

"Intimidation. Hmmmph," Kelly said. "Ask me."

"Look at it this way," Annette continued. "Say you're the animal feeder at the zoo. You're used to the animals, and they're used to you. But one day a small gorilla looks at you and beats his chest. What do you do?"

"Get the hell out of Dodge," Casper said.

"Sure. You'd find a safe place." Annette stood up from the desk. "But why? That gorilla didn't hurt you, or even touch you. Didn't even step toward you."

"I'm gone, not studying what that gorilla's doing," Darla said.

"I wouldn't wait for him to hurt me 'cause I know he could do it," Kelly said.

"See, physical force wasn't necessary for you animal feeders to vamoose," Annette said. "Something you saw as a threat was just as effective."

Ginger let her mind wander back to Texas right after Casey was born. Mike had pinned her backwards over the dryer, his fist balled against her chin and dared her to say another word. And she hadn't. She gave in and from that moment on Mike knew all he had to do was threaten. The threat didn't even have to be physical. Any threat would do because she knew physical violence was possible. That made sense now. *What if I had known it then?*

The shelter required that Ginger show she was taking steps toward her own independence, but she had to be pushed out of the nest like a fledgling bird. With Laine's help, she made a To Do list.

The least scary task she chose to do first: helping the boys resume their schoolwork. It meant she had to talk with their teachers. She'd need to go to the school to get their books and assignments. Could she count on the school not to tell Mike she was coming? She'd have to ask. And she'd have to be careful what she revealed about where they were. Laine helped her script the conversation and they role played until Ginger felt comfortable.

Laine checked the car phone for new messages from Mike. Then Ginger drove out of the gates—her first time outside their protection since she'd arrived.

At the old farmhouse that served as the school, she sat in the principal's crowded office, knee-to-knee with the boys' teacher. She'd chosen the long-sleeved navy dress for this meeting.

"I need to get my boys' assignments," Ginger said. "I'm not sure when they can come back to school. And I can't tell you—"

"Mrs. McNeil, please don't tell me anything at all," the teacher said, placing her hand on Ginger's arm. "Your husband came to my house, and I don't want him to come again."

"We'll be glad to work with your boys as best we can," the principal said.

Ginger thanked them and returned without incident.

Back in her room with the boys, she switched off Nintendo and spread open social studies workbooks.

"We're homeschooling again," she said.

Mike continued to search and leave messages. Mrs. Dunn was tangled in a lawsuit against a cousin and already distraught, Mike said. When he told her Ginger and his boys were missing he said Mrs. Dunn had collapsed. If Ginger didn't come to see her and she died…

He told an elderly woman who'd bought bread from Ginger that Ginger had died.

He phoned Trent's grandfather in Texas, saying Ginger was deranged and suicidal, that he had to wrest a gun away from her as if the 1998 incident had happened recently, and that he was afraid for his boys.

Ginger dreaded opening the car door and seeing the message light flash. She had to answer; she had to play the messages. She had to.

She wanted to collect some of her and the boys' personal belongings, so she spoke with Wayne and a neighbor to help make the arrangements. Mike agreed. When she talked to the neighbor again, he said, "Mike said to tell you he put your things in the Layton house down by Black Creek. He thought you'd rather not come back to the cabin."

"The Layton house?" she said. "That abandoned house near the fishing hole? Tell him no sirree. How do I know he won't be hiding there, waiting for me?"

It's okay to say No, Ginger wrote in her journal. Kelly and another woman had asked her to watch their children one morning, as she had done many times, and she turned both down. *I won't be a doormat ever again.*

chapter fourteen

Ginger checked off the To Do list until at last she faced its highest mountain—applying in court for a protection order against Mike.

"What's a protection order?" Casey asked when he looked over his mother's shoulder at her list.

"It's what your mother gets at the courthouse that says your dad can't come around or the police will come get him," Greg said. He visited their room often.

"Is that right, Mom? You're going to sic the police on Dad?" Casey asked.

"No, I'm not, and yes, it does, sort of." Protection orders were new to Ginger also, but they'd been well-discussed in group meetings and the shelter recommended its residents file for them so they could legally keep abusers away. Nevertheless, the process, its formality, going before a judge, all of it scared Ginger to her bones. She read from the notes in her journal: *A protection order is a court order designed to prevent assault.*

"I have to go to the courthouse up in Waynesboro since we live in Tennessee," Ginger said. Waynesboro was a sixty-mile drive from the shelter.

"Ordinarily a staff member from the shelter would go with you," Laine had told her. She said staff members called court advocates stand beside residents to translate court jargon or simply be a familiar face in a strange setting. "But an Alabama advocate can't go to Tennessee. I'm afraid you're on your own."

Again, Laine scripted and rehearsed with Ginger, and the other residents shared their experiences at the Alabama courthouse.

On October 12th, Ginger slipped on the yellow dress with the capped sleeves and laced up her boots while the sun came up, hoping an early start would give her a jump on her apprehensions. Laine gave her a hug.

She set out for Tennessee, retracing the thirty miles that brought her to the shelter. She looked for Mike's brown Chevy Caprice with each approaching car. She watched her rearview mirror and tensed at every side road, intersection, and parking lot, the entire sixty miles to Waynesboro.

The courthouse, a gray brick fortress, presided over the center of the town. Stone stairs led to a two-story vestibule where the business of the county took place behind closed doors. "Office of the County Clerk" read black stenciled letters on the clouded glass of one door. That was the one Laine told her to find. Ginger cracked the door and peered inside before she stepped into a cramped space in front of a wooden counter. Two men and one woman leaned against the counter while they each talked with a woman on its other side. Ginger pressed against the back wall, waiting, trying not to listen to the conversations.

Waynesboro, May 2007

I leaned across the same counter seven years later and addressed the three women at work at their desks, "Do you remember a woman named Ginger McNeil?"

All three looked up at me, at each other, and back to me.

"How could we forget her?" asked the woman at the largest desk. A name plate read Carolyn Mathis, Clerk and Master of the General Court for Wayne County, Tennessee. She came to the counter to talk.

"I noticed her when she came in the door. She looked broken down, like an old hollow-eyed woman in a faded cotton print dress. I could see she was frightened to death."

"Genuinely scared," added Deputy Janet Staggs, shaking her head.

"That's right," said Willa Blackwell, the third clerk in the office. Like Ms. Staggs, she stopped her work to add her impressions. "She wouldn't look you in the face, she was so timid. And thin like she wasn't well-fed."

"I began helping her," Mrs. Mathis said, "but soon all three of us were hovering over her, walking her through the paperwork. Her hands shook when she wrote."

Ginger swore out a warrant for a protection order to be issued against Mike. In it she alleged that he shoved and pushed her, poured coffee over her head, threw rocks at her on September 29, whipped her with his belt on Mother's Day, 1998, and abused her physically on other occasions. A hearing was set for October 19, 2000, before a judge of the General Court. In the meantime, Mike was forbidden to have any contact with Ginger.

After it was done, Ginger sat in the car for ten minutes waiting for the thumping in her chest to subside before she turned the key in the ignition. She drove back to the shelter, mindful always of running into Mike, and eager to be behind locked gates when the deputies served him with notice of the hearing.

Mike described the deputies as respectful when they served the notice. He said after they left, "I found myself on the floor on my knees in a pool of tears like Job. It was another pile-on, like on the football field, more weight to the pile, added stress."

A local hairdresser set up a makeshift beauty parlor in the group room at the shelter. Ginger stood third in line, running her hand through her hair, lifting it off her neck. "I can't wait to chop this hair off," she said to the women behind her.

Her turn came and she took the chair. She stared at her image in the round mirror while the hairdresser slipped a black plastic cape over her shoulders.

"Now, how do you want it cut?"

Ginger searched the mirror's image. Her heart pounded under the cape. She opened her mouth to speak but her words stuck in her throat. *I'm the body. I'm not in charge. I even made a public statement of submission when I covered my hair with a cloth.* Tears rolled down her cheeks.

Casper pulled up a chair to sit close beside her.

The hairdresser handed her a tissue. "When someone has really long hair, I don't like to cut it short all at once. What do you think about cutting it at your shoulders?"

"Let's just cut it a little."

They all—Ginger, the hairdresser, Casper, the other residents waiting their turn—settled on trimming it by six inches. Ginger watched as each lock hit the floor. She began to smile.

"I'm taking charge," she said.

When it was done, her buddies let out a cheer. Ginger swirled and danced down the hall into the rec room to show everyone. "It's just six inches this time. Next time we'll cut more."

She'd left the boys working on a history assignment, so she went back to the room to check on their progress. They were sprawled across their beds, books open. Casey looked up when Ginger entered. "You've cut your hair."

Cody turned to see. He uncurled from the bed and stood up, almost shoulder to shoulder with his mother, his freckled little-boy face drawn tight. "Who told you to cut your hair?"

A lump rose in Ginger's throat. So did anger and it loaded her voice with authority. "Young man, you have no right, neither of you do, to question me. You will not play the role of your father in his absence. Is that clear?"

Late that night, while the boys slept, Cody's words rolled over and over in Ginger's head.

On the morning of October 19, Ginger climbed the stairway leading to the second-floor courtrooms of the Wayne County Courthouse. She had decided the navy dress with its long sleeves and dark color would be most suitable for court. Despite being rehearsed, prepared, and primed for what to expect, her mouth felt like cotton. She hadn't even tried to hold food in her stomach all day.

She looked around, seeking someone who should be looking for her. The Alabama shelter had managed to make arrangements for a court advocate in Tennessee to be with her for the protective order hearing. *Maybe she's waiting inside the courtroom.* Ginger opened the double doors of the court room.

The minute she stepped in a woman approached her, holding out a brown paper sack.

"He said to give it to you."

The woman pointed—there was Mike, leaning against the far wall. He nodded at Ginger. His white beard fell like a bib over a clean white shirt that tucked into his jeans.

Ginger took the sack. It held two wrapped packages. She removed the red tissue from the first and caught her breath. It was a framed 8" x 10" picture of Trent, enlarged from the last snapshot she had of him. The other package contained a box of Kleenex.

Ginger clutched the picture to her chest and shivered. If Mike hoped to throw her off balance, he'd made her angry instead.

"Mrs. McNeil?"

A woman tapped Ginger's arm. She turned out to be the court advocate from Tennessee, a matronly woman with a ruddy complexion in a navy suit.

"All rise," the bailiff called out. The room fell quiet, and everyone rose to their feet.

The judge came in, his black robe flowing unfastened behind him. White hair curled above a thin face with weathered skin. When he spoke, his voice filled the room. He explained that Ginger would speak first, since she applied for the protection order. After that Mike would answer what she said and could question Ginger. He directed them each to chairs behind the two tables.

Ginger stood when the judge asked her to. Her voice shaky, she began to speak. Before she finished two sentences, Mike jumped up from his chair.

"That's not the way it was—"

"Mr. McNeil, take your seat." The judge rapped his gavel.

Ginger started again. She held the picture tight to her chest. The court advocate nudged her.

"She said to tell you my husband gave me this picture to upset me, your honor."

"What's the picture of?" The judge peered down at Ginger.

"My son."

"Your son? And why would that upset you?"

"He's dead. It's the last picture I have of him before he shot himself. It was just a snapshot, but my husband had it enlarged and put it in this frame.

He gave it to me today when I came into the courtroom, the picture and a box of Kleenex."

"I see."

The judge's expression did not change. He made no comment about the picture.

"Go on."

Ginger felt cold, as if she were encased in ice. Her teeth chattered.

"I was afraid for my life on the day I left for the shel—"

"You planned it." Mike jumped up from his chair. "You picked a fight—"

The judge banged his gavel. Hard. "Take your seat, Mr. McNeil."

The third time he rapped his gavel he said. "You sit down and shut up. This is not your turn. Take a pencil and write down any questions you have. I'll get to you."

When Mike's chance came, he grilled Ginger for forty minutes. She took a deep breath before she answered him and pressed her lips together so as not to speak out of turn, just as she'd practiced over and over at the shelter. *Let the court do its job.* She kept their instructions at the front of her mind. Nevertheless, tears rolled and her teeth continued to chatter.

Carolyn Mathis, the Clerk and Master of the General Court, the one who had helped Ginger fill out the papers petitioning for the hearing, didn't ordinarily attend hearings, but this one she wanted to observe. Mr. McNeil tried to put words in Ginger's mouth, she told the other clerks later. Also, he was hostile and didn't respect authority, and that wasn't lost on the judge.

Mike accused Ginger of abuse. "You hit me in the chest, you remember?"

He stood between her and the judge, looked from one to the other, and paced while he talked. "In the camper, you remember that?"

"Yes, I remember. That's when you threw me to the floor."

"Judge, she hit me then and another time she hit me with a wet dish rag—"

"A dish rag? Did you say a dish rag, Mr. McNeil?"

"A wet dish rag, and it hurt. A wet dish rag hurts. It hit me in the eye and scratched my eyeball."

The judge smiled. "That'll be enough, Mr. McNeil. I'll grant the protection order."

He awarded $170 to Ginger to help her with expenses for the next month, after which he ordered Mike to pay $480 of his disability check each month toward child support. The boys were to resume their schooling. Mike would pick them up at the school on Fridays and return them on Monday mornings. He was not allowed to ask them where they were staying. They could phone him twice during each week.

"As for you, Mrs. McNeil, I'm not awarding you any support. You don't need to be supported. You can do this."

He rapped his gavel to signal the hearing had ended.

Mrs. Mathis gasped when she heard what the judge said to Ginger. She ran down the steps to report to the two other clerks manning her office. They were all horrified.

"He's marching her right back to him," Mrs. Mathis said.

"She'll have no choice but to go back," Deputy Staggs said.

"She'll be killed." Ms. Blackwell said aloud what they each thought.

Ginger had an hour in the car on the return trip to contemplate the judge's words. Back at the shelter, she bounced down the hall to find Laine.

"Guess what?" she said. "The judge didn't give me any support. He said I could do it. The judge said I could do it."

"You bet you can!" Laine said. "You can get a scholarship to the community college if we hurry. Classes start in two weeks."

Mike returned to the cabin after the hearing to wallow in his sorrow and frustration, alone except for Samson. Eight days before he could bring his boys home where they belonged. He had them only on weekends, the judge had said. It wasn't right, but he had no choice.

When school let out the next Friday, he was there, arms outstretched as first Casey, and then Cody ran into them. They hugged and cried there on the sidewalk, despite the curious stares of the other kids. Back at the cabin, the boys burst from the car and ran into the woods. When they came back, they ran again. All weekend they ran and howled. Cody carved another smiley face on the hickory tree by the swing. On Monday morning, Mike returned them to school, as the judge had ordered.

As they got out of his car, he handed them each a letter.

Ginger didn't have to ask about their weekend when she picked them up later that afternoon. The two boys talked all over each other in the car, telling what they did and what had changed since they left.

"Guess what, Mom? Dad's got a phone and gas heat," Cody said.

"What? Say that again."

"See," Casper said when Ginger told her buddies this news. "Told you so. That self-sufficient outdoor crap was just crap."

Ginger sat at the table in the kitchen, still incredulous. She held one hand with the other in her lap to keep them from shaking.

"Looks like isolating you was his purpose," Laine said.

"I'm flabbergasted. Why to think…." Ginger shook her head. "This opens my eyes for sure."

Just before supper, Cody asked, "How did Turner trick you at the fair?"

"What? What are you talking about?" Ginger was folding laundry on her bed. She stopped to face Cody.

"Dad said to ask you." Cody sat on his bed with his schoolbooks opened. Casey slid to the edge of his bed.

"He said you'd remember."

"Turner tricked me at the fair…." She hesitated. "Wait a minute."

"You mean in the letter?" Casey asked Cody. "Show Mom."

Cody handed his mother the letter Mike had given him that morning. In it he poured onto paper how much he loved them. Then he added: *Please forgive your Mom for being such a Horses rear-end….Ask her to tell you how Turner tricked her into taking Trent to the Fair. She'll remember.*

Ginger remembered. Sure, Trent could go to the fair that night. Turner would bring him to her the next morning. But instead of her baby, a deputy sheriff stood at her door.

And now Mike had put a phone in the cabin.

She lay in bed that night staring at the ceiling.

The boys came home with letters from Mike after each weekend visit. always filled with his love and prayers for them and admonishments to love and obey God. Sometimes he enclosed letters for Ginger. Sometimes the boys' letters bore messages to her.

One week he said he could hardly stand not having Ginger with him, though "I imagine I'll start looking for a new wife to take her place…but not her place in my heart."

The next letter filled five legal-sized pages with talk about God and prayerful confessions of falling short of God's law. Divorce is wrong under God's law, it said. "I want you to clearly understand my next statement. I knew Trent, all but his first year of life. I loved him. God allowed Mom to divorce Trent's Dad…He knows her loss in Trent and He knew the price she would have to pay the day she left and divorced Turner."

He neglected to mention that he too was divorced yet God had not exacted the same price from him on his sons by his first marriage.

"Your Moms' heart is as hard and as cold as a cold Tennessee creek stone…and there's nothing we can do except pray, so let us pray."

Enclosed with the letter was a poem for Ginger about a king who lost everything and a plea that she talk with him.

The Big little King
(By me About me)

I once Knew a King,
who was mighty and strong.
Young and Brave as the Day was long.
His decisions came easy,
they were obstacles to win.
He counted them proudly,
with a satisfying grin.
Oh, but the day came
when he met his defeat.
He had met his match,
and he felled with great grief.
As he started reviewing the
shame that he bore and
counted his Battles he Rose
with a Roar…Bring all
The armor and bring it to
Bear, get all the weapons.
and call all those that care.
He sat and he planned the great battle to come
He added totals and pondered the sum
With great study and thought

he planned the attack
He grabbed his large gavel
To declare the wars start
But found himself alone,
The truth was quiet stark.
He had lost all

M.

Ginger,
Please, recognize the foolish little boy I was, and forgive and allow the father and
husband I should have been to come forth. Please, let us talk.
Mike

Ginger set the poem on her bed table after she read it. She read it once more later that night. *Too late, Mike. I know honeymooning when I see it.*

Wayne said Mike talked about what he could do to get Ginger back.

"He wanted to trick her back, to hurt her, but financially, not physically. I thought he was crazy but not dangerous. He abused her mentally. I never saw anything physical toward Ginger. He said he was going to give her enough rope and she'd hang herself.

"Those boys didn't give squat about being with Mike. They ran to my house every time Mike had them."

Like young lions, Casey and Cody were uncaged on the weekends, free to roam the wilds. Monday the cage door slammed shut again, penning them between its walls. Like caged animals, they paced.

They argued with Ginger. They had witnessed little of the physical abuse and what they *had* seen paled in comparison to tales they heard from other children at the shelter and the black eyes and bruises they observed among its residents.

"Dad was a saint by comparison," Cody told his mother.

"I think you overreacted," Casey said. He hated being at the shelter. "It wasn't as if Dad was going to kill you."

From the very first, neither of the boys liked going to the weekly group meeting for kids. All of them had to gather in the rec room with two counselors, doors closed, television off, for what the counselors called "sharing" time.

"All they do is poke at you," Cody said after the second session.

"Let's talk," Casey said in falsetto, mocking Annette. "What do you think about—"

"Toe cheese." Cody poked Casey in the arm, and both boys collapsed into giggles.

"Whoa, there, don't be disrespectful," Ginger said. And each week since she had pushed, prodded, and shoved them into their meeting until the last week of November.

"Time to go," she said while she pulled on a sweater in their room. Her group met the same time as theirs and she wanted to be on time.

Casey sat on his bed, his head in a book. Cody was lying on his bed with a pillow covering his face. Neither boy moved.

"Come on. You hear me?" Mid-stride to the door, she stopped. "Boys. Casey. Cody. Up and at'em."

No reply. Barely a stir.

"What's going on here? Your mother is speaking to you, and I expect an answer."

Cody swung his legs to the floor and stood up.

"We aren't going."

"What did you say?"

"We aren't go—"

"Oh, yes you are." Ginger said. Her hands flew to her hips and her eyes bore down on Casey.

Casey pushed his book aside and stood up. "I'll go. But I don't want to, and I don't like it."

"Well, I'm not going," Cody stood, arms crossed at his chest, his feet planted apart.

Ten minutes later she marched both boys into the rec room, and they took their seats. She whispered to Annette, "Sorry. We hit a brick wall this morning. If you have any trouble, come get me."

Ginger yanked open the door to her own group and stormed in, her lips pinched together and her hands balled into fists at her side. As she related what had happened, her voice became shrill with anger.

"My boys have never been defiant before. Never."

"You talking about teenagers?"

"Surprise, surprise!"

"Thought you lived in the woods," Lu rolled her eyes. "Sounds like La La Land to me."

"Casey caved in, but Cody stood up and defied me to my face." Ginger was still mad.

"Law, honey, not a day goes by at my house without somebody telling me no," Darla said. "You been lucky if you put it off till now."

Tears filled Ginger's eyes and rolled down her cheeks. "It *hurts*."

"What are you going to do?" Lu asked.

"I don't know." Ginger wiped her eyes and thought a minute. "Call their dad."

"What?"

"Surely not."

"You don't mean…"

"Why on earth would you call him?"

"Because he'll set them straight," Ginger said. "He will not abide defiance."

"Even to you?" Lu asked.

"Why do you think he's going to make them respect you when he didn't?" Caspar shook her head. "He's set that example."

"I'm going to call him. That's what I'm going to do."

And she did.

"I'll take care of it," Mike said.

When they returned from their next visit with their dad, both boys, but especially Cody, apologized to Ginger for being disrespectful. They did not resist going to group again. They still didn't like it and said so. They still objected and complained about other rules, but they didn't defy their mother.

From some of her group members, Ginger sensed a shift. She thought of it as a questioning, a perplexity. How could she have asked the enemy for help?

Like a rope bridge over a chasm, Ginger's call opened a tenuous link between the parents of two teenage boys. Whatever hostility, rage, or hurt Ginger and Mike felt with each other they could set aside long enough to deal with the boys. One topic only. Neither veered off course.

Ginger remained at the shelter for two months, secure in its structure. She tackled the challenges of moving on, but challenges weren't strangers to her. The judge had said she could do it. She was determined to prove him right.

Overall, she felt a beginning. Nightmares had come in the woods in the middle of the night when there was nowhere to go for help. At the shelter she felt free, as if a tailwind were sweeping her along. Where, she couldn't say, not yet. But it felt right.

Running a vacuum, loading dishes in a dishwasher, and clothes in a dryer—she must be in Disneyland, she thought.

She wrote daily in her journal and slipped pages under the door each night for her caseworker. She made her Safe Plan. She applied for a Pell Grant for school and low-rent housing for an apartment.

The Pell Grant came through. Her application for the apartment did not. She was turned down due to a bad credit rating.

"Bad credit?" Ginger cried, "I've never had bad credit. I pride myself on my credit record. There must be some mistake." She trotted to SunTrust Bank to have them correct her record.

There was no mistake. The credit card she'd used in Texas carried a one-year overdue balance of $6,000 she knew nothing about. Anger flooded through every blood vessel. She sank onto a bench inside the bank until she could pull herself together. In her mind she railed at Mike: *My credit was my honor and my avenue of escape, and you stole both from me. Stole them. I feel like a dirty lowlife. I can't even move into a house just one step above the government projects.*

When she returned to her car, she saw the message light flashing on the car phone. Mike again. *He's with me everywhere I go.* She reached toward the phone and pressed Delete. *Why didn't I do that a long time ago?*

More hardened than ever in her resolve to put Mike behind her, she drove back to the shelter.

The shelter owned a transition house. She and the boys moved there in December.

chapter fifteen

It wasn't easy—going to school, working, mothering two teens, and stretching their $543 Social Security Disability check until the end of each month.

Funny. She'd never dreamed about college or what she might become until the possibility arose at the shelter. In fact, she wasn't even sure why she enrolled at first. But college quickly became affirming, and she threw herself into her studies to the point of exhaustion. The book learning lent structure to what she observed at the shelter, and soon her goal grew crystal clear.

"You're very perceptive," Laine had told Ginger very early on. Though Laine may have nudged and steered in the beginning, Ginger was instinctively drawn to the study of human behavior. Why do people do what they do? Why did she do the things she had done? And most important, how can we change? If something passes down through families, can we bring it to an end?

Change was possible. Of that she was convinced. She had only to look at herself.

The boys transferred to public school. Casey tested at above twelfth grade level and Cody at eleventh, yet they were placed with their age group—Casey in the ninth grade and Cody the eighth. They didn't fit, socially or academically, nor did they care for formal schooling.

Casey was liked well enough on the school grounds, but he wasn't in the clique. The isolation he'd enjoyed in the woods now separated him from his peers. In nearly three years, only one person ever invited him to do anything outside of school.

For Cody, it was rougher.

"You threw me out in the world and the world didn't want me," he told his mother. "I had nowhere to go."

Ginger and Mike divorced in January 2002.

Through his attorney, Mike offered to pay Ginger $8,000 for her share in the cabin and its 45 acres.

"Outrageous! That's below its value," Ginger told her attorney. "He's trying to weasel a bigger share for himself. All I want is an equal division, equal, nothing more but nothing less."

"Then you'll have to sell the cabin and split the proceeds."

"Sell the cabin? That could take months, a year even. I don't want to put this divorce off any longer."

"Then make a counteroffer to Mike. He'll come back with another offer, and we can negotiate from there."

Sell the cabin? She'd never thought about selling the cabin. *Why not? What is it about selling the cabin that's making my stomach flip-flop?* She shook the thought aside.

"Okay, I'll counter with what Mike offered me. Tell him if $8,000 is a fair price for him to pay me, then I'll buy his half for $8,000. We'll see how fast he squirms around that."

The next day her attorney called to say the cabin would be hers.

"What? But I didn't...I didn't think he'd *accept* it."

As the initial shock wore away, Ginger remembered how she'd harped about the unfairness of Mike's $8,000 offer and how she wanted only her equal share. She called her attorney back.

"I can't take advantage of Mike. It's not right. Tell him I'll pay him $8,000, but he can continue to live there while I finish school. That should make it fair."

Ginger hadn't wanted the cabin. The only time she'd been back was with the police when she collected her belongings. But when she thought about selling it, about her boys not being able to go back to their familiar haunts in the woods, she didn't want that to be taken from them.

She could see them building the smoke house, barefooted and mud-streaked, measuring, pouring concrete, setting blocks, and putting their handprints in concrete at the water faucet

Casey and Cody weren't the sole reason she changed her mind. *It's my last grasp at the days when that world was intact. I can still see Trent standing outside the window nailing up trim. I can almost reach him through that window. The cabin is where I was last with him; it's my last connection to him. It's where the sycamore tree grows.*

After a time, Mike grew tired of living all alone at the cabin, so he rented a house in Muscle Shoals.

One day Samson bounded out to greet the animal control truck and earned a ride to the pound. Dogs not claimed by their owners or adopted into new homes were euthanized after a number of days. Someone notified

Mike, and he brought Samson home. It happened a second time. This time Mike had had enough with Samson's running off.

With graduation in sight, Ginger finally set out to take possession of the cabin. For twenty miles she kept smiling when she thought about it. Then apprehension set in. *What will it be like to go back? What will it hold for me now?*

When the cabin came in sight, she hit the brakes. Weeds, tall grass, oil cans, weathered cardboard, trash, and debris everywhere. The washhouse window nothing but jagged glass. A soggy McDonald's cup by the door to the cabin. She got out of the car and felt lightheaded.

The front door had swollen. It opened with a jerk and Ginger stepped inside the house she'd hammered together. An amber light filled the room, a surreal glow that illuminated the memories flooding her mind. She shook them away and looked at the rubble around her.

The dust of years. *It looks as if it'll fall down with the next breath. And that light…*She traced it to sunlight shining through windows thick with a brownish film of cigarette smoke. She opened a small walnut cabinet by the sink that had been her safe place to store things. The dented canned goods stood just as she left them. All but one. One can of beans had burst open, spilled out, and dried.

In the bathroom her toiletries were ready for use. *It's as if I never left.*

She reached overhead to a cedar plank that served as a shelf over the shower. There in a Tupperware container lay the sanitary pads she'd made from flannel baby blankets. The pad on top was so thick with dust she could barely make out its pastel figures, but those underneath were as white as the day she bleached them.

She cried.

In June of 2004, Ginger Mitchell McNeil walked across the dais in cap and gown to receive her BS degree in Behavioral Science from Athens State University in Athens, Alabama. Casey and Cody were there, proud as they could be of their mom. Her friend Nell and Nell's husband drove from Texas to see her receive her diploma. Laine and Annette from the shelter were there with others who'd encouraged her.

She had told her family the date, time, location. None of them came.

A court advocate at last. A duckbilled platypus, Laine called the work— an officer of the court but paid by the shelter. Ginger traded in the Honda before it collapsed from age. She bought a life insurance policy and paid her living expenses.

"Whoopee, boys, come look," she shouted at the end of July. "We've got money left over. We're not poor anymore."

chapter sixteen

"Where'd you get the tomatoes?" Ginger asked Cody. She kicked off her shoes, ready to relax after Sunday duty at the shelter. Thick red slices of tomatoes floated in their juice on a blue plate on the table.

"Dad sent them. I stopped by his house this morning." Cody squirted ketchup on two buns. He sat opposite his mom. June 2005 and she and the two boys lived in a four-room house in Tuscumbia. Mike lived ten miles away in Muscle Shoals. "He said to tell you the Old Goat died."

"What?" Ginger's hand stopped in mid-air above the mustard jar. "When?"

"I don't know, maybe this morning," Cody said with a mouthful of hot dog. "Somebody called him early this morning."

"Was he upset?" Ginger asked.

"Nah. He worked on the car."

"That figures." Ginger bit into her hot dog.

"Why'd somebody call Dad about the Old Goat?" Cody asked. "He was a mean old man. I mean, who cares, really?"

"Your dad cares. After all, the Old Goat was his father. And your grandfather."

Later that evening, Mike phoned. Ginger expected his call. They talked occasionally now. They had spent seventeen years as a family, all their sons' lives, and they couldn't erase that history.

Mike was well out of Ginger's system, yet she didn't hate him. She hadn't figured that out until she spoke to a church group.

A woman asked, "Don't you think men who have beaten their wives and harmed their families deserve to be locked up in jail?"

"Many people think so," Ginger said, "and often I do, too." But something gnawed at her, something she'd always known and felt but never put to words. A hush hung over the room. All at once the thought crystallized and the words came.

"I believe in every person there resides something—call it a soul, or humanity, but something that gives us hope and allows us to change. Whatever it is allowed me to change. And if I can change, so can other people. So, I don't demonize batterers. Besides, I loved one for a very long time."

Now on this night she knew Mike needed to tell someone he didn't care that the Old Goat had died.

"Come on over," she said.

She met him outside and showed him to chairs in the backyard. She'd changed into khaki shorts and tied her hair off her neck. Mike wore a white shirt loose over jeans. A mustache curled across his upper lip, more gray than blond.

"When's the funeral?" Ginger asked.

"I'm not going." He exhaled blue smoke. "You know I don't go to funerals."

Ginger flinched. The pain from the last time he'd said that struck her afresh.

"You need to go, Mike."

"The Old Goat's had his last punch at me. I vowed I'd stay out of his reach when I left home, and I only broke that vow once."

"You've said all along your dad could go hang, that you didn't care if he was alive or dead. Now's your chance to put him in the ground."

"If he's dead, he's gone. The end."

"Not your dad. He's Plastic Man. Either you see him off or he'll reach out at you from the grave, just like he has all your life."

Ginger stopped. She'd said enough. She squeezed a slice of lemon into a glass of tea and drank a big swallow.

Mike wandered around the yard, puffing on his cigarette. He flicked it into a shrub by the back fence and came back to Ginger.

"The funeral's Wednesday. In Beaumont."

"Beaumont? Why?"

Mike sat down in the folding chair. "Grandpa gave them burial plots. I know my dad never put out any money on a hole in the ground."

"And your mother?"

"Still in the nursing home in Baycross. Doesn't know one day from the next."

"Beaumont's not as far to drive as Baycross," Ginger said.

"I didn't say I was going to Beaumont."

Mike stood. He walked behind his chair. Lit another cigarette. Exhaled. Sat down again. He rested his head on his hands, the cigarette between the fingers of one hand.

Ginger curled her feet under the swing and drank more tea.

"The hard school of knocks," he said when he spoke again.

She knew what was coming. The orange glow of sunset was fading to purple. Mike talked until the sun set and mosquitoes chased them indoors.

Ginger began drying supper dishes at the kitchen sink. Mike dropped into a chair at the kitchen table beside a stack of brochures from the shelter. On top lay the Power and Control Wheel Ginger used in her work.

He picked up one of the brochures and tapped the table with it while he told Ginger about his father's turning the power meter upside down.

"Dang it, Ginger. Why was my dad such a scalawag?"

Ginger smiled at "scalawag." Mike slapped the brochure against the table, then seemed to notice it for the first time. He read the heading, unfolded it, and shoved it aside.

"Are you asking why your dad was so mean?" Ginger had seen Mike holding the brochure. "Think back when you were a little boy. How'd your dad treat your mother?"

"No better than he treated anybody else. What do you mean?"

"Pick up that brochure you had in your hand—yes, that one, the Power and Control Wheel. Look at the questions it asks."

Mike opened the brochure and studied it.

Ginger began to ask the questions she knew by heart.

"Did he treat her like a servant?"

"Lord, she waited on him hand and foot." Mike glanced at the brochure.

"Did he limit her involvement outside the house?"

"Yeah, wouldn't let her get a job." Another glance.

"Did he make her ask for money?"

"Sure. Hey, I did that." He looked up from the brochure to face Ginger. "You always asked me if you could spend money."

"Did he make her afraid by using looks, actions, or gestures?" The countertop separated Ginger from Mike and she rested both elbows on it, leaning toward him.

"You mean like this?" He scrunched his eyebrows together and glared at Ginger. "I did that to you." He chuckled. "Where's this going?"

He turned the wheel in his hand and began to read aloud. To one question after another he answered, "I did that...and that...yeah, another one.

Ginger, I did all this to you. What's this saying? Does this make me like my dad?" He closed the brochure and tossed it onto the table.

Ginger circled behind Mike and took a chair across from him at the table. "Mike, it's what you learned. You learned it from your dad. Don't you see? And what's learned can be unlearned."

"I never wanted to learn anything from my dad." Mike buried his face in his hands. When he looked up again, tears filled his eyes. "I said I'd never be like my dad. I vowed I'd never hurt my kids like he hurt me, and I didn't. I hurt you instead. Oh, my God! Oh, my God!"

Ginger took Mike's hand in hers and squeezed it. They sat at the table talking quietly for a long time. When at last they said goodbye, Mike had accepted Ginger's offer to ride with him to Beaumont to the funeral. She would ask the boys if they wanted to go, too.

Ginger's new assignment, the Peace program for batterers, met Tuesday nights in the southern end of the county. When it ended at nine sharp, Ginger bounded from the courthouse to the car where Mike and Casey waited outside. A twelve-hour drive lay ahead, from north Alabama across Mississippi and Louisiana to Beaumont, Texas. With tag team driving and sleeping in shifts, they'd arrive Wednesday morning in time for the services. Cody chose not to say goodbye to a man he didn't know.

The road stretched south past drive-through eateries, Dollar General stores, and mobile homes before it doglegged onto a long corridor through scrub pines and black night.

"Those starched shirts'll Rotor-Root that cemetery when the Old Goat goes down beside them," Mike said. "My grandma especially. That's Grandpa's joke on Miss Fancy-Schmancy."

"Is the house still standing?" Ginger asked. She sat in the back on a towel spread over the stained seat cover. Casey fiddled with the radio from the passenger seat, trying to pick up a signal.

"Somebody said they tore it down." Mike flicked his cigarette in the ashtray. "Lots of places to hide in that house."

"And that's where you went to a funeral?" Casey asked.

"Yeah, at the cemetery. I was a kid." Mike rolled down the window and flicked his cigarette into the wind. "The only reason I'm going to this funeral is to drive you two."

The next morning the three travelers washed up and changed clothes at a run-down motel outside of Beaumont.

At Forest Lawn Cemetery, Mike slowed the car to a crawl between the stone posts bracketing the entrance. On his left squatted a yellow stone building.

Another stone building with a steep roof housed the chapel. Behind the chapel, a green tent canopied a dozen folding chairs. Mike pulled into a patch of shade under a hickory tree and turned off the motor. "Come on, let's get this over with," he said. "Only reason I came here was to drive you."

Several people dribbled from their cars toward the chapel. Others clustered on the front steps. Ginger recognized Mike's brother, Lawson, in a brown coat, standing with his mother. Mike hadn't seen his mother or his siblings in years and hadn't spoken to some of them the last time he saw them.

Lawson reached out and hugged Mike tight. As they embraced, Mike's mother threw her arms around Casey.

"I know you," she said. "Look at you."

Mike opened his arms toward his mother.

She stepped back. "I don't believe we've met."

Mike froze. His arms fell to his sides.

"Mama's got Alzheimer's, you know," his sister reminded him. She hadn't spoken to Mike the last time they were together. Roy, Jr. had declined to attend his father's funeral.

"Welcome to the All-American family," Mike said to Casey as they entered the chapel. He stopped inside the door. "It looks smaller than last time and it's cold."

Cool air rushed with a rattle from an overhead vent. Emerald velvet cushions lined rows of honey-colored pews, only a few occupied.

Roy McNeil's open coffin stood in front of the chapel, flanked by urns of white gladiolas, much like Mike remembered his grandfather's casket. He strode down the center aisle to the coffin and elbowed Ginger.

"Look," he said. "His face looks soft, like he never snarled. Bet that took a tub of make-up."

Mike stared down at his dead father. He could not have said what his feelings were or even if he had any feelings.

He took his seat with his siblings on the front pew.

"Let us pray," said a man in a dark gray suit.

Mike had never known his father to be religious, even after Roy's heart-attack-conversion.

"Oh, how he loved his Lord," the pastor intoned. Mike rolled his eyes at Casey. At the graveside the pastor offered another prayer, then a recording played "Taps."

Mike didn't know what came next. He glanced around. Almost out of sight, a grass cloth covered a mound of black dirt, a backhoe, and a stack of shovels. Shovels.

His dad swinging a shovel at him and hitting his mother instead.

He jerked, startled. The preacher stood before him with his hand extended. He shook Mike's hand, as he had shaken the hands of the other family members. They all stood, dry-eyed, except for Carol, who sniffled into a handkerchief. Soon whispers rose to chatter mixed with laughter and men mopped sweat from their foreheads. In twos and threes they trickled back to their air-conditioned cars.

Ginger saw Mike hurry away down a path that wound among other graves. After a time, she went looking for him. She found him on his knees in the grass, crying and beating both fists against the ground.

"I'm mad with him at what he did to me. I'm mad because he didn't have the right to do this to me."

His face reddened with each strike. Tears rolled down both cheeks, and his nose dripped.

"And if I'm mad at him because he didn't have the right, then I didn't have any right to do it to you. And I'm mad."

He stopped pounding.

Ginger handed him Kleenex from her purse. She stooped down to sit on the concrete curb around a grave.

"He doesn't deserve forgiveness," Mike said, looking up at her. "But if I don't forgive him, then how can I expect you to forgive me?"

Ginger didn't answer. The question belonged to Mike.

He shuddered and let out a long sigh. He started to get to his feet and Ginger reached out her hand to him.

"Let's go," Mike said.

Back in the parking lot, his mother waited with Lawson beside Mike's car. Mike put his arms around her and hugged her.

Ginger took the first turn driving home. Mike was twisting the radio knobs, looking for zydeco music since they were in Cajun country. It seemed to her that Mike had cracked into little pieces, then reassembled himself as good as new. She hoped he'd buried his pain and anger with his father.

Somewhere in Mississippi, Mike asked Ginger about the Peace program. He was driving now, on the home leg.

"It means Tuesday nights and more money, for one thing," Ginger said. "It's a court-system program to help batterers learn how to change."

"You think you can do that?" Mike asked. "Work with batterers?"

"Yes." Ginger grinned. "I had a good teacher."

Mike said, "Good? Just good?"

Hours later he left Ginger and Casey at their house to drive on home. A thought had been playing in his mind and suddenly it took form—she thinks I'm like those men in that program.

chapter seventeen

I never knew the submissive, stringy-haired Ginger. The Ginger I met was the woman from the sandwich shop, tall, stylish, vibrant, and confident in her work.

I learned to read Ginger's feelings as they crossed her face and hear them in the timbre of her voice and the words she chose to recount her memories. The counselor who could hold her own in the courtroom became the little girl when she talked about fishing with her daddy.

His approval, in my opinion, remained her greatest need.

"I was forty-seven years old and still feared the steel of my father's eyes drilling through me," she said.

She and her father spoke on the phone, and she visited her parents occasionally, all the time walking a fragile tightrope, fearful the least misstep might send her tumbling out of her father's good graces. The connection, such as it was, was too precious to risk. She hadn't told her family about the man she was seeing, whose ring she wore except when visiting them. She didn't dare.

She hadn't gone looking for love. In fact, she'd avoided, dodged, run, and hid until he finally convinced her he was the gentle, caring man he appeared to be. Despite the diamond on her left hand, there were no specific wedding plans.

She had come so far, put so much behind her, yet tentacles from the past still lodged somewhere deep inside. Church, or her faith, whatever that tangled knot was, twisted and turned but never loosened.

"I can't accept its teachings." She pinched her lips together and shook her head, struggling to explain the only church she'd ever known.

"I can't tell you. We have to go. You have to see for yourself."

We selected a Church of Christ from the phone book and set a time to meet next Sunday. Ginger had been in her mid-twenties when she left the church. Going back after more than twenty years, if only for a single service, would not be easy.

She grew less talkative as we neared the church, a rambling one-story maroon-brick building. By the time I parked the car, her face looked as tight as if she held a stone in her throat.

We were welcomed from the parking lot to the pew. Once seated, I read the church bulletin which announced leadership classes open to teen-age boys. Except for the lack of musical instruments, the service reminded me of the Southern Baptist services of my childhood. Ginger knew nearly every song by heart, and she joined in the singing, seemingly calmer until the hymn, *It Is Well with My Soul*.

"That hymn was a favorite," she said later while I spread sandwiches in my kitchen. "But it was disturbing to sing when all is not right with my soul. It was fearful."

Her eyes glistened. "I looked at the ring on my finger, and it ran through my mind that I'm playing with fire. The two paths collided and put me at odds with myself. I thought, I have to be very careful about how much of this I let in today—if I let it in, it destroys me."

She twisted the ring on her finger, wandering somewhere alone for a few minutes.

"I wore my armor today. I'm afraid of the power of the church from inside—it's so deep in me. Just going there was awesome. All I have to do is open up my arms—that's what I did before, opened my arms, and they withdrew from me. And after all that, this church still feels like the only way to God and that's stressful. It's like something was put inside me and it's still there."

~~~~~~

I needed to learn more about the Church of Christ. What Ginger experienced was so devastating, I had to know if her childhood church was typical of the denomination. Most of all, I wanted to know about the actions of the church in Hackleberg that demanded the pregnant Ginger and newly baptized Mike divorce or live as brother and sister.

I already knew Ginger's Church of Christ and The United Church of Christ were totally separate and that many denominations carry similar names. Ginger's was first officially recognized by the 1906 Religious Census.

A small university in Florence serves people called to ministry in this Church of Christ. It confers graduate and undergraduate degrees on students who major in Bible, the only major offered. I sought my answers there. The vice president took my questions in his office on campus.

"Churches of Christ are autonomous Christian congregations. Since there is no central authority, the churches may vary greatly in practice and beliefs. What's customary in one may be forbidden in another."

I related Ginger and Mike's experience with the church in Hackleberg.

"Many churches would have taken a different view," he said. He paused, put his hand to his chin. "Had I been in that situation, and knowing God's word, I would have chosen to divorce."

In February 2006, eight months after Mike's father's funeral, Mike pocketed a check for $77,500. In one commercial real estate deal, he earned almost five times his annual income from the disability check.

"I was a success that day," he told me the next week at the Waffle House. He shrugged his shoulders. "Money's just a way to keep score. The score matters, not the money."

He'd sent word to me the previous week, "This isn't Ginger's story to tell, not hers alone. I'll have my say."

Mike was a wheeler-dealer then, a big-shot juggling meetings, clients, offers, phone calls, text messages, always racing to some place and somebody more important. I learned to expect interruptions.

He interrupted me mid-sentence at our first session. "I don't want to worry you."

He leaned across the silver-speckled table almost in my face. "You better get your eye seen to. Something looks wrong about it."

"My eye's okay." I'd had an eye exam the day before, so I was certain. *Strange*, I thought, but I went on with what I had been saying.

He asked about my eye again from time to time, regardless of how I responded. I didn't catch on until I learned about the mind games he'd played with Ginger. He wanted me to think he had knowledge of me that I didn't have, and I wasn't playing the game.

Despite his success, and almost before the $77,500 check cleared the bank, Mike rejected the idea of reinvesting in real estate to chase a new venture.

The man who ripped the television from the wall and dashed it in the front yard, who removed his family to the woods to protect them from society's "garbage," now leased a barn-sized lounge, secured a liquor license, and booked live bands every night. With Casey as a partner, he lined up DJs and sound and light specialists. Cody moonlighted around another job to pitch in. Young people lined up three hundred deep to pay the cover charge and ring the cash registers in the bars.

"It wasn't no Sunday School," Wayne said. "Mike sitting around drinking Hot Damns with *Girls Gone Wild* booked in at night and still talking out of the Bible all day."

Ginger stopped by at Casey's insistence. The sea of gyrating kids reminded her of a *National Geographic* show about frogs copulating.

As loud and wild as the lounge could be at night, it was almost deserted in the daytime. Mike and I eventually shifted our meetings from the clatter of the Waffle House to the lounge's quiet and relative privacy. A small alcove off a dance area served us well despite the bottles, cans, and spills of the night before, or the cleaning crew mopping up. Fans drew in enough fresh air to mask the smoke and beer odors.

We still dealt with interruptions, if not from the crew, then from Mike's phone and text messages. His wheeler-dealer days were gone. He was scrounging by then to find people who'd work for him.

Our conversations took a turn at the lounge. For one thing, Mike was not confined to a booth. With space to move about, he talked more freely.

Some people talk with their hands. Mike talked with his face and his feet. He lifted his eyebrows or squeezed them together in a scowl or peeped out from under them with his head lowered. He jutted his head forward or dipped his chin to punctuate. He jumped to his feet, paced while he talked, and spoke without regard for who might overhear.

Frequently he reminded me, "I'll have my say."

~~~~~~

One windy day in November, we met in the alcove, looking out through a framed hole in the wall to the abandoned dance floor. The far wall held windows and a door to the outside. Somewhere music played, the base over-powering the melody.

Mike had been talking for half an hour about how frustration boiled up inside him until it spilled out as abuse when he and Ginger were married.

"I'll admit I'm guilty. I did all those things. Any man would be a kindred spirit to me because men know how the program goes. Sixty to eighty percent of men are closer to me than not. If I had it to do over, I'd do it all again just the same. We came out at a good place, and we had to go through it all to land where we are now."

He stood up to peer out at a cola delivery man leaving through the back door, then sat back down again.

"Ginger and I are to a safe place in our relationship now. We still care for each other, but we're no good living together. We can set the past aside."

Ginger had told me they could talk about the abuse now as if it were something they gave birth to and it died. They were very open and candid about it. She thought they might be unique that way.

"You were married before. Was there any abuse in your first marriage?"

I knew little about his experience with women other than Ginger.

"No, I told you she stayed depressed all the time."

"And there was nothing physical, no abuse?"

"No," he said. His brow furrowed. "Only once. I'd given her a new suit. She said something and I threw her down against the bed. It ripped the jacket. I can't remember another time."

"So, what does the word 'batterer' mean to you?"

We'd used that word many times. Maybe it didn't carry the same meaning for Mike as it did for me.

He clasped his hands behind his head, leaned against the wall and stretched out his legs.

"My absolute supreme definition would be someone that would have a basic routine. That's my definition of a batterer."

"A basic routine of what?"

He gave me a quizzical look.

"Whether it be drinking or accelerated by drinking or whatever."

"Have you ever seen yourself as a batterer?"

"No."

Then with a slight shrug of his shoulders, he said, "Frustrated, maybe. Ill-taught, ill-trained."

The distant music shut off. I listened, expecting it to start again.

Mike leaned toward me in the silence, as if he were going to whisper a secret. "Do you know what a governor is? On a car?"

I nodded yes.

"The governor's set in the wrong place."

"What do you mean?"

"Like in your car if somebody put something under the accelerator, then you'd have limited control. If you're taught you don't play by the rules, then you have no governor."

He shook his head side to side, side to side. "I never wanted to be like my dad. But when accosted—assaulted—provoked—angered—frustrated, I don't have boundaries firm enough in place to resist certain things. I'm tapped out. It's not a meanness issue. Don't you see? I was taught by the chief."

He stood up. Sat back down. Twisted in his seat, as if he were searching for something to hang his thoughts on.

"It's like if I try to pick up something tender, like a butterfly, once I've touched it, it'll never fly again."

He lifted his face and held out his palms to me. "When you're upset, you have no awareness of your grip. Times I grabbed Ginger's arms and she'd have a bruise. Of course, she bruised easily. Not me. I don't bruise."

He was quiet for a long minute.

"No, there was never any routine. What I did was only at the high anxiety point. Nobody knows what anxiety and fear goes through your mind when you see somebody you've lived with for fifteen years come out of the bedroom holding a loaded pistol and saying, 'Don't you stop me.' I was on the other side of the room, and I grabbed the pistol from her hand, threw her over my knees and whipped her before I knew what I was doing. The next day she showed me her behind and I cried, because it was blue, I mean just blue.

"You just don't realize how your grasp is bruising someone you love." His eyes brimmed with tears.

"But it was just a few times over seventeen years. Just like a skirmish leads to bombs, we had some serious clashes that accelerated, but Ginger's life was never in danger."

"Did you ever think about that? About Ginger's life? Because there were some people who thought—who were afraid for Ginger."

I had to tell Mike what I'd been told, hard as it was for me to broach. He'd opened the door and I had to pursue the issue.

"I don't know who that would have been. Must have been somebody Ginger knew that I didn't. I don't know who it is, but it doesn't make any difference. Only somebody who had a limited relationship with me. Because everybody who knew me would never have thought that. So that's my challenge to that."

"You never knew of a time when Ginger was afraid?"

He laughed. "Ginger was afraid if I scrunched my eyebrows."

He drew his eyebrows together and thrust his head toward my face to demonstrate. Quite an effect.

"She was never—the only thing we had was once—the Trenton deal was kind of like throwing gas on a fire. Like squirting lighter fluid in the barbecue pit, that's what Trenton's suicide did to her, number one, and to us."

He went on about how Trent's death affected Ginger. I asked if he'd noticed Trent's being depressed. We were long past fear for Ginger's life.

I hadn't anticipated this conversation nor was I afraid of Mike. We weren't alone in the lounge. There were cars parked outside. I could hear trash being emptied into garbage cans, and we were expecting Casey at any time. Mike had never threatened me in any way and didn't frighten me when he leaned toward me and thrust his chin out as he had just done. Leaning toward his listener, thrusting his head forward—these were his mannerisms.

Even so, I felt he'd crawled under his skin that day, possibly for the first time, and let me go with him. I wondered what he would tell me when he "had his say."

If Mike and Ginger were at a good place, then why not all meet together?

The three of us gathered in the carpeted alcove on a blistery hot August afternoon. Ginger came straight from work in her business clothes. Mike wore jeans, ready for his work to begin much later. Noises of people preparing for the evening performance floated through the open door.

What began as idle reminiscing funneled like a tornado toward September 29, 2000, the day Ginger left.

"That was a set-up. Premeditated plan." Mike was standing, propped on the door frame.

"I didn't plan to leave you," Ginger said. She sat on the carpeted built-in bench.

"Oh, yes. You knew what you were doing." Mike's voice rose. He yanked a chair up to the table and sat down opposite Ginger. "I talked to people. I know. They told me."

"No, it wasn't planned, not at all," Ginger said. The pitch of her voice inched up. She leaned toward him, facing him straight on.

"I know. Terri told me left-handed." Mike spoke slowly, emphasizing each point with a dip of his chin. He didn't shout but his voice was still raised. "You talked with her on the phone the week before and told her all about it."

Ginger's eyes zeroed in on Mike, but she leaned back from him.

"I didn't, Mike. I never said a word to Terri."

Mike turned to me. "You talked to Terri. What did she say?"

I preferred to remain a fly on the wall, but I'd spoken with Terri. "Terri said she knew nothing about Ginger's leaving."

"She's covering up."

Mike glanced from me to Ginger and back to me. "I know what she told me."

He twisted around to the wall behind him. Turning back, he braced one arm against the table and leaned across it toward Ginger. "You picked a fight with me just to have an excuse; you knew just what buttons to hit to provoke me. You had it planned all along."

"Very well." Ginger maintained eye contact but pressed her back against the carpeted wall behind her. "That's not what happened but believe what you choose. It's history, so it really doesn't matter. It's okay that we don't agree."

Her voice was soft but steady. She folded her hands in her lap. "Weren't we talking about money decisions?"

She shifted to what I considered her counselor voice and backed away from the argument. When she disengaged, Mike was defused. He responded at once to her lead. The remainder of the afternoon was pleasant and productive.

I made a mental note to ask Ginger later about what she'd done.

~~~~~~

The club shut down three months later. Too many bills, too little cash, too few cool heads, a suspended liquor license. Casey and his dad parted company. Most of the other partners had bailed out earlier, some charging that Mike ran them off.

Mike put the lounge behind him.

"I've always treated a job as a learning experience," he told me back at the Waffle House. "When I've learned what I want to know, I move on. The Social Security folks dug up twenty jobs I'd held when they granted me disability. To them, changing jobs proved I had a problem. But when I changed to selling real estate, they cut off my check. Said they'd overpaid me, so now they're making me pay them back."

"You're paying back the disability money?" I asked. That was a shocker.

"It was my money in the first place. I paid it in taxes." He fidgeted in his seat. Tossed his pack of cigarettes onto the table.

"What about when you told Ginger you were going to die? Were you sick then?"

"I knew something was wrong, something very terminal was coming in my life. It was probably blood sugar. I took Zyprexa for five years, an antidepressant, and that's caused me now to be diagnosed with serious diabetes. I'm in a class action lawsuit about that."

He lit a cigarette and blew the smoke away from me.

"Or maybe I was just anticipating the demise of my marriage, but I thought God was telling me something. I was face down in the dirt—like Job." His face wore a pained expression.

"Ginger always thought I was cold when I was crucifying myself in turmoil. What appears on the outside isn't a good indicator of heart of hearts."

chapter eighteen

Before the dust settled at the lounge and without the disability check, Mike picked up the pieces of a business around the corner from the lounge. It sold rebuilt appliances and closeouts, akin to an indoor flea market, except that some of the goods sat outdoors under a green funeral tent in front of the store.

Mike and I sat in unmatched vinyl chairs with price tags dangling from their arms. A table between us supported Mike's ashtray and my recorder.

One day when rain blew sideways with a wind that threatened to take down the tent out front, Mike announced he was ready to have his say. He stood, looking down at me in my chair. His shirt lay open at the neck and gray chest hair showed, as bushy as his eyebrows.

"God made women to be subservient. That's why there're more women nurses than men nurses. It's their job. It's what God put in their nature. God put men in charge."

He peered out at the storm. Rain slapped leaves against the glass door, and the wind rolled a metal lawn chair into the street. He took the chair next to me and lit a cigarette.

"Because of who Ginger was and who I was, there was constantly a conflict. We were raised different. I see gray, she sees black and white. Different upbringing. She was taught under a heavy hand to be subservient, but she wanted more. She tried to straddle the fence. For us to survive, I had to become like her dad. She put me in that position.

"What I'm saying is, Ginger causes friction. She put on that head covering and argued right on."

He pointed his index finger, as if to underline what he was about to say.

"It takes two to tango. The street runs both ways. Short of restraining or penning somebody up, the only way one person can control another person is through the willingness of that person to be controlled. If that person gives over control, he or she is giving their consent to the control."

"And you think Ginger did that, gave her consent?"

"I do. She expected me to make decisions and then she'd get mad at what I had decided."

He swiveled his chair in my direction.

"She's a self-martyr who gives and gives and gives and then gets frustrated. Once she hit me on the chest when we were in the camper. She had fire in her eyes, and she come at me. I grabbed her wrists and threw her to the floor and dang if the carpet didn't burn her knees."

He wiped his hand across his mouth.

"I felt bad about it, but I'm not a batterer."

"Then please tell me what 'battering' is?" I asked. So far, I'd only been listening.

"A batterer is a man who routinely gets drunk every night and beats up his wife. And I don't drink."

He dipped his chin. "Besides, it didn't happen that often. It wasn't habitual and it only happened at very volatile times. Stress comes in many fashions and when you have stress, you don't know what you're going to do. Nobody does."

He took a long draw on his cigarette and placed it on the tin ashtray.

"I can't comprehend getting drunk and beating up a woman. However, I can equate the fight or flight scenario. If the core of your being is threatened, you're going to fight. If your life is tied up with somebody and you lose control, you're going to fight.

"For a man, losing control is a threat. It's not the same for a woman because she's got a safety net. She can say *I'm not in charge.*

"God told women to yield to their husbands. To submit. If it had been left up to women, this world would never have got populated the way it has, the way God intended it to happen."

He fidgeted. The cigarette on the ashtray had burned down, so he stubbed it out and lit another.

"Like I said, for a man, losing control is a threat."

"So, what does that justify?" I asked.

"Not anything. But you're going to have to play Mexican Sweat."

"Play what?"

The telephone rang. Mike jumped up to get it, throwing his answer to me over his shoulder.

"Mexican Sweat. A poker game. And dare the consequences."

Dare the consequences? Was this another game? What did he mean?

Mike put the phone down to check bar codes on cans of motor oil. I listened to the wind whip rain against the windows. When he returned to our conversation, I picked up with a question.

"How far would you have gone to keep Ginger under control? We've talked about this before. There were people who thought you would kill Ginger."

I had come back to the question left hanging from the day at the lounge when Mike talked about catching a butterfly, that once he touched it, it would never fly again. I looked him straight in the eyes and waited for his answer.

He looked away, put his hand to his chin, but gave no reply.

He was hard of hearing, I remembered. Was it possible he didn't hear the question? I repeated it.

"Mike, people thought you would kill Ginger rather than let her go."

"That's what somebody told you?"

"That's what several people suspected or feared."

"I don't know who would have told you something like that. No, I don't know."

He turned to meet my gaze. "Who would that have been?"

We could have been back at the lounge.

"Who doesn't matter, Mike."

Mike tapped his fist twice against his leg. Smoke curled from his nose.

"No. Absolutely not."

He flicked his ash, stared at the cigarette, and rolled it between his fingers. Then he ground it into the ashtray.

"Twenty years of turmoil and always a storm brewing underneath. I got roped in and hung in the end." He held his head with his hands above each ear and his fingers meeting at his crown, as if his head ached with memories.

A blue haze of smoke filled the room. Through the glass door I watched the sun pierce the clouds. The rain slacked. Steam began to rise in wavy lines off the pavement.

He stirred the ashes in the glass ashtray with his forefinger. With his chin almost touching his chest, he looked up at me, his blue eyes locked onto mine.

"Am I a misfit?"

I wanted to answer, to say something, but I didn't have a ready response, and Mike didn't wait.

"Maybe I'll go to the moon and drive a sign in the ground, stake out someplace right for me. Buy me a ticket on a spaceship."

"That would be an adventure," I said, eager to say anything. The rain had stopped, it was time for me to go, but I didn't want to end on this note. If a door had cracked open at the lounge, I felt it closing today. Not shut tight but closing. Maybe he would look inward again. Maybe he needed to go forward and back up. Whatever his needs, I didn't want "misfit" to be among our parting words.

I remembered something he'd told me.

"What was it Reuben Welch said to you?"

"My baseball coach? My gosh. Don't you remember? That night at church camp?" Mike settled back into his chair. "We were walking down the road, and Mr. Welch threw his arm around my shoulders. Then he told me I had more potential than any kid he knew. More than any kid he knew."

A smile lifted Mike's features, dropped years off his face.

"That was the best thing that ever happened to me, when Reuben Welch said that. That was the best day of my life."

Encouraging words and a hug. The best day of his life. When he was fifteen.

When I left, Mike leaned out the door to say goodbye. The rain had cleared out and left a sauna behind. I was about to pull my car out into traffic when Mike called out to me. "Hey!"

I rolled the window down. "Yeah?"

"It wasn't all bad, Ginger and me."

chapter nineteen

No signs marked the low brick building where Ginger worked. No windows broke its front façade. I looked all around before rapping on the door where I'd stood many times before, each time aware anew of the security this work required. Ginger admitted me and we walked down the corridor to her office, passing posters citing statistics about domestic violence.

Ginger sat at her desk, its top coated with glass-covered family snapshots. I opted for the wingback chair. Behind me bookcases flanked a blue couch and a rocker.

I wouldn't be in this office again. Ginger was moving. A promotion meant greater responsibilities but less space in a different city.

"You were in the courtroom yesterday," she said.

"I wanted to peek. All this time and I'd never seen you at work. Pretty impressive."

I left ahead of her and was crossing the street when I heard Ginger's voice on the courthouse steps. She was bantering with an attorney and a judge about homemade pickles. Self-assured, briefcase in hand, just like the day I met her.

"When you stand before a judge with your client, do you sometimes see yourself?"

"Oh, do I! I was a shaking hollow shell back in Judge Jones' courtroom in Tennessee. I opened my mouth to speak and nothing came out."

"The woman without a voice now speaks out for others, in court and—"

"Anywhere an audience will listen. I've always been a talker." She laughed, then grew serious. "Judge Jones gave me quite a gift when he didn't award me support money. He challenged me and, hard as it was, I was determined to make it. And I did."

I only had one question. A poster in the corridor cited a really grim statistic: Six of every ten boys who grow up in a home where there is abuse will become an abuser. Was she worried?

"I know there's a high likelihood my sons will batter," Ginger said. "It's very sad, what my choices mean for their tomorrows."

Her boys are grown now with good jobs that take them far from their mom. Nevertheless, Ginger has spoken pointedly with them about growing up around abuse and what it may mean for them.

"I made a promise to each of them," she said, tapping her fist on her desk. "If ever I learn you have abused your wife or children, I will intervene. That includes going to the police and taking your kids from you. That's not a threat, it's my promise."

Her jaw was set, her voice rang with conviction. I believed her.

"Six out of ten become abusers," Ginger said. "That means four don't. I find hope there. And my boys witnessed little of the physical violence between Mike and me. Maybe that will matter.

"This legacy can end. People can change. I know. I changed."

September 2007

Almost two years to the day since I first traveled up the Natchez Trace to the cabin, the day I was bested by a chicken plucker, I rode back there with Ginger. Leaves still clung to the trees, but the hummingbirds were back, hundreds of them. Every September ruby-throated hummingbirds make a stopover on the Trace on their migration south. A sure sign of summer's end, whatever the temperature on the thermometer.

Almost seven years since Ginger raced down this same highway toward the shelter in Alabama. I wondered if she was thinking about that day now.

She had something at the cabin she wanted to show me.

On our way, I mentioned the exchange she had with Mike when the three of us met at the lounge.

"You blew out the fire that day."

"All I did was what I do with batterers every day. It's what I've learned how to do." She passed a tractor.

"It's like walking on a spider's web and not getting caught. What I've learned protects me. I know warning signs of abuse, how to prevent it, what to do about it. And anybody can learn what I know. That's why I speak to groups—given the chance, people can learn." She sighed.

"I often wonder, had I known more, earlier, before I fell in love with Mike...."

With a quick shake of her head, she said, "That's why I care so much about my work. We can end this legacy—for some people, it can end."

We had come to the turn-off to the cabin. She drove up the road and stopped her car beside the sycamore tree. We both got out.

"Here's what I wanted you to see. Sycamores grow like weeds."

Ginger stood beside the tree to gauge its height and we guessed fifteen feet. Its mottled gray trunk had already peeled to white near the lower branches.

"I can't believe how tall it's grown," I said.

"And how strong." She pushed against its trunk, and it didn't budge. She gave it another push, then stepped away to gaze at its yellowing leaves. The sticky green buds of next year's leaves had already formed at their base.

"I call it Trent's tree," Ginger said. "Strong already and still growing. It's his gift, but it's really me." Her smile seemed equal parts joy and mischief. "It came up out of a compost pile."

EPILOGUE

More than twenty years have passed since Ginger sped her wrecked car past the gate to make her escape. She left behind abuse, poverty, and despair to become a forceful advocate for victims of domestic violence everywhere.

The woman too scared to speak for herself found her voice. Speaking became part of her job, and she was dynamic in telling her story to audiences.

Telling the story was a way to repay the people who had prepared a place for her at the shelter when she arrived. It was also a way to keep others from falling into the snares of domestic violence, and to break the cycle of abuse.

Her story almost reached a national audience in 2004 when *Dateline: NBC* filmed it. It was set to run, promos were out, and then breaking news bumped it to the archives.

I came into Ginger's life a year later. I proposed a book and Ginger was willing to do the tedious, sometimes painful, work that a book requires. Hence, *As the Sycamore Grows* came to be. It allowed Ginger's story to reach a broad audience.

First, we put books in all the women's shelters in Alabama and Georgia. Ginger was still working in the Alabama court system, both with victims and batterers. She lobbied the Alabama legislature and came away with the funding she asked for. Her reputation as a speaker grew, and soon she was the keynote speaker at conventions in surrounding states.

I did radio and TV shows from Montreal to Chicago to Seattle and San Diego. A network of more than 500 book clubs chose *As the Sycamore Grows* as *Bonus Book of the Year* in 2012. Kappa Kappa Gamma recognized me and *Sycamore* at its national convention in 2014. The book was awarded six other literary awards.

Ginger and I both spoke for domestic violence prevention. On every occasion without fail, at least one person, maybe more, whispered to us afterward that she had a similar story, or her friend did, or sometimes that Ginger's story had led her to find safety.

Domestic abuse continues to grow, which is why we have reissued this book. Domestic abuse surged during the pandemic. The latest statistics from the National Coalition Against Domestic Violence show:

- From 2016 through 2018 the number of intimate partner violence victimizations in the United States increased 42%.
- 1 in 4 women and 1 in 10 men experience sexual violence, physical violence and/or stalking by an intimate partner during their lifetime.
- Approximately 1 in 5 female victims and 1 in 20 male victims need medical care.
- Female victims sustain injuries 3x more often than male victims.
- 1 in 5 female victims and 1 in 9 male victims need legal services.
- 23.2% of women and 13.9% of men have experienced severe physical violence by an intimate partner during their lifetime.

Ginger's story reaches these people who need to hear it. And more.

Ginger and I teamed up to present workshops that offered Continuing Education Units to first responders, social workers, and law enforcement officers. Ginger wrote a training program specifically designed for law enforcement.

We learned that *As the Sycamore Grows* was used in a women's prison ministry in Alabama and another in Alaska; that a government agency used it for training social workers in Augusta, Georgia; that a program for homeless women in Golden, Colorado, read it; and that the Methodist Church in Alabama used it in their Walking to Emmaus programs.

Georgia Public Radio contends that the story goes beyond abuse and applies to whatever might be holding a person back from reaching their potential. Thus, they read it over the air to the blind and handicapped.

We answered questions from readers. The question most often raised by readers concerns the root cellar. If it was a threat, if Ginger feared it, then why didn't something happen in it? Why introduce it if it wasn't going to figure into the story later on?

Very good questions. If this were a book of fiction, then the root cellar would have been the scene of something sinister. This story was true, though, and the truth was nothing bad came of the root cellar. Thank goodness. It easily could have.

Mike built the root cellar as a bunker back during the Y2K scare. Its walls measured 10 x 12 feet and were eight inches thick reenforced concrete. Its metal door was heavy and got stuck at times.

The root cellar was set into the low side of a slight rise in a wooded area. Its entry was small and hidden behind overgrowth. There was no road, no path, nothing to mark its existence. No way to be heard if someone were inside; no one to hear or help on the outside.

Would Mike have closed Ginger inside? There were people who thought Mike would kill Ginger. I asked him once but had second thoughts about my own safety so didn't press. Ginger sensed danger in her bones.

What she learned at the shelter after her escape crystallized her fear. The most dangerous time for a woman is from the time she decides to leave until she makes her escape. If her abuser suspects his control is slipping, he will do whatever it takes to hold on to her. Ginger is fortunate that she got away.

I'm claustrophobic, but I had to see inside the root cellar. Ginger held the door open, and I stepped inside. In the low light, I could see wooden shelves lined with her canned soups and vegetables. We were the only people on the property, so I didn't fear getting shut up in there. Nevertheless, I was in and out within a minute. Ginger had goose bumps.

She retired after eleven years with the shelter and then returned for another year during the pandemic.

Ginger is married now to a fine man who adores her, and they are very happy. Her boys are well into their thirties. Casey grew into the explorer, living aboard his 48-foot sailboat that carries him from one wonder to another. Cody's fearlessness has led his life into uncharted territory where he continues to test his limits, preferring to explore the world on a more philosophical level than the physical world his brother chose. Both are accomplished but in entirely different ways.

Mike died in 2019 in Oklahoma following a long struggle with lung cancer.

Now a grandmother to Cody's five-year-old son, Ginger runs beside his bicycle, chases lightening bugs, body surfs at the beach, plays hopscotch, picks plums to make jam, and collapses into bed each night that he visits, all while harvesting a million tomatoes with her husband.

"Every day is a wonderful adventure," she says.

PHOTOGRAPHS

The sycamore tree

The house in Hackleberg with plywood walls
and camper attached.

Mike and the boys on the staircase
in the Hackleberg house.

Cody, age eight, at the
house in Lutts, TN

Casey, age ten, Lutts, TN

Ginger with Trent at age 2.

Trent wearing his white hat,
Ginger with her head covering
in Lutts , TN in 1997

Building the Cabin.
Mike teaches Casey and Cody
how to fit floor joists.

Door to the root cellar.

The Cabin in 2009.

Four pictures for a quarter in a coin-operated photo
kiosk in 1999. Mike had just trimmed his beard.

Ginger between Cody and Casey, ages 12 and 14,
at the Florence library after she left Mike.

Ginger along the Natchez Trace, 2009

Ginger heads into the courthouse to go to work.
She attends court in six counties in northwest Alabama.

Safeplace billboard.
Ginger memorized the phone number and remembered
it for two years before she fled to the shelter.

Ginger and Jennie at the Liberty Luncheon sponsored
by Safeplace in July 2010, Florence, Alabama.

AUTHOR'S NOTES

In telling this story, I have relied on interviews with Ginger, Mike, family members, friends, co-workers and court officials; court records, letters and journals written at the time, and other research.

Some memories were lost or had faded with the passage of time. Several times Mike was unable to recall specific times and details. He said Ginger's memory was ten times better than his, so he deferred to her and once to the neighbor called Wayne in the book.

Ginger did remember in great detail. In addition, she had letters, poems, mementoes, yearbooks, journals, and church bulletins to back her up. Thus, many accounts came from her.

At one time Mike wanted to write "his say" and I encouraged him to do so. Later he changed his mind.

SOURCES AND DOCUMENTATION

Prologue. "I slapped the fool out of her." Direct quote from interview with Mike at the Waffle House. Also, alleged by Ginger in Petition for Orders of Protection in the Chancery Court for Wayne County, Tennessee, Civil Action No. 10745, Oct. 12, 2000:

The Order of Protection was granted Oct. 19, 2000 after a hearing before Judge Robert L. Jones in Wayne County, Tenn. Mike was present and participated in the hearing. The Court found that Mike represented a credible threat to Ginger's physical safety. The Petition and Order of Protection will be referred to jointly in these notes as Protection Orders.

Chapter 1. Incidents based on Protection Orders and interviews with Mike in which he says Ginger "ticked him off"; he "doesn't remember why now, maybe temporary insanity"; he "poured coffee over her head"; "chunked rocks" at her and her car; and admits the same things in a joint interview with Ginger.

The same incidents are also in Ginger's account. The same scene is told from Mike's viewpoint in Chapter 12.

Chapter 5. The scene in the mobile home where Mike knocked Ginger into the coffee table and to the floor. I did not verify this specific incident with Mike. He admits to shoving Ginger and throwing her to the floor on several occasions. For example, "All I did was just grab her wrist and throw her to the floor and it skinned up her knees…"

Ginger described this scene in an interview.

Writing checks. I asked Mike if he had ever written a check when he didn't have money deposited to cover it. "Oh, yeah, we did it all the time. I had to beg her to do it." I used the term "kiting checks" and he corrected me. Then he said, "Now, there're still other ways—you can run a magnet over a check and it lifts the magnetic reader, so they've got to put it aside and later they put a little white strip on the bottom of the check. [do a lot at once and they send you a letter]…do one at a time you can slow it down a day or two." I asked if he had ever done that. "Oh, absolutely."

Threatening Ginger. Mike admits threatening Ginger on more than one occasion. He did not say what words he used. His words when he bent Ginger over the washer are what Ginger recalls. The Protection Orders also allege threats.

Chapter 7. Throwing Ginger to the floor. "Once I was standing in the camper, and she balled up her fists and started pounding me on the chest. I took her by the arms and threw her across the floor. She got all upset because the carpet burned her knees, but I had to do something to stop her."

Chapter 8. Slapping. Alleged in the Protection Orders. Mike said to me at our initial meeting at the Waffle House, "I slapped the fool out of her."

Scene where Mike chased Ginger and broke the necklace. Mike says Ginger ran, he chased her, "grabbed her collar and got the necklace at the same time. Saw what a red mark it made and let her go." Ginger attests that the blouse tore. Janey, the friend who took Ginger in for the night, recalls the imprint of a hand on her face and later a bruise.

Mike admits he knocked Ginger to the floor, pinned her with his knee, and forcibly detained her. The admission is not specific to this incident. He did it more than once. The words of the threat are from Ginger. Mike did not say what words he used.

Bruises on Ginger's wrists. "Times I hit, grabbed Ginger's wrists and she'd have bruises." Interview with Mike.

Pulling hair. Ginger alleges Mike pulled her hair in the Protection Orders and Mike admits it. Cody remembers his father pulling her hair.

Incident with police. Ginger, Mike, Casey, and their friend Terri recounted this incident. Terri told me she drove to their house and watched from her car. However, the local police department has no record of an arrest.

Mutilating the picture of Ginger. Mike admits to mutilating the picture. "Yeah, I broke it and cut her picture out."

Chapter 10. Mike admits to pinching Ginger. He did not say where he pinched her and I did not ask.

Chapter 12. Mother's Day, 1998. Ginger and Mike disagree as to what Mike said to Ginger that morning and whether or not he looked at her bruises. She alleges in the Protection Orders that he whipped her with a belt on her lower back, buttocks and legs, leaving stripes that were purple for several days. Mike admits whipping Ginger with his belt. "I grabbed the pistol from her hand, threw her over my knee and whipped her before I knew what was going on—[the next day he cried when he saw her bruises] blue, I mean just blue."

Mike's account of September 29, 2000. Sources are the Protection Orders and interviews with Mike.

Mike told me he didn't remember what he did that afternoon.

COPY

IN THE CHANCERY COURT FOR WAYNE COUNTY, TENNESSEE

Angie E. McNeil
PETITIONER

FILED

VS.　　　　　　　　CIVIL ACTION NO. _10745_ OCT 12 2000

Michael D. McNeil
RESPONDENT
P. O. Box 9
Cooper Ridge Rd.
Cypress Inn, Tn 38452

Time _10:55 A·M_
Carolyn Mathis
CLERK & MASTER
WAYNE COUNTY, TENN

PETITION FOR ORDERS OF PROTECTION

7. Respondent has abused and/or threatened to abuse petitioner. Specifically,
respondent has: (Write what happened, when it happened, and where it happened on
the following lines.)

On September 29th, 2000 at about 2:30 PM, at our residence
poured coffee on my head and put his face close to mine and
screamed at me to leave saying that I had better go to a
shelter, or something because he was going to hurt me. He
threw a large sand bag at me as I walked to the car and
then threw rocks at my car. He hit the car at least twice
and was screaming at me to go. (See attached)

On May 10th, mother's 1998, at our residence "d in the
afternoon, I was very sick with asthma. He accused me
of being a bad mother (I had lost a son two months
before this.) He whipped me with a belt on my buttocks,
upper legs and lower back leaving stripes that were purple
for several days

On several occasions he has slapped me, pulled hair,
spit in my face. These generally began with his throwing hot
coffee at me or on me

Handwritten portion from Petition for Orders of Protection reproduced here:

Petition for Orders of Protection in the Chancery Court for Wayne County, Tennessee, Civil Action No. 10745, Oct. 12, 2000

7. Respondent has abused and/or threatened to abuse petitioner. Specifically, respondent has: (Write what happened, when it happened, and where it happened on the following lines.)

On September 29th, 2000 at about 2:30 p.m., at our residence poured coffee on my head and put his face close to mine and screamed at me to leave saying that I had better go to a shelter or something because he was going to hurt me. He threw a large sandbag at me as I walked to the car and then threw rocks at my car. He hit the car at least twice and was screaming at me to go. (See attached).

On May 10th Mothers Day of 1998, at our residence and in the afternoon, I was very sick with asthma. He accused me of being a bad mother (I had lost a son two months before this.) He whipped me with a belt on my buttocks, upper legs and lower back leaving stripes that were purple for several days.

On several occasions he has slapped me, pulled my hair, spit in my face. These generally begin with him throwing hot coffee at me or on me.

COPY

IN THE CHANCERY COURT FOR WAYNE COUNTY, TENNESSEE

FILED

GINGER E. MCNEIL
PETITIONER

OCT 19 2000

VS.   CIVIL ACTION NO. __10745__

MICHAEL D. MCNEIL
RESPONDENT

Time _12:46_ _P._ M
[signature]
CLERK & MASTER
WAYNE COUNTY, TENN

ORDER OF PROTECTION

This cause came on to be heard on the _19TH_ day of __OCTOBER__ , 20 _00_, before Judge ROBERT L. JONES_____ pursuant to T.C.A. Section 36-3-601, et seq., at which time the Court found as follows:

1. The respondent represents a credible threat to the physical safety of __GINGER E. MCNEIL__ .
2. Respondent received actual notice of the hearing.
3. Respondent had an opportunity to participate in the hearing.

Jennie Miller Helderman placed copies of
As the Sycamore Grows in all the women's shelters
in Alabama and Georgia when it was originally
published in 2010.

Please consider donating a used copy to
a shelter nearest you. Please support domestic
violence programs financially.

Contribute to your shelter or to:

Safeplace, Inc.
P. O. Box 1456
Florence, AL 35631

U. S. National Domestic
Violence Hotline
1-800-799-SAFE
1-800-799-7233
TTY-1-800-787-3224
www.thehotline.org

RESOURCES

The National Domestic Violence Hotline
 1-800-799-7233 (SAFE)
 www.ndvh.org

National Dating Abuse Helpline
 1-866-331-9474
 www.loveisrespect.org

National Child Abuse Hotline/Childhelp
 1-800-4-A-CHILD (1-800-422-4453)
 www.childhelp.org

National Sexual Assault Hotline
 1-800-656-4673 (HOPE)
 www.rainn.org

National Suicide Prevention Lifeline
 1-800-273-8255 (TALK)
 www.suicidepreventionlifeline.org

National Center for Victims of Crime
 1-202-467-8700
 www.victimsofcrime.org

National Human Trafficking Resource Center/Polaris Project
 Call: 1-888-373-7888 | Text: HELP to BeFree (233733)
 www.polarisproject.org

National Network for Immigrant and Refugee Rights
 1-510-465-1984
 www.nnirr.org

National Coalition for the Homeless
 1-202-737-6444
 www.nationalhomeless.org

National Resource Center on Domestic Violence
1-800-537-2238
www.nrcdv.org and www.vawnet.org

Futures Without Violence: The National Health Resource Center on Domestic Violence
1-888-792-2873
www.futureswithoutviolence.org

National Center on Domestic Violence, Trauma & Mental Health
1-312-726-7020 ext. 2011
www.nationalcenterdvtraumamh.org

National Runaway Safeline
1-800-RUNAWAY or 1-800-786-2929
www.1800runaway.org

CHILDREN

Childhelp USA/National Child Abuse Hotline
1-800-422-4453
www.childhelpusa.org

Children's Defense Fund
202-628-8787
www.childrensdefense.org

Child Welfare League of America
202-638-2952
www.cwla.org

National Council on Juvenile and Family Court Judges
Child Protection and Custody/Resource Center on Domestic Violence
1-800-527-3233
www.ncjfcj.org

Center for Judicial Excellence
info@centerforjudicialexcellence.org
www.centerforjudicialexcellence.org

TEENS

Love is respect
Hotline: 1-866-331-9474
www.loveisrespect.org

Break the Cycle
202-824-0707
www.breakthecycle.org

College Campus Safety Guide
www.affordablecollegesonline.org/campus-safety-guide/

DIFFERENTLY ABLED

Domestic Violence Initiative
(303) 839-5510/ (877) 839-5510
www.dviforwomen.org

Deaf Abused Women's Network (DAWN)
Email: Hotline@deafdawn.org
VP: 202-559-5366
www.deafdawn.org

WOMEN OF COLOR

Women of Color Network
1-800-537-2238
www.wocninc.org

INCITE! Women of Color Against Violence
incite.natl@gmail.com
www.incite-national.org

LATINA/LATINO

Casa de Esperanza
Linea de crisis 24-horas/24-hour crisis line
1-651-772-1611
www.casadeesperanza.org

National Latin@ Network for Healthy Families and Communities
1-651-646-5553
www.nationallatinonetwork.org

IMMIGRANT

The National Immigrant Women's Advocacy Project
(202) 274-4457
http://www.niwap.org/

INDIGENOUS WOMEN

National Indigenous Women's Resource Center
855-649-7299
www.niwrc.org

ASIAN/PACIFIC ISLANDER

Asian and Pacific Islander Institute on Domestic Violence
1-415-954-9988
www.apiidv.org

Committee Against Anti-Asian Violence (CAAAV)
1-212- 473-6485
www.caaav.org

Manavi
1-732-435-1414
www.manavi.org

AFRICAN-AMERICAN

The Black Church and Domestic Violence Institute
1-770-909-0715
www.bcdvi.org

LESBIAN, BI-SEXUAL, GAY, TRANSGENDER, GENDER NON-CONFORMING

The Audre Lorde Project
1-178-596-0342
www.alp.org

LAMBDA GLBT Community Services
1-206-350-4283
http://www.qrd.org/qrd/www/orgs/avproject/main.htm

National Gay and Lesbian Task Force
1-202-393-5177
www.ngltf.org

Northwest Network of Bisexual, Trans, Lesbian & Gay Survivors of Abuse
1-206-568-7777
www.nwnetwork.org

Trans Lifeline
877-565-8860
www.translifeline.org

ABUSE IN LATER LIFE

National Clearinghouse on Abuse in Later Life
1-608-255-0539
www.ncall.us

National Center for Elder Abuse
1-855-500-3537
www.aginginplace.org

MEN

National Organization for Men Against Sexism (NOMAS)
1-720-466-3882
www.nomas.org

A Call to Men
1-917-922-6738
www.acalltomen.org

Men Stopping Violence
1-866-717-9317
www.menstoppingviolence.org

LEGAL

Battered Women's Justice Project
1-800-903-0111
www.bwjp.org

Legal Momentum
1-212-925-6635
www.legalmomentum.org

Womenslaw.org
www.womenslaw.org

National Clearinghouse for the Defense of Battered Women
1-800-903-0111 x 3
www.ncdbw.org

Legal Network for Gender Equity
nwlc.org/join-the-legal-network

Domestic Violence Legal Empowerment and Appeals Project
www.dvleap.org

Source: National Coalition Against Domestic Violence

ACKNOWLEDGEMENTS

Ginger escaped. She could find safety in a women's shelter, and her gratitude to those who provided the shelter inspired her to tell her story in this book.

Shelters haven't always been there. The first in the United States opened in 1974. Nor have we had laws protecting women, or even awareness of domestic abuse. My appreciation goes to those who have prepared the safe places, made and enforced the laws, and helped people, yes, men and women, know the warning signs of abusers.

Back in 2005 Rick Bragg began teaching at the University of Alabama in Tuscaloosa and I sat on the front row of that class. The nontraditional student, I begged my way into the class and commuted 2 ½ hours to get there, because I knew Rick and what I could learn from him. He gave me an assignment for a magazine story that grew into this book, so I am forever indebted to him for the assignment, his guidance as I wrote, and his support and friendship since then.

I'm also indebted to all who shared their memories with me. To my writing buddies who critiqued and told me what I needed to hear: Joyce Finn most of all, Fiona Benson, Kathryn Anzak, Nancy Kopp, Maureen Rogers, Sarah Fogarty, Molly Flowers, Barb Warman, Harriet Cooper, Miho Kinnas, and all in Writers and Critters (WAC), my online critique group. And to my editors Renni Browne and Shannon Rogers. And to others who encouraged, read, or listened: authors Sue Williams Silverman and Jedwin Smith, friends

Sandra Berman, Mary White, and Joanie Leach, and my daughter Catherine Markwalter.

And to Arneda Heath who connected me with Ginger; Janet Smith, my volunteer publicist; Evelyn Muskett and Martha Jax, booksellers extraordinaire; Rachel Hackworth, Rocky Stone, and The Sigma Gentlemen of the University of Montevallo for their support.

My love and appreciation go to Frank, my husband, my protector and supporter, who withheld his advice until I asked. Frank and I met at the Saturday picture show when we were twelve years old, and we were married sixty-two years. Frank died in March 2022.

Had there not been a billboard with a telephone number, a shelter, a pantry, funds for the billboard and shelter, this story would have a different ending. There's much left to do.

Jennie Helderman

ABOUT THE AUTHOR

Jennie Miller Helderman championed women's and children's issues from the grassroots to national levels, beginning with a call to a crisis center that led to the first women's shelter in her hometown. She helped add a forensics component to a children's advocacy center; chaired the boards of a statewide advocacy organization and later Alabama's Department of Human Resources, (DHR). Charged with oversight of all the state's social programs, DHR saw 5200 clients per month. Jennie worked with a national organization to develop personal safety and leadership training for women.

Jennie has taught school in rural Alabama, worked in a congressional office, and been photographer on an archeological research team at Pompeii.

She is also a *Pushcart Prize* nominee who writes both fiction and nonfiction. *As the Sycamore Grows* is her third book. Her fifth book, a memoir, has a 2023 publication date. An Alabama native, Jennie is a resident of Atlanta.

AS THE SYCAMORE GROWS
DISCUSSION QUESTIONS

1. The story opens with Ginger's escape. Why do you think the author opens with that scene, and how does it set the stage for the rest of the book?

2. Ginger's fondest memory of her father was when they went gigging for flounder. What does this scene show about their relationship? How did their relationship affect the rest of the story?

3. Mike often talked about their upbringing. How was their upbringing alike and how did it differ? How did their experience affect their parenting?

4. Mike said over and over he never wanted to be like his dad. How did he succeed and how did he fail?

5. What was Ginger seeking when she married Turner? Discuss their marriage.

6. What were the red flags in her relationship with Mike?

7. Why didn't Ginger just leave?

8. Ginger's spiritual needs were shaped by her family and her experience in two congregations. Mike came to religion late. What role did religion play in their relationship?

9. Discuss the metaphor of the sycamore tree. What did the tree represent? Was it fitting in the title As the Sycamore Grows?

10. Where did Ginger turn for help? What resources are available in your community? How would you help someone in a similar situation?

The National Domestic Violence Hotline is available throughout the United States and will give anonymous, confidential help, 24/7 at 1-800-799-7233. If someone is in immediate danger, they should phone 9-1-1. You can help by passing along this information, or this book, to someone who may need help, provided you can safely do so. Also, you can support your state or local shelters financially.